Thinking Differently about Leadership

NEW HORIZONS IN LEADERSHIP STUDIES

Series Editor: Joanne B. Ciulla, *Professor and Coston Family Chair in Leadership and Ethics, Jepson School of Leadership Studies, University of Richmond, USA*

This important series is designed to make a significant contribution to the development of leadership studies. This field has expanded dramatically in recent years and the series provides an invaluable forum for the publication of high quality works of scholarship and shows the diversity of leadership issues and practices around the world.

The main emphasis of the series is on the development and application of new and original ideas in leadership studies. It pays particular attention to leadership in business, economics and public policy and incorporates the wide range of disciplines which are now part of the field. Global in its approach, it includes some of the best theoretical and empirical work with contributions to fundamental principles, rigorous evaluations of existing concepts and competing theories, historical surveys and future visions.

Titles in the series include:

Thinking Differently about Leadership

A Critical History of Leadership Studies

Suze Wilson

Senior Lecturer, School of Management, Massey University, New Zealand

NEW HORIZONS IN LEADERSHIP STUDIES

Edward Elgar
PUBLISHING

Cheltenham, UK • Northampton, MA, USA

Published by
Edward Elgar Publishing Limited
The Lypiatts
15 Lansdown Road
Cheltenham
Glos GL50 2JA
UK

Edward Elgar Publishing, Inc.
William Pratt House
9 Dewey Court
Northampton
Massachusetts 01060
USA

Paperback edition 2017

A catalogue record for this book
is available from the British Library

Library of Congress Control Number: 2016931735

This book is available electronically in the **Elgar**online
Business subject collection
DOI 10.4337/9781784716790

Printed on elemental chlorine free (ECF)
recycled paper containing 30% Post-Consumer Waste

ISBN 978 1 78471 678 3 (cased)
ISBN 978 1 78471 679 0 (eBook)
ISBN 978 1 78811 680 0 (paperback)

Typeset by Columns Design XML Ltd, Reading
Printed and bound in the USA

Contents

Models

Tables

Acknowledgements

My thanks go first to Professor Stephen Cummings and Dr Sarah Proctor-Thomson at Victoria University of Wellington who provided invaluable support during the conduct of this research. While finalising this manuscript, colleagues at Massey University kindly ignored my distracted state of mind and offered encouragement to sustain the effort: my thanks go to Damian Ruth, Craig Prichard, Jo Bensemann, Andrew Dickson, Fahreen Alamgir, Ozan Alakavuklar and Shirley Barnett in particular. Professor Joanne Ciulla of the Jepson School provided me with delicate but insightful editorial guidance, while the team at Edward Elgar Publishing, including Alan Sturmer, Erin McVicar and Elizabeth Clack, have been a pleasure to work with. My family and friends have evinced absolute belief in my ability to succeed, even when I have doubted otherwise. For this my sincere thanks go to Mum and Dad, Jennifer, Des, Richard, Linda, Kathryn, David, Tony, Fiona, Chris, Sammi, Daniel, Logan, Holly, Georgia, Sandra, Nigel, David, Ashleigh, Pete, Rosemary, Leeann, Lucy, Jessie, Oscar, Bella, Pixie and Muffin. Finally, the person who both literally and figuratively sustains me on a day-to-day basis and who knows best of all what this endeavour has required is my darling partner, Steve Harris: thank you, thank you, thank you, for none of this would have come into existence without your support.

1   Why leadership?

The object was to learn to what extent the effort to think one's own history can
free thought from what it silently thinks, and so enable it to think differently.
(Foucault, 1985, p. 9)

Leadership is not a 'mystical or ethereal concept'. Rather, leadership is an
observable, learnable set of practices. Certainly leaders make a difference.
There is no question about it. (Bass, 2008, p. 10)

AN INVITATION TO THINK DIFFERENTLY

We have come to live in an age where leadership is the solution,
regardless of the problem. Pre-eminent leadership scholar Bernard Bass
is even willing to declare that 'there is no question' about just how vital
leadership is. As part of this, managers are now routinely expected to be
'visionary', 'charismatic', 'transformational' and 'authentic' leaders, creating 'breakthrough strategies' and 'inspiring' employees to ever higher
levels of performance.[1] Leadership, it is now widely thought, is *the* vital
ingredient which enables organizations to achieve their goals and have a
highly productive, engaged workforce. These days, whatever the challenge, we are presumed lost without leadership. But *with* leadership,
anything and everything becomes possible – anything, it seems, except
thinking differently about leadership itself, because its value, its potency
and what we expect from it are now beyond doubt: whatever the issue,
leadership is the answer.

Research on leadership has grown rapidly in recent decades, simultaneously reflecting and feeding our intense interest in this topic.[2] The
efforts of academics in promoting 'visionary', 'charismatic', 'transformational' and 'authentic' approaches to leadership means that these ideas are
typically understood as modern, enlightened and grounded in scientific
research. Yet, in the vast, confusing and often contradictory body of
recent literature on leadership, only rarely is the confidence we have that
leadership constitutes the panacea for all manner of organizational and
social challenges questioned.[3]

Because of this state of affairs, because of this intense faith in the potency of leadership and the demanding expectations we have of managers-as-leaders, my concern here is to examine how and why we have come to understand leadership in this particular way – and what these understandings *do* for and to leaders, followers, their relationship and society more generally.

An important proposition being advanced here is that the conventional understanding we have of leadership today is profoundly limited, limiting and problematic. However, the overarching argument threading through this book is that whatever else leadership might be, it is fundamentally a *social invention* – and hence wide open to re-invention, if we only but free ourselves to think differently about it. I argue that this thing we call leadership, so commonly assumed a timeless, universal 'fact' of 'human nature', has, rather, been invented and re-invented in many different forms over a long period of time. Each particular 'form' of leadership has its own unique history, relies on a particular set of assumptions, incites a particular set of effects, serves a particular set of interests and is implicitly designed to address a particular set of problems. Paying attention to these particulars and examining different forms of leadership from the past and the present, as I do here, enables us to grasp that 'leadership' is something malleable, something that we can (re-)form in a manner which reflects *our* priorities and *our* values, should we conclude that existing forms don't serve our interests well. Rather than being held in sway to the faith that leadership is and always has been the answer to our problems, we can instead critically assess its varying forms and what each form does for and to us.

Given all this, one thing this book offers is an appreciation of the varied ways in which leadership has been thought of, allowing you to expand your sense of what leadership can be. More than this, though, I hope this examination of what ideas about leadership can *do* to our sense of self, as leader and follower, and the wider social function such ideas serve, will encourage you to think carefully about what you expect of yourself and others, as leaders and followers, and how leadership can best be formed in ways that serve shared notions of a good society. In particular, the framework for re-thinking leadership which I offer in Chapter 8 can support you to invent, in your community, a uniquely tailored theory of 'leadership' which reflects its shared values, needs and concerns, this being in sharp contrast to the generic, context-free 'recipes' that constitute the nature of most contemporary leadership theories.[4]

To try to make sense of how and why we have come to understand leadership in the way we now do, what follows is, in part, an intellectual history of Western leadership thought, examining Classical Greek, medieval and modern ideas about leadership. It is a history of scholarly ideas on the topic of leadership, tracing developments in thought over time and connecting those developments to the context in which they arose. However, in order to also understand what these ideas about leadership *do* for and to leaders, followers, their relationship and society more generally, these ideas are treated as *discourse*, in the sense developed by Michel Foucault – meaning, basically, that I examine how these ideas *construct* specified, disciplined ways of being and particular ways of ordering relations between people. This perspective also means that I am not testing here whether the ideas about leadership which I examine are 'true', in the sense of asking if they accurately reflect a 'reality' which exists beyond the page of the text. Rather, my analysis looks at what is incited by these ideas irrespective of their truthfulness – because history teaches us that irrespective of their scientific credibility, ideas are powerful if they are believed.

This stepping aside from questions of truthfulness allows me to treat leadership knowledge as, in and of itself, a socio-political act, as an attempt to say something about how the world ought to be. I treat the statements scholars make on the topic of leadership as responses to what they hold to be the problems of their day, as imbued with the assumptions of the time in which they are written and as offering prescriptions to leader and followers on how they should act and relate to others. Viewed in this way, leadership knowledge can be understood as enabling and requiring certain specific ways of being and doing leadership, a configuration whose dimensions we can then examine and ask 'what does this do to and for us?' and 'whose and what interests are served by this approach?'. With this perspective, we can bring into focus the context in which leadership ideas emerge and which informs those ideas. We can look at the micro-level effects of these ideas for leaders' and followers' sense of self, and for their relationship. And, we can look at the macro-level effects of a given form of 'leadership' for society more generally. That, in a nutshell, is the nature and scope of the analytic moves I work through as I examine how leadership has been thought about at different times.

My process of inquiry into this topic, however, didn't begin in my head but in my gut. More precisely, it began with a churning in my gut as time after time, as an executive in a large government-owned company (17,000 employees and contractors), I felt my own leadership efforts were somehow lacking, despite my best efforts. In my role as a General Manager of Human Resources, I would work hard at role modelling the kind of leadership I and my fellow executives said we wanted to see in the organization. We drew on ideas of leadership as involving 'vision', 'transformation' and 'authenticity' with confidence that these were credible, proven, modern approaches. Being New Zealanders, a culture where, traditionally, 'showing off' and fine rhetorical flourishes are viewed with some suspicion, we were somewhat less inclined to promote expectations of 'charisma' – but we also weren't averse to rewarding and promoting those seen as being charismatic.

I took the expectations we had of managers in our company seriously and considered it crucial, both in ethical and instrumental terms, for me to practice what we preached. So I tried to be 'visionary', 'transformational' and 'authentic', and if others perceived me as 'charismatic', then all well and good. Yet, it seemed that no matter what I tried, someone, somewhere, was not satisfied with my leadership; 360-degree survey feedback would tell me I was doing too much of 'x' or not enough of 'y'. Employee engagement surveys would indicate 'gaps' in areas that I, as 'leader', was expected to have acted on. It came to seem that if I was to be a 'good leader' I needed to be perfect, but I knew I wasn't and couldn't ever be, and so I felt trapped and overwhelmed by these seemingly impossible expectations. I thought I generally did a pretty good job at 'leading', and I was lucky to have a lot of supporters, but I also thought that relative to what people seemed to expect of leaders I was never going to be good enough.

As part of my role as a member of the executive leadership team (ELT) at this company, I would also regularly visit some of our 500-plus worksites spread throughout New Zealand. During these visits, employees would frequently raise good ideas about how to solve issues affecting their worksite or about doing something new and different. However, even when they held the necessary authority to implement their ideas, staff would commonly ask for ELT sponsorship and endorsement for their initiatives, appearing to believe that matters could not improve without this. I found this confusing. The ELT at that time consisted of just 11 people. How could 11 people possibly hope to know everything that was going on in a company of 17,000? How could the ELT possibly be expected to make every decision or assess every idea for improvement? It seemed as if the more 'leadership' was emphasized as the key to success, the more dependent on leaders we were making everyone else, and that, I felt, could not be a good thing.

These two lessons – that the expectations held of leaders were impossible to live up to and that emphasizing leadership somehow resulted in others becoming dependent on leaders – stuck with me for a long time. In subsequent work I've done in many different organizations, I have found these same patterns of thought and behaviour: whatever the nature of the problem or opportunity, 'leadership' is seen as being necessary to make progress. Not just clever people working well together. Not just good ideas. These alone are not seen to be sufficient. Instead, 'leadership' is called upon as the default requirement, the magic ingredient, the vital necessity, without which nothing good will eventuate. And so from these experiences, over a period of time, I developed the sense that somehow we just weren't *thinking* about leadership in the right way, that our *ideas* about leadership were somehow deeply problematic. It was this sense that I carried with me into the research process which gave rise to this book.

Importantly, these lessons mean that while I engage here in a determined critique of influential contemporary leadership theories, what you will not find is something that is anti-leader or anti-leadership. I am not 'against' anyone in a leadership role who, as I did, is trying their level best to cope with the demands of their role. Nor am I opposed to the existence of leadership roles. This is not some wildly idealistic, anti-authority polemic. My concern is the particular, onerous, inflated, impossible expectations we have built up about leadership and what it can do for us, expectations that I have come to see as deeply problematic and in need of challenge. My worry is that our conventional understanding of 'leadership' is causing harm and giving rise to problematic effects, matters which can be avoided, or at least minimized, if we think differently about leadership. My aim is, unashamedly, to expose the nature of the harm our present thinking can create – as doing so is necessary to motivate change. I also trace why and how this situation has come about, identify the key assumptions which it rests on and offer ideas for what we can do about it. If you have tried to lead others and found it profoundly challenging or have become disillusioned with the efforts of those in leadership positions, then this book offers a basis for reflecting on the assumptions and expectations that society today has about leadership, such that you can begin to think differently about leadership. That is the provocation and the invitation on offer. What follows may delight or infuriate. You may disagree strongly with some or even all of what I have to say. But chances are that you will still look at leadership through different eyes as a result, and that, I believe, is all for the good.

LEADERSHIP TODAY

In recent decades, leadership has been extensively promoted by management scholars and practitioners alike as a vital force for good, crucial to overcoming the myriad challenges facing groups, organizations and even societies, and securing a better future.[5] Such is the confidence of proponents of this view that Bass can even claim that the value of leadership is now beyond debate.[6] However, while it has recently been argued that 'the fundamental question we must ask is, what do we know and what should we know about leaders and leadership',[7] I contend that the emphasis and expectations now placed on leaders and leadership instead demand analysis of *why* and *how* it is we have come to constitute 'leadership' as the answer to all our problems.

Effective leadership is commonly understood in the modern West as having 'visionary',[8] 'charismatic',[9] 'transformational'[10] and, more recently, 'authentic'[11] qualities. Collectively, these ideas are known as the 'new leadership' school.[12] Leadership of this intense, powerful and compelling nature has, over the last quarter century, come to constitute the expected standard for managerial performance and to be widely accepted as something which employees, 'followers', both need and benefit from.[13]

With the development of 'new leadership', leadership is now generally understood as valuable and desirable for every situation and context.[14] Leaders are held up as admirable persons in possession of highly desired and valued qualities or skills.[15] Effective leaders are said to generate quantitatively and qualitatively superior results.[16] Central to the credibility of these claims has been the understanding that our grasp of leadership now derives from robust, scientific methods of inquiry.[17] As a consequence of all these factors, the confident expectation that we must have 'leadership' in order to overcome whatever challenge a group, organization or society faces and to achieve our individual and collective potential has become naturalized and normalized, perhaps even automatic. The critical scholarly tradition, however, demands that any social practice, norm or value that is 'taken for granted' needs careful scrutiny, because its dominant hold on our thinking and behaviour limits us. This is especially important when dealing with something involving unequal power relations, as leadership typically does.[18]

Critically informed interest in leadership has certainly grown in recent years, often drawing attention to the difficulties managers have in living up to the hype that now surrounds leadership.[19] Existing critical studies, broadly speaking, also build a case that the 'gap' they routinely find between leadership theory and leadership practice is not typically grounded in bad leadership practice but, rather, in bad leadership theory – theory which fails to grapple with the contradictory, complex, relational nature of our selves and the ambiguous, contested contexts in which we work. Indeed, a notable feature of the most influential contemporary leadership theories is their absolute refusal to engage with postmodern understandings of the self and the context-blind nature of their prescriptions.[20] However, despite these insights into the current state of leadership theory and practice, research on the 'culture- and discourse-driven nature' of how leadership is conventionally understood is something that remains 'neglected in most of the literature'.[21] In other words, the question as to why and how we have come to be so captured by these particular ways of thinking about leadership needs more attention – which is where this book comes in.

The approach taken here is motivated by three key concerns with the current expectations we have of leadership. First, current thinking places expectations of almost super-human capability and performance on people in leadership positions. This creates enormous, distressing and harmful pressures on those striving to meet these expectations,[22] as well as encouraging hubris by those who come to see themselves in such grandiose terms.[23] Second, it both relies on and reinforces the idea that the vast majority of people are somehow lacking, incapable of overcoming challenges without the exceptional few leading the way.[24] This, worryingly, undermines the values necessary for sustaining a liberal democratic society, such as the importance of active participation from all citizens on issues of common concern and egalitarian attitudes being central to interactions between people.[25] Third, the more this positioning of leadership as 'the solution' to every challenge comes to seem normal and natural, the more difficult it becomes to think both critically and creatively about leadership.[26] Thought itself is disciplined, channelled in a particular fashion, constrained, when a given set of ideas (a discourse) exerts such a hold on our understanding of what is real, true and good.[27] Cumulatively, then, the current understanding and positioning of leadership as the solution to every challenge poses multiple problematic consequences in diverse matters such as producing harmful effects for leaders' and followers' sense of self, facilitating power relations which favour the 'gifted' minority ('leaders') and diminishing the role and status of the 'ordinary' majority ('followers'), thereby damaging the values needed to sustain a democratic society and, through its sheer hold on our thinking, inhibiting theoretical innovation.

Importantly, leadership has not always been held up as the answer to every problem. Early 20th-century management scholars, for example, gave leadership little attention, focusing instead on structured, routinized systems and processes as key drivers of organizational performance.[28] Earlier, Enlightenment era political philosophers were deeply concerned to limit the power and influence of leaders, claiming that individuals and society as a whole were better served by so doing.[29] They wanted leaders to have less influence. From their perspective, leadership was a problem to be managed, not a solution. How, then, did we end up where we are now, seemingly at the very opposite end of the spectrum to some key founding assumptions of modernity?

FOCUS AND SCOPE

To analyze this state of affairs, the overarching question which I examine here is 'how and why has our understanding of leadership come to take the form it now does?' Clearly, this implies both a historical ('how') and theoretical ('why') dimension to the analysis. However, to provide a richly layered account of these developments there are five supplementary questions which I also address. First, to situate developments in leadership thought in the context in which they first arose, I ask, 'what issues deemed "problematic" shaped the development of the leadership discourses examined here?' Second, to understand what the ideas I examine rely on, intellectually, I ask, 'what key themes and assumptions inform them?' Third and fourth, to consider what these ideas do for and to us, I ask, 'what subjectivities and relationships are incited?' and 'what is the social function of these discourses?' And, finally, to consider long-term patterns in leadership thought, I ask, 'what changes and continuities are notable when comparing these discourses?' These questions provide the basis for a multi-dimensional analysis, dimensions informed by the work of Michel Foucault.[30]

Philosophically, the approach I take rests on an understanding of language as *constitutive* of our reality, rather than merely being a tool to represent in words things that already exist.[31] This means that the words we use to make sense of the world do not merely describe more or less accurately some pre-existing objective reality. Rather, through language we actually create that reality, in the sense of creating a set of categories, definitions and meanings through which we then interpret the world and act in it. This understanding implies that we can only 'be' and 'do' that of which we can speak intelligibly, meaning possibilities for being and doing which cannot be spoken of intelligibly are rendered impossible and unacceptable.[32]

As particular ideas (expressed in language) come into vogue and become accepted as legitimate and truthful understandings, they inform and motivate particular social *practices*, generating routinized ways of acting that are deemed appropriate and shaping our sense of self and others. Combined, both the language used and the associated practices in relation to a particular topic form a *discourse* or, more bluntly, a *discursive regime* – a particular way of ordering human activity.[33] This disciplining effect of discourse, of what is deemed acceptable and intelligible,[34] provides a compelling reason to examine leadership theory, understood here as a discourse/discursive regime, to examine how and why it constitutes, defines and disciplines 'leaders', 'followers' and 'leadership' in particular, limited and often problematic ways.

The book offers a series of case studies examining scholarly texts from different times which address the topic of leadership. I focus on specific periods in Western history when leadership has been an active topic of scholarly debate: Classical Greece of the 4th and 5th centuries BC, 16th- and 17th-century Europe, and the modern (mostly Anglo-American) West, beginning from around the middle of the 19th century and through to the present day. As a comprehensive account of every leadership text within these periods is far beyond the scope of one book, I focus on those ideas about leadership which dominated the scholarly literature in these periods. While understanding the diversity of opinions about leadership in each period is of inherent value, I look at the prevailing scholarly understanding of leadership of a given time based on the pre-supposition that these dominant ideas had, or have, the most influence.

As a result of its design and focus, this study reaches into times and spaces not previously subjected to analysis of the type offered here, revealing previously unacknowledged connections between the past and the present in leadership thought. Contemporary leadership ideas are placed, here, within a much broader historical context than has previously been done, enabling a more fulsome assessment of the 'progress' that has been made in recent decades. This strategy is intended to achieve a critical distance from the present in which we are normally embedded in order to 'free thought ... and so enable it to think differently'.[35] The subsequent comparative analysis arising from this approach enables the assessment of both change and continuity in thought, further supporting the achievement of critical distance from current norms.

This book proceeds on the basis that recourse to comforting narratives which simply assume an ever-increasing state of enlightenment as regards our knowledge of leadership[36] will not suffice in accounting for our way of thinking about leadership. However, a critical history of the type offered here not only explains how and why we have come to this understanding. It can also enhance our ability to develop new approaches. Consequently, I use my key findings to explore new ways of conceptual- izing leadership in a manner which seeks to address the pitfalls and tensions I identify in current and past models. Specifically, I set out a flexible framework which can be used to invent forms of leadership uniquely tailored to specific circumstances and reflecting different norms, values and assumptions.

In showing why and how different ideas about 'what is leadership' have prevailed at different times, the book foregrounds the vital influence that time, place, circumstances and assumptions have on both past and current versions of the truth about leadership. My analysis reveals, moreover, that our current understanding of leadership ought not to be seen as grounded in an approach more enlightened and truthful than anything that has come before. Rather, just as at other times in the past, it is contemporary problems, politically informed processes of idea formation and the broader intellectual preferences of our age which profoundly shape what we today see and accept as constituting an accurate account of 'what is leadership'.

From these findings I extend my argument to a questioning of the very ontology of leadership. Through showing how leadership has been thought of at different points in time, this book argues that far from being a stable, enduring 'fact' of 'human nature' now revealed to us by modern science, as is typically assumed, leadership is most usefully understood as an unstable social invention, morphing in form, function and effect in response to changing norms, values and circumstances. What I show is that the 'truth' about leadership currently so widely accepted is an elaborate but contingent, constructed and ultimately fragile invention. Other truths about leadership have existed in the past and have been similarly elaborate, contingent, constructed and fragile. From understanding these developments, however, we are much better placed to make choices about the way in which we might re-invent leadership to suit current concerns and values. My central thesis, then, is that the conventional understanding of leadership now prevailing is profoundly problematic, not least for its hegemonic hold on our thinking, but that, being a contingent construction and not something grounded in nature or science, this situation is open to change.

My theory is that the phenomenon we call 'leadership' is fundamentally a social, political invention. Its ontology is fluid, unstable and not something fixed in 'human nature'. What leadership is, therefore, is open to adaptation. What we call on leadership to do and to be depends on what problems we ask it to address, the assumptions we make about 'leaders' and 'followers' (if we choose to conceive of such roles), and what we value. In whatever form it takes, what we understand as 'leadership' will be shaped by relations of power and power/knowledge dynamics which discipline what is deemed 'acceptable' and 'truthful', yet these, too, are ever changing.[37] Leadership, then, is an invention – and hence open to re-invention.

This way of thinking about the nature of leadership runs entirely counter to that which dominates contemporary leadership studies where priority is given to determining universal truths about leadership, something assumed to have enduring characteristics and capable of being assessed in objective terms.[38] Here, in contrast, the proposition is that there is no singular, objective truth about leadership 'out there', waiting to be discovered by the deployment of the scientific method. As a consequence, we need to change how we typically go about our thinking about leadership.

Taking on this challenge, I show how adopting this perspective enables theoretical innovation, offering new approaches to leadership which seek to overcome or ameliorate the problematic consequences of current understandings for leaders and followers identified already[39] and explored further here. Liberating leadership thought from the discursive frame in which it is currently trapped, as I seek to do here, therefore supports recent calls for leadership practice that also seeks to liberate.[40] The end result is that this book not only explains why we ought to think differently about leadership but also offers a framework for how we can do just that.

The major limitations of this research pertain to its scope in respect of the periods studied, the data sources used, the themes I focus on and the theoretical framework used to interrogate the data. In all these matters, the research is partial and not comprehensive. While I contend that the conclusions I reach are grounded in a plausible, carefully considered and reasoned interpretation of the data using the theoretical framework I adopted, the material I reviewed is limited in scope and my questions were such as to direct my attention only to some aspects of that material. All research suffers from limitations of this nature.

The major contribution of this research is to place the form and formation of contemporary leadership scholarship in a wider historical context than other studies have done, such that its apparent grounding in modern, scientific and enlightened thinking now seems questionable. The analysis presented here calls into doubt what has been so widely promoted and accepted as truthful and positive in recent decades. My findings give us pause to ask ourselves: have we got it right? Is this approach to leadership really what we need? Denting and de-familiarizing the naturalized, normalized status of contemporary leadership discourse is, thus, the major contribution of this research.

HOW THE BOOK IS ORGANIZED

So far I have offered only an introductory overview of the topic of inquiry and how it is addressed in this book. I have also previewed in summary form what is to be argued. Looking ahead, in Chapter 2 I examine the current state of the leadership literature in considerably more depth, providing a wide overview of different types of leadership knowledge before honing in to highlight the limited and problematic nature of existing, dominant understandings of organizational leadership. Chapters 3 to 6 then offer four 'case studies' of leadership thought at different times. Chapter 3 focuses on the leadership thought of the Classical Greeks, the era of the Athenian democracy. Chapter 4 looks at leadership thought in 16th- and 17th-century Europe, the time of the Renaissance and the Reformation. Chapter 5 examines the origins of modern leadership science found in the work of Thomas Carlyle and the subsequent trait theorists. Chapter 6 then examines the post-World War II period, looking at the dominant theoretical developments from then through to the present-day era in which 'new leadership' thought prevails.

For each of these periods, I look at the problems informing leadership thought and trace how the ideas emerged. I explore the key assumptions the ideas rely on and the key themes being promoted, as well as what the ideas do to and for us. This 'time-travelling' also makes it possible for me to identify both change and continuity over time in leadership thought, so it is this issue which forms the specific focus of Chapter 7. In Chapter 8, I consolidate the key findings in respect of the research questions and offer a new approach to theorizing leadership which arises from the preceding analysis. For readers unfamiliar with the work of Michel Foucault, the Method Notes at the end of the book may prove helpful to explore before you start on my case studies, to familiarize yourself with the Foucauldian concepts and approach shaping my analysis.

WHO THE BOOK IS INTENDED FOR

The book is intended to offer an intellectually rigorous and challenging but still accessible analysis of leadership thought. It does not require or assume any prior knowledge of the periods it examines. It does not require or assume any prior knowledge of leadership theory or of the work of Michel Foucault. Technical terms are kept to a minimum. If you have by and large followed this first chapter then you should encounter no major issues in coping with the rest of the book.

Consequently, then, the book is intended to be suitable for student, scholarly and practitioner audiences as a work whose primary purpose is to get you thinking about leadership by examining how others have been thinking about leadership. For students, the book offers a wide-ranging analysis of influential leadership theories, past and present. It can therefore serve to orient you to the leadership studies field, as well as to enable you to think critically about leadership knowledge more generally, something your teachers will, in all likelihood, actually appreciate and reward.

For critically minded leadership and management scholars, the study here extends existing critique via its examination of times and issues not examined previously, as well as offering a framework to enable localist approaches to leadership theorizing. For more mainstream leadership scholars this book will likely be confronting, for it may challenge many of your key assumptions. However, I hope you find this helpful in sparking reflection on how you approach future research efforts, for if nothing else this book highlights the crucial influence of scholarly assumptions in generating leadership knowledge.

For practitioners in leadership roles, this book does not offer you tips and tactics on how to be a 'better' leader: for that, your local airport bookshop is probably already filled with many such offerings. However, if you have found the expectations held of you as a leader challenging to fulfil, or you are looking for ideas on how to tailor your leadership approach to your own circumstances, then this book should help with those concerns. For practitioners not in leadership roles, this book reveals the problematic assumptions that may be limiting your freedom of action and influencing what you expect of yourself and those who 'lead' you.

For all readers, this book provides a basis for reflecting on what leadership means for you and what expectations you have for it in relation to the diversity of challenges which our communities and organizations encounter. After reading this book, leadership may no longer seem as if it should constitute the answer to every problem, given what I suggest is its typically vexed character. Maybe you will pay greater heed to the trends and events that are simply *far beyond the control of our leaders* no matter how capable they are, this reality being played out in the news every day, if only we care to look. Maybe the development of effective laws and policies to govern behaviour, maybe mass action on the issues we care about, maybe these things will come to seem more potent means of achieving enduring change than the frenetic search for the exceptional few to save us from ourselves. Perhaps too, if our expectations about leaders and leadership become more modest, more accepting that they don't offer us the solution to every problem, we may ask more of ourselves as community members, and at the same time ensure that those we allow into leadership roles are properly held to account against standards that are realistic, not godlike. Leadership is ours to invent, I argue here, so let us invent it with care, seeing it as but one mechanism, one means that may, sometimes, help in addressing our needs, but not the answer to every problem.

NOTES

1. See, for example, Bass, 1985a; Bennis and Nanus, 1985; George, 2003; Kouzes and Posner, 2007
2. Bolden et al., 2011; Jackson and Parry, 2011
3. Alvesson and Kärreman, 2015; Sinclair, 2007
4. Osborn, Hunt and Jauch, 2002; Schruijer and Vansina, 2002
5. See, for example, Bass, 1985a; Kotter, 1996; Kouzes and Posner, 2007
6. Bass, 2008
7. Avolio, Walumbwa and Weber, 2009, p. 423
8. Bennis and Nanus, 1985
9. House, 1977
10. Bass, 1985a
11. Luthans and Avolio, 2003
12. Bryman, 1986; Jackson and Parry, 2011
13. Alvesson and Spicer, 2011a; Bass and Riggio, 2006; Jackson and Parry, 2011
14. Bass, 1985a; Heifetz, 1994; Kouzes and Posner, 2007
15. See, for example, Bass and Steidlmeier, 1999; Bennis and Nanus, 1985; Zaleznik, 1977
16. See, for example, Bass, 2008; Bennis and Nanus, 1985; Kotter, 1988
17. See, for example, Antonakis, Cianciolo and Sternberg, 2004; Bass, 2008; Yukl, 2012
18. Alvesson and Deetz, 2000; Collinson, 2005, 2006
19. See, for example, Alvesson and Sveningsson, 2003a, 2003b, 2003c; Ford, Harding and Learmonth, 2008; Sinclair, 2007
20. Alvesson, 1996; Sinclair, 2007
21. Alvesson and Sveningsson, 2012, p. 209
22. Ford et al., 2008; Sinclair, 2007
23. Kellerman, 2004; Kets de Vries, 2003; Schruijer and Vansina, 2002; Tourish, 2014
24. Alvesson and Sveningsson, 2003a, 2012; Sinclair, 2007
25. Alvesson and Willmott, 1992; Parker, 2002; Russell, 1984
26. Alvesson and Deetz, 2000; Foucault, 1985
27. Foucault, 1972, 1977, 1978
28. See, for example, Fayol, 1930; Taylor, 1919
29. See, for example, Locke, 2010 [1690]; Mill, 1989 [1851]. Original dates of publication are noted in square brackets
30. Foucault, 1977, 1978, 1985, 1986
31. Foucault, 1972; Hacking, 1999
32. Foucault, 1972
33. Foucault, 1972
34. Foucault, 1985, 1986
35. Foucault, 1985, p. 9
36. Alvesson and Deetz, 2000; Dean, 1994
37. Foucault, 1980
38. Alvesson, 1996; Alvesson and Spicer, 2011a; Alvesson and Sveningsson, 2012

39. See, for example, Alvesson and Sveningsson, 2003a, 2003b, 2003c; Ford et al., 2008; Sinclair, 2007
40. Sinclair, 2007

2 Questioning leadership knowledge

[T]he leadership field over the past decade has made tremendous progress in uncovering some of the enduring mysteries associated with leadership . . . The period that leadership theory and research will enter over the next decade is indeed one of the most exciting in the history of this planet. (Avolio et al., 2009, p. 442)

Perhaps one day people will wonder at this . . . People will wonder what could have made us so presumptuous. (Foucault, 1978, pp. 157–158)

INTRODUCTION

My overarching purpose in this chapter is to explain why we ought to wonder about the triumphant stance, exemplified in the quote from Avolio et al. above, which is being taken by mainstream leadership scholars today in respect of leadership and our knowledge of it. I begin, however, by providing an overview of the Western leadership literature so as to orient you to the overall scope and nature of the different approaches to generating leadership knowledge in the Western tradition. Following this, I turn to the social science literature, for which I also provide an orienting overview, before then critically reviewing the state and focus of mainstream contemporary leadership studies. I then adopt a problematizing approach[1] to the assumptions informing this mainstream thought, thereby further building the case for the approach taken in this study. After that, I examine alternative perspectives on leadership and prior analyses of the history of leadership thought, these being the two key literatures from which this study draws and to which it makes a contribution. Finally, I identify how the key findings which arise from this questioning of the literature link directly to the research questions which inform this book.

THE NATURE OF WESTERN LEADERSHIP KNOWLEDGE

Leadership has been studied and analyzed in the West for literally thousands of years.[2] Many of the West's most influential thinkers, scholars such as Plato, Aristotle, Plutarch, Erasmus, Luther, Hobbes and Locke, have turned their minds to the question of who should lead and on what basis – and we will look at some of these contributions in this book. From ancient times till quite recently, moral and political philosophers, historians and practitioners were the primary generators of knowledge about leadership. These days it is social scientists, in particular those with a grounding in psychology, who now produce most of our scholarly leadership knowledge.[3] While these disciplinary divisions are themselves a quite recent way of categorizing knowledge, each of these approaches does, nonetheless, produce particular *kinds* of knowledge and this, in itself, is an important influence on how we approach our thinking about leadership today.

Philosophers have tended toward prescriptive or normative accounts of what leaders should do, or analytic accounts of what leadership entails. Traditionally, many of these scholarly efforts had leaders as their intended audience, as philosophers sought to offer guidance on how leaders should approach their role.[4] Some, such as Plato and Erasmus, took on teaching and mentoring work with leaders, experiences which likely influenced their thinking. This philosophical knowledge is, conventionally, drawn from the philosopher's own reading, observation, experience and reflection. It seeks to use reasoning and argumentation to advance a particular viewpoint, rather than statistical or other empirical evidence.

Historians, meanwhile, have tended to produce accounts of leaders' lives and deeds, with a particular focus on monarchs, politicians and military leaders.[5] In more recent times, business leaders have also become of interest to historians, reflecting and reinforcing the ever increasing influence of business organizations in our lives. The resulting knowledge arising from such efforts is usually richly descriptive, albeit that what is deemed worthy of attention typically reflects the historian's personal assessment as to what they consider interesting. However, historians do not typically seek to produce or advance a theorization of leadership for wider application, focusing instead on describing the case at hand.

Practitioners have also long offered analyses of leadership grounded in their personal experience. Texts of this nature by business leaders are now very popular,[6] whereas in the past political and military leaders tended to be the source of practitioner texts. This literature tends, however, to be anecdotal, idiosyncratic and, at times, hagiographic or self-serving.[7] Where a theorization of leadership is offered, this is normally rooted in the individual experience of the leader, meaning that its wider relevance is untested.

Despite the important contributions that the skills and experiences of philosophers, historians and practitioners can bring to our understanding of leadership, since around the turn of the 20th century it is social scientists who have come to dominate the production of leadership knowledge. This is a dramatic shift in the leadership knowledge-production landscape, moving the centre of the leadership studies field away from a tradition which had prevailed for over 5000 years. Our contemporary thinking about leadership is, moreover, primarily shaped by that tradition within the social sciences which looks to the natural sciences for its inspiration as to what constitutes valid knowledge and how it can be produced.[8]

As a consequence of this orientation, most leadership researchers now seek to produce knowledge which is 'objective' and 'value-free', aiming to identify law-like regularities which are assumed to exist in the social world by use of the hypothetico-deductive method. Practically, this results in a reliance on structured survey instruments that seek to statistically measure and identify relationships between some aspect of leader behaviour and followers' response as the primary means of advancing leadership knowledge.[9] The results of these efforts are expected to be robust, reliable and a matter of 'fact not opinion'.[10] Leadership scientists today, the majority of whom have a grounding in psychology,[11] thus largely focus on the empirical testing of theories which themselves comprise a series of formal hypotheses and, through this, they seek to continuously plug gaps in our understanding of the causes, effects and dimensions of leadership.[12] In amongst all this 'science', the assumptions and political dynamics that I and many others argue unavoidably shape all forms of knowledge production get lost from view, hidden behind a mass of statistical tables. The fundamental limitations of these scientific approaches to generating knowledge in respect of what is a highly contested and complex phenomenon are rarely considered.[13] The interpretivist and critical social science traditions sit largely at the margins of the contemporary leadership studies field.

THE SOCIAL SCIENCE LITERATURE ON LEADERSHIP

The sheer dominance in contemporary leadership studies of social science generally, and psychology-based studies particularly, in and of itself means that our current thinking is limited, or oriented in a particular way. While conventional, positivist social science is very useful for measuring aspects of the social world that are fairly clear and unambiguous, scholars lack broad agreement on the key characteristics, basic nature and origins of leadership and how it may be defined. Questions about what practices or processes it entails generate a multiplicity of competing, irreconcilable views.

As a result of this lack of agreement about fundamental issues, leadership scholars commonly 'adopt' a particular leadership theory which holds some appeal for them and then work at advancing knowledge of that theory: the challenge of which theory, of the many we now have, has the greatest explanatory power is left unexamined. Efforts to develop a general theory of leadership have been abandoned.[14] At best, there is broad agreement that leadership constitutes a relationship or process of influence.[15] However, given that salespeople also influence others this hardly takes us very far.

Despite these serious problems which characterize the mainstream social science literature on leadership, the production of knowledge using the hypothetico-deductive method combined with complex statistical analysis serves to give us a sense that we do now know a lot about leadership and that this knowledge is fundamentally reliable. Numbers reassure us, these days, in a way that a wordy interpretation grounded in reading, observation, experience and reflection struggles to compete with. In pushing the value of philosophical and historical inquiry to the margins of contemporary leadership knowledge, we have, however, turned our backs on over 5000 years of thinking about leadership.

There are, to be clear, three main disciplines which inform the contemporary social scientific study of leadership: political science, sociology and psychology.[16] This *could* imply significant diversity in thinking about leadership and the common use of a multi-disciplinary approach. In the study of organizational leadership, however, psychology constitutes the primary, and often exclusive, disciplinary underpinning.[17]

Political science certainly treats political leadership as a topic within its disciplinary ambit. Specific issues of interest include leaders' strategies, tactics and use of power, analyzing leader styles and specific leaders, the effects of leaders on voter behaviour, and analyzing the formal roles of leaders in different political systems.[18] But while the political science literature makes some limited use of psychological concepts and theories, there is minimal interaction between the political-science-based leadership literature and the psychology-based, organizational leadership literature.[19]

This may in part be due to the much greater use of qualitative research methods within political science, which the psychology-based leadership scholars typically do not favour.[20] Such theory as is produced by political scientists in respect of leadership tends to be conceptual or heuristic in nature,[21] rather than comprising the formal statements of hypothesized relationships which form the basis of most psychology-based leadership theories. Because of this separation between the disciplines, the heightened sensitivity to issues of power in both its structural/institutional and interpersonal dimensions that is typically encouraged via a grounding in political science is absent from most organizational leadership studies and theories.

Meanwhile, the primary contribution from sociology to the modern study of leadership has been Weber's account of charisma.[22] His broad depiction of charisma has subsequently been 'operationalized' according to the standards of psychological research and developed into various formal theories of charismatic leadership.[23] More recent sociologically informed research on leadership tends to be qualitative or conceptual in nature, yet this work, while of growing interest and offering intellectually provocative accounts, has nonetheless had limited influence in the area of organizational leadership.[24] Concerns with power, domination, inequality and exploitation which inform critical studies of leadership are typically founded in sociological understandings of these matters.[25]

Turning to the discipline with the most influence on contemporary understandings of leadership, then, the psychology-based leadership literature, which focuses mostly on leadership in and of organizations, draws primarily on social psychology concepts, constructs and theories, with the key issue of interest being to identify the effects of leaders on followers.[26] Psychological theories and research on personality, behaviour, cognition, motivation, adult development, influence and social process are key influences on this body of literature.[27] Because of its focus on organizational leadership, most of this literature constitutes a specialist area within the broader field of organizational behaviour.[28]

Empirical studies typically focus on testing the effects that formally designated leaders (i.e. managers) within a work organization have on subordinates (designated 'followers'),[29] with the legitimacy of managerial authority going largely unquestioned.[30] Measuring the correlation between leader behaviour and follower motivation, commitment or performance constitutes the primary focus for this body of literature.[31]

The research undertaken by these scholars is mainly survey based and designed to test a specific hypothesis, consistent with the underpinning positivist epistemology being deployed.[32] Psychiatric and psychoanalytic theories have been used in a small number of leadership studies.[33] Some scholars have also adapted formal, quantitative research into prescriptive or heuristic models, often then illustrated by way of case studies. This work is then distributed via books and through consulting work,[34] thereby spreading scholarly ideas to a much broader, practitioner audience.

As with any disciplinary lens, psychology has its strengths and its limitations. It can precisely measure behaviour against a specified model. It can identify patterns in individual and group behaviour for us and then explain these in relation to other psychological factors such as cognition, learning, personality, group psycho-social dynamics, and so forth. Such work serves to identify common patterns in human behaviour. But a psychology-based approach to understanding leadership is not well placed to grapple with the complex and dynamic nature of our broader social context, nor does it routinely generate theories which are sensitized to contextual factors,[35] even though leadership inevitably occurs within and is shaped by these factors. Via its scientistic techniques, psychology offers knowledge which *appears* robust because of its precision, but this same precision is simultaneously blind to contextual influences. One cannot see the wider world through a microscope, but in studying leadership most psychology-based studies deploy a microscopic focus which addresses one or two dimensions and excludes everything else. As a consequence, then, there is a considerable gap between the precision of psychology-based leadership theories and the more messy and ambiguous reality of leadership practice: one disciplinary lens alone cannot offer us an holistic view. The proposition that the detailed analysis of correlations between highly specified constructs offers much by way of genuine insight for action, given that all action is contextually constrained, is therefore one that I question. To take seriously the wider context in which leadership is practiced, we are better off turning to sociology, political science, history and philosophy, yet today most of our thinking about leadership does not draw on these traditions.

Instead, the common aim of much work on organizational leadership is to test and refine formal, psychological theories of leadership and address gaps in existing knowledge, so as to produce greater predictive and prescriptive accuracy and validity.[36] My estimate is that 80 percent or more of contemporary leadership research comes from within this perspective or relies on it. It is this body of literature which therefore constitutes what I term the 'mainstream' of leadership studies and to which I now turn to examine in more depth.

MAINSTREAM LEADERSHIP STUDIES TODAY

Many leaders of world religions, such as Jesus, Mohammed, and Buddha, were transforming. They created visions, shaped values, and empowered change. (Bass, 2008, p. 618)

[E]ffort was being made to reverse this monotonous discourse. (Foucault, 1977, p. 288)

The mainstream of contemporary studies of organizational leadership is the specific literature which concerns me as someone working in the broader field of management and organization studies. This mainstream can currently be characterized as one which is in a state of Kuhnian 'normal science',[37] with scholarly acceptance of key assumptions, theories and methods of inquiry being a marked feature, other than amongst those at the margins of the field who draw on different research traditions. 'New leadership' theories, which emphasize a leader's 'visionary', 'transformational' and 'charismatic' qualities and behaviours, have achieved widespread acceptance amongst mainstream leadership scholars as being fundamentally sound, desirable and valid.[38] The sheer 'monotony' of this discourse, of this way of thinking about leadership, however, makes it particularly worthy of critical scrutiny.

While there is continuing debate over both key concepts and finer points of detail,[39] 'new leadership' thinking nonetheless strongly coheres around the positioning of leaders as highly influential persons capable of bringing about dramatic changes in both followers and organizations.[40] In the various 'new leadership' theories, leaders are said to produce an intensity of impact and connection with followers which unleashes enhanced performance.[41] As the quote at the beginning of this section demonstrates, 'new leadership' thinking has sought to associate itself with the most famous, divinely gifted and revered of persons in all of human history. 'New leadership' is presented as comprising a blend of intellectual, moral and emotional influence, such that followers are moved to pursue the goals articulated by the leader with selfless enthusiasm and determination.[42] Through this experience, followers are said to experience personal growth,[43] facilitating the presentation of 'new leadership' theories as progressive in nature.

The common implication is that what 'new leadership' thinking presents to us is a true account of leadership, a model which is of enduring significance, which has grasped hold of some essential aspect of human nature, where this is assumed to itself be timeless and unchanging.[44] Because of its reliance on these same factors, the development of authentic leadership theory over the last decade[45] can be seen as a continuation of 'new leadership' thinking.

Following an initial period when different 'charismatic', 'visionary' and 'transformational' versions of these theories and their key concepts, constructs and measurement instruments underwent constant development, acceptance of their validity became and remains widespread.[46] Quantitative measurement of the positive effects on followers arising from the leader characteristics and behaviours described in these theories now constitutes the core focus of many empirical studies.[47] Theoretical refinement proceeds incrementally, with the basic ideas, constructs and underpinning assumptions now largely accepted with demur by those applying these theories. Authentic leadership theory, which has only emerged over the last decade, is still in a state of active development. However, it has quickly attracted the attention of influential scholars such as Avolio and Gardner[48] and is being actively promoted to practitioners, despite very limited empirical support to date[49] and significant concerns being raised as to its morality.[50]

With the advent of 'new leadership', the community of leadership scholars saw its field as having reached new heights of theoretical sophistication well in advance of what had been previously achieved.[51] The widespread appeal which 'new leadership' has had with practitioners has been critical in sustaining scholarly support.[52] While the key ideas of 'vision', 'transformation' and 'charisma' are no longer actually 'new', I suggest this framing of these theories as such remains in use because scholars largely believe that 'new leadership' offers approaches to leading which are attuned to the modern organization and business environment. While these theories have 'matured', they have not been seen to have 'aged' or become outdated. Given all this, accounts of developments in the field commonly offer a narrative of current confidence and success as a result of 'new leadership', leaving behind an earlier period of struggle for both credibility and relevance.[53]

The emergence of 'new leadership' has been widely presented and understood as enlightened and modern thinking.[54] Traditional conceptions of management or, for some commentators, management without leadership, have been positioned by proponents of 'new leadership' as constraining, rule-bound, mundane and out of step with the contemporary context.[55] 'Management' alone has thus been held to be incapable of responding to increasingly dynamic market conditions. It is said to be unable to contend with employees seeking to be 'empowered', customers expecting innovation or shareholders demanding dramatic improvements in returns.[56] 'Leadership', in contrast, has been positioned in this literature as liberating for both leader and follower alike, as unleashing the latent potential of both managers and employees which 'management' had suppressed.[57] Leadership has been held up as what is now needed to succeed in this more demanding operating context. A new foundation for the manager–subordinate relationship is said to have been established, one which relies on mutual trust, mutual benefit and the personal growth of both leader and follower.[58] From this, it is claimed that only good things follow.

Interest in leadership amongst both scholars and practitioners has grown rapidly since the mid-1980s with the advent of 'new leadership' thinking.[59] Leadership studies now number in their thousands.[60] Government and business expenditure on leadership development has grown rapidly since the mid-1980s, as have university research and teaching programmes and consulting firms' interest in leadership.[61] The sought-after return on this investment is an increase in both the quantity and quality of leaders who are said to be capable of moving organizations and societies forward in a positive direction and manner.[62]

In reviewing the state of the field in the mid-1990s, Alvesson argued that while 'thousands of studies have been conducted ... (the) outcome of these enormous efforts has been meagre'.[63] He concluded at that time that the 'field fails to meet its own criteria of knowledge accumulation'.[64] He called for a 'radical re-thinking' of the philosophical assumptions and methods used by leadership scholars.[65] Despite this, Jackson and Parry recently concluded that 'hard evidence about the impact of leadership is surprisingly and tantalizingly hard to find',[66] indicating that little has changed since Alvesson's 1996 review. In a more recent assessment, Alvesson and Kärreman go so far as to depict the mainstream of leadership studies as an intellectual failure, one whose appeal and success are founded in ideology alone.[67] However, while leadership is certainly now attracting more critically informed attention, the mainstream view remains remarkably dominant and it is this view with which practitioners are most familiar.[68]

Beyond the academy, conventionally accepted truths about leadership appear strongly tied to the mainstream of leadership scholarship: practitioner discourse, if not practice, has been found to draw heavily on the 'new leadership' terms, concepts and ideas used by researchers.[69] The 'new leadership' theories which have dominated the scholarly literature in recent decades have been very widely disseminated through texts and university programmes aimed at practitioners and have, by and large, become part of the accepted discourse of contemporary managers.[70]

It is, thus, now commonplace to speak of 'management' as being something different from, and inferior to, 'leadership'.[71] Concepts and ideas such as 'visionary' leadership,[72] 'charismatic' leadership,[73] 'transformational' leadership[74] and the leader as 'modelling the way'[75] have become common parlance amongst practitioners.[76] While there are undoubtedly differences in how practitioners may interpret or apply these terms from the precise propositions developed by researchers, practitioners nonetheless have strong reasons for believing that their understanding of leadership is one based on science and all that would normally imply in terms of rigour, objectivity and ethics.

This widely accepted ideal of the manager-as-leader now goes largely unquestioned. 'New leadership' ideas today provide a generally understood and accepted standard against which managers are measured.[77] This approach has, therefore, become both a hegemonic and a disciplinary discourse from which it is increasingly difficult to escape in order to consider alternatives.[78] It is hegemonic in the sense that, despite a proliferation of alternative theories of leadership which have been developed in recent years, the leader as visionary, charismatic, transformational agent remains not just the dominant way of thinking about leadership but also, for many scholars and practitioners, the only way of thinking about leadership.[79]

It is also a disciplinary discourse[80] in that it provides norms and standards of behaviour against which 'good' managers are expected to measure themselves and to then act to close any gaps. Variation from this norm is seen as constituting failure on the part of the manager/leader,[81] while an exploration of different ways of leading is subtly discouraged via the positioning of this account of leadership as 'natural', 'normal', 'modern' and 'progressive'. These expectations are not simply 'a procedure of heroization' in which some are set up as superior to others; they also function as 'a procedure of objectification and subjection', treating leaders and followers as objects of analysis, rendering them subject to, subjectivated by, a specified version of what constitutes an acceptable way of being.[82] Multiple studies conducted by critically oriented scholars, moreover, show us that people cannot live up to these prescriptions – and that they suffer in trying to do so.[83]

Ideas which rely on asserting the naturalness and normality of inequality between persons need to be treated with considerable caution.[84] For centuries, inequalities between men and women and between people of different ethnic or cultural backgrounds have been subject to the defence that these differences are 'natural' and 'normal'.[85] Today, it has become widely accepted as 'natural' and 'normal' that 'charismatic' leader-managers should develop 'visions' which will 'transform' their organizations and their 'followers'. Yet, implicit in this is the idea of leaders as superior beings to whom others ought to defer. What is constructed with 'new leadership' discourse is not only the idea of someone who can both conceive of and execute radical visions for change which others will find inspiring, but also the idea and the ideal of the exceptional few directing the ordinary many. What is implied for most of us is deference and dependence, not democracy, not participation and not self-determination.[86]

With this way of framing the role and potency of leaders, no sector and no issue appear to be beyond the bounds of where leadership might usefully reach, be it climate change, the 'Global Financial Crisis', the performance of your favourite sports team or the election of parent representatives for the school board, leadership is today promoted as being of central importance.[87] Dissemination of these ideas, at least in part via the imprimatur and authority of the university system, makes it seem highly likely that practitioners believe this emphasis on leadership to be one founded on scientific evidence.[88] This way of thinking about leadership is thus presented as 'enlightened' but, at the same time, appears to be quite 'natural' and 'normal' due to its alleged status as a feature common to all times and places; the evocation of great leaders from the past to serve as endorsements for current thinking is a common enough rhetorical move in mainstream accounts of leadership.[89]

In these mainstream studies, doubt is rarely cast on the value and potency of leadership. Bernard Bass, for example, a prominent 'new leadership' scholar, argues that 'in industrial, educational, and military settings, and in social movements, leadership plays a critical, if not the most critical, role'.[90] However, the influence of factors such as organizational systems and processes, technology, competitors, and economic and regulatory conditions are hardly ever accounted for in studies of leadership.[91] The effects of leadership are hardly ever compared with other ways to organize collective effort, such as teamwork.[92] The authority of leaders to influence and potentially change others is almost always treated as an unproblematic imbalance of power in mainstream leadership studies.[93] A unity of interests between leaders and followers is typically taken for granted,[94] despite the obvious political naïvety of so doing.

Mainstream leadership studies are, then, very partial and partisan while claiming to be objective and unbiased. Critique from the margins of the field is largely ignored and has had little impact to date in shifting the mainstream of the field.[95] Leadership typically takes centre stage in formal studies, examined in splendid isolation, largely oblivious of other factors which could affect how people behave and immune from politically informed analysis and critique.[96]

The development of an agreed definition of leadership has proved impossible, despite decades of scientific research.[97] From his analysis of definitions put forward by numerous scholars, Yukl suggests that there is a common theme of conceiving of leadership as an influence process.[98] However, salespeople and advertisers also enact influence processes and they are not normally thought of as leaders. It would therefore seem that this vague consensus definition is unable to distinguish leadership from other influence processes and is of little value. The field of study is, thus, one which examines something it cannot define but which it nonetheless is convinced has the power to overcome everything that troubles us.[99]

Perhaps as a consequence of its ubiquity, the conventional approach now taken to leadership has come to seem natural, normal and self-evident: it simply seems obvious that leadership is important and desirable and that leaders are both entitled and able to bring about change in their followers. This way of thinking, this reification and valorization of leadership, has become so persuasive, pervasive and normalized that it effectively disarms the credibility of any dissenting view.[100] This context is, however, deeply problematic if one expects an objective, impartial scientific approach to the topic: leadership scholars are not removed from, or immune to, societal norms and values, and, indeed, the knowledge produced by these scholars may serve either to reinforce or to challenge those norms and values.[101]

Leadership has, then, come to be portrayed as the solution of choice for every problem facing organizations and societies. It is seen as valuable and desirable for every context, a key driver of results and potent in its effects. Despite the proliferation of definitions even within mainstream leadership literature, leadership is most typically conceptualized as 'leader-ship': what leaders do or who they are. This 'leader-centric', heroic notion of leadership, while regularly criticized, continues to dominate most leadership studies and practitioner understanding. Whether born or made, therefore, it hardly matters, so long as there are leaders to inspire, guide and transform the vast majority of people, who need to be led, whose role is to follow, to be made better than if left to their own devices. The stark inequality in the status, rights and powers of leaders and followers invoked by this way of thinking hides in plain sight, there for all to see but accepted without question. Such is the state of our contemporary truths about leadership.

KEY ASSUMPTIONS IN MAINSTREAM LEADERSHIP STUDIES

Leadership is part and parcel of the human condition. A mystery as modern as the nation state and as ancient as the tribe, it brings together the best and worst in human nature: love and hate, hope and fear, trust and deceit, service and selfishness. Leadership draws on who we are, but it also shapes what we might be – a kind of alchemy of souls that can produce both Lincoln's 'better angels of our nature' and Hitler's willing executioners. (Harvey, 2006, p. 39)

This quote is drawn from a collection of essays written by highly regarded leadership scholars who jointly explored the possibility of developing a general theory of leadership.[102] Hence, it can be read as expressing a view which would likely be taken seriously by mainstream leadership scholars, despite its colourful language. I particularly like that Harvey appreciates that leadership has sometimes been used for nefarious purposes, a recognition lacking in most studies which consider only positive effects,[103] a one-sidedness I continue to find disturbingly naïve. If we accept his ideas at face value, then leadership is enormously important to social well-being and warrants the most serious of attention. However, Harvey also positions leadership as something derived from human nature, as something enduring, timeless, fixed and essential and this, I argue, is problematic.

Like Harvey, most mainstream leadership scholars treat leadership as a natural phenomenon, as part of human nature, which itself is taken to be largely fixed, rather than something malleable and shaped by different cultural milieu.[104] Leadership is also commonly assumed to comprise universal and timeless qualities, to have an 'essence' which is constant and unchanging. Bennis and Nanus argue, for example, 'leadership competencies have remained constant, but our understanding of what it is, how it works, and the way in which people learn to apply it has changed'.[105] Bass asserts that 'leadership is a universal phenomenon. It is not a figment of the imagination'.[106] Given Bass' critical role in advancing transformational leadership theory, it is hardly a stretch to conclude that when he argues that 'leadership is a universal phenomenon', what he is also implying is that transformational leadership is similarly universal.

These assumptions are, however, at odds with the simultaneous claim of mainstream scholars to have discovered brand new approaches to leadership which are of specific practical relevance, right here, right now. They logically lead to the unasked and, for mainstream theorists, extremely awkward question of how far human nature might be flexed to respond to current demands. This a priori expectation that leadership exists *because* it is part of human nature and hence presumed to be enduring, may be so influential in shaping what is observed that leadership is discovered time and time again simply because that is exactly what researchers are primed to see.[107]

These assumptions that leadership is part of human nature and comprises universal and timeless qualities, however, rarely stand alone. Instead, they are typically combined with contradictory assumptions that modern approaches to leadership are new because leadership is amenable to scientific manipulation and able to be adapted to current conditions.[108] These latter assumptions, taken alone, warrant the proliferation of theories and models that exists in the contemporary literature. However, taken in combination, as they typically are, surely demands that attention be paid to determining what it is about leadership that can and cannot be changed, providing a potential boundary for the field of inquiry. This is not so, however, as these contradictory assumptions, which sit at the very heart of contemporary mainstream leadership research, have been left largely unquestioned. The mainstream approach thus effectively seeks to have a dollar both ways in accounting for the basic nature, the ontology, of the phenomena it studies, which is a shaky foundation for a field claiming the status of a science.

It is, of course, very appealing to believe that one is studying something timeless, enduring and essential to the human condition, just as it is very appealing to believe one is at the cutting edge of a scientifically informed approach to shaping leadership for the modern context. However, the two views are logically at odds. They cannot both be true unless one was to (perversely) treat human nature as being endlessly flexible, begging the question as to what value the concept of human nature then adds to our understanding. Nonetheless, mainstream leadership scholarship proceeds by drawing on both of these contradictory assumptions about the very nature of leadership.

This logical contradiction is not the only concern. When it is assumed that leadership is a natural phenomenon, then leadership knowledge produced via the scientific method can be presented as a *discovery*, in the same sense that a biologist might discover something about the functioning of bumblebees and wasps. This conception of leadership knowledge as scientific discovery has the effect of shaping what then constitutes credible, intelligible critique: to critique a 'scientific fact' for its 'facticity', one must proceed along the lines of assessing ontology, epistemology, hypotheses, methodology, methods, data sources, data collection and analytic techniques for their technical and logical rigour.[109] This is a privileged conversation in which only a few can participate. Questions about rights, values and power, for example, may be dismissed as illegitimate in the face of 'scientific discoveries': one cannot argue with credibility that bumblebees should have more power relative to that of wasps.

By conceiving of leadership as a natural phenomenon about which discoveries ought to and can be made, leadership knowledge, and the production of that knowledge, is positioned as an apolitical activity, insofar as nature has no politics and seeking the truth about nature is just good science.[110] The interest given to leadership and our ideas about it can also be seen as natural, constraining both critique and the exploration of alternatives. History also disappears in this perspective, as developments in knowledge are framed as the progressive accumulation of evidence, rather than being understood as moves which act to construct social reality and which are informed by their socio-historical context.

In contrast, if leadership is conceived of as a contingent construct, something fashioned through individual and collective effort in response to a particular social context, knowledge claims about leadership can also readily be seen as contributing to its ongoing construction.[111] Such knowledge claims then have the status of being *inventions*, not discoveries, rendering their unavoidably partisan and partial perspective open to scrutiny.[112] Questions about whose interests are served by a particular invention, why it is relevant now and what effects it creates become legitimized and the ability to ask them is less reliant on specialized knowledge.[113]

Grint has argued that leadership is not amenable to scientific measurement because 'what counts as a "situation" and what counts as the "appropriate" way of leading in that situation are interpretive and contestable issues'.[114] Ford et al., using Derridean methods of analysis, claim that leadership is an empty signifier, a word which can be loaded with different meanings as it bears no direct relationship to some definite object but, rather, exists in discourse, subject to competing claims over its meaning.[115] Ford et al. also suggest that talk of leadership is best conceived of as identity work. Alvesson,[116] and Alvesson and Sveningsson,[117] have also objected to claims of leadership as having fixed, essential qualities or as involving definite practices, suggesting it be understood as a discursive resource and regime. However, to date these findings have not impacted on mainstream leadership studies.

The bulk of contemporary leadership research, then, proceeds on the basis of problematic assumptions which it compounds through its claims to have *discovered* the truth about the nature of leadership. Here, I am seeking to demonstrate an alternative view: that 'leadership' is contingently constructed.[118] The proposition is that leadership scholarship contributes to the ongoing *invention* of leadership. The book explores the pathways such inventions have followed, analyzing what has triggered them, what they entail and their effects. The value in considering what scholars thought was the truth about leadership at different times from our own is that it provides a comparison for seeing more clearly our contemporary constructions as such.[119]

The various problems I have indicated which arise from the adoption by mainstream leadership scholars of a naturalistic, essentialist and scientistic conception of leadership and its study constitute a key reason for the approach taken here. If it is assumed that leadership is given by nature and the aim is to discover facts about its nature, important questions will simply elude us. Moreover, if we treat leadership today as something both natural (and therefore old) and, simultaneously, as something new, then we are trapped in a logical contradiction that cannot be reconciled. If, instead, we treat leadership as something that is contingently constructed and seek to understand its construction, then we are better placed to question the received wisdom of our own time.

ALTERNATIVE PERSPECTIVES ON LEADERSHIP

There is a small but now rapidly growing body of literature which conceptualizes and studies leadership in ways that seek to avoid the problems which plague mainstream leadership studies. Some of this work is overtly critical in its orientation, by which I mean it is strongly informed by sociological and political theories and concerns about such matters as power, inequality, identity, subjectivity, exploitation, oppression and domination. It often forms part of a wider project to critically analyze contemporary workplaces and managerialist and capitalist discourses and practices with a view to promoting fundamental change in the way in which society is presently organized and functions.[120] Other work that offers alternative ways of thinking about leadership is more interpretive in orientation, meaning that its goal is to enhance our understanding of the complex, ambiguous nature of the social world and the people who inhabit it, focusing on the meanings we draw from our experiences.

The critical/interpretive distinction I make here is, of course, quite fine-grained and certainly not rigid: some work may be both critical and interpretive in orientation. Nonetheless, if we may speak of there being two strands of alternative thinking, despite the differences in their research goals both frequently draw on post-structuralist and postmodern understandings of the self as something that is always under construction, which is shaped by relations with others and which is fragmented rather than unitary in its character.[121] Both strands tend to emphasize interaction and communication as central but always contested features of human life. And for both, language is typically understood not as representative of reality but as constructing reality.[122]

Looking first at critically oriented leadership studies, these alert us to various troubling effects at macro (societal), meso (organizational) and micro (individual) levels which arise from mainstream understandings and approaches to leadership. Of basic concern is a tendency toward 'talking up' the value and impact of leadership in a way that simplifies and distorts reality. This 'romantic' bias results in the habitual attribution of positive outcomes to leaders, irrespective of other influences on the results achieved and evidence about those influences.[123] Negative outcomes are also less likely to be attributed to leaders, again irrespective of evidence.[124] This bias constitutes a societal/cultural norm which routinely distorts our understanding of leadership. It means we commonly credit leaders with having more influence over events and results than they really do,[125] and we incline to letting leaders off the hook when they do err, attributing failure or problems to factors other than the leader.[126]

We cannot simply assume that leadership researchers are immune to this bias, indeed the marked tendency to research the expected positive effects of leadership and only rarely consider its potentially negative effects[127] suggests there is no such immunity. There is a clear risk, moreover, of a reinforcement effect as the body of leadership research grows: the more we speak of the positive effects of leadership, the more likely we become to think of leadership only in respect of its positive effects and the more likely we are to think that leadership is only ever a positive thing. Thought itself thus becomes disciplined in a particular vein and alternative perspectives become harder to imagine, much less implement, when a particular way of understanding and organizing the world has such a hold on us.[128]

Perhaps as a consequence of this distorting cultural norm, the emphasis on the heroic individual which we see in contemporary leadership discourse has a strong, seductive appeal, one which incites managers to produce themselves as exceptional, compelling individuals.[129] This same seductive appeal arises in leadership development, where aspiring leaders are incited to feel 'transported out of the ordinary' and to 'feel blessed' by the experience of becoming leaders.[130] Fantasy and grandiosity thus prevail as a consequence of these forces, not humility nor a shared sense of reality grounded in dialogue with diverse others. To think of oneself as a leader implies crafting a self-image as one who is not just different from others but also better than others, one who is blessed, exceptional and compelling, no longer weighed down by the sufferings and frailties of the non-leader. Leadership practice, however, is a site of ongoing struggle, where the dialectics of consent/dissent, control/resistance and men/women are continuously in tension,[131] hence striving to sustain this blessed state is a fraught experience. Cult-like organizational cultures, risky decision-making and the suppression of dissenting viewpoints are, moreover, what arise when leaders' self-image and self-belief are distorted in this narcissistic manner.[132] The logical consequence of our current way of thinking about leadership, then, is to encourage leaders to develop a grandiose self-image and to lead in dangerous and damaging ways.

Simultaneously, people encounter many difficulties in living up to the idealized, distorted accounts of leadership which are foisted upon them. Managers, for example, have great difficulty in describing coherently what they actually do as leaders and what leadership is.[133] Talk of 'leadership' constitutes a discursive resource to help bolster a fragile sense of professional identity, as well as enhancing managerial legitimacy and status,[134] even at the same time as it constitutes a source of existential pressure, as managers struggle to maintain a leader identity in the face of theories which offer an image of perfection to which they are expected to aspire.[135] The validity and utility of 'leadership' as a useful way of understanding the prosaic and often mundane daily reality of managerial work, where budgets, rosters and solving practical problems of production and service delivery are so central, are doubtful.[136]

Gendered assumptions and expectations embedded in conventional understandings of leadership mean that female leaders commonly engage in behaviours which conform to stereotypical expectations of women, so our conventional ideas about leadership harm what would otherwise constitute an important 'source of self-esteem' for women.[137] Growing calls by mainstream scholars for leaders to display their 'authentic' self, a self which is to be manufactured to align to a specified model of what is deemed to constitute authenticity, are existentially impossible demands, placed on managers who feel they must comply with them.[138] The generation of such unrealistic and harmful expectations by scholars is deeply problematic and arguably immoral.[139]

Critical scholars, then, argue that mainstream thinking about leadership is commonly both distorted and distorting.[140] Some people are seduced by the hype of this (distorted) thinking about leadership,[141] such that they (distortedly) come to see themselves and act as if they are 'God's gift', and in doing so create harm and danger for others.[142] Others strive and struggle to live up to the hype, seeking to prop themselves up by recourse to the (distorted) belief in the potency of leadership, but also repeatedly falling short of that ideal and then judging themselves as deficient beings in consequence: the experience of trying to be a 'leader' thus repeatedly distorts their sense of self and their self-confidence.[143] As a result of all this, we may conclude that these current ideals about leadership are a source of danger and harm.

Examination of how this state of affairs has arisen has had some attention from critically oriented scholars.[144] Crucial connections between leadership thought and contemporaneous social, political and economic trends have been identified, pointing to a dynamic relationship between the broader social context and how leadership is conceived at different times. Simon Western links shifts in leadership thought to different stages of industrial development throughout the 20th century, revealing a relationship between modes of production and modes of leading.[145] Knights and Morgan connect the focus on strategic leadership which emerged in the 1990s to wider managerial debates and practices in vogue at that time.[146] Sinclair links the growth in interest in leadership in the latter half of the 20th century to its connection with business interests more broadly, resulting in a situation whereby 'capitalism and the managerial agenda have installed many assumptions into leadership, focusing it especially on the heroic performance of the individual'.[147] However, Trethewey and Goodall Jnr highlight how these linkages are not normally acknowledged, arguing that

> theories of leadership provide a story that is largely ahistorical. Divorced from the social and cultural discourses that shaped them, disconnected from the political and economic realities that surrounded their making, and seemingly immaculate in their conception as ideas, these free-floating signifiers we call theories of leadership are the bastard children of all that has been omitted from their lineage.[148]

As historians have long argued, if we do not know our past then we likely cannot make sense of our present in order to seek to influence our future. These existing critical histories suggest that there is a much richer story that we need to understand if we are to make sense of where we now find ourselves and identify ways of bringing about change.

Overall, critical leadership studies reveal that difficulties and dangers are associated with trying to live up to the heroic ideals which characterize 'new leadership' thought,[149] as well as highlighting how the relationship between leadership theorizing and the wider social context is often ignored.[150] Meanwhile, direct attempts to shift the field's focus away from its leader-centricity has seen 'leader*ship*'[151] being increasingly examined for its complex, emergent, discursive and relational characteristics.[152] These, mostly interpretive, efforts offer a fundamentally different foundation for theorizing than has dominated leadership studies to date, so I turn now to consider this strand in the literature.

From this perspective, leader-centric theories are inadequate explanations of the leadership phenomenon, with their universalist, leader-focused lens unable to grasp at the dynamic, contextually specific interplay between leaders and followers, in which influence flows in multiple directions and sense making is co-constructed in an emergent manner.[153] These alternative bases for understanding leadership are typically grounded in social-constructionist assumptions and often privilege interaction, or 'small-d' discourse,[154] as both the basis for studying leadership and as the key medium through which leadership is enacted.[155]

Deploying this approach, leadership can be understood as a continually negotiated relationship, with the capacity to influence others an unstable dynamic entailing actions and interactions which shape how reality comes to be understood.[156] This forging of a shared understanding and determining priorities for action are, then, seen as being co-created in such a manner as to indicate that leadership is an emergent process.[157] More commonly, here, the self of the leader and the follower are understood as being always in a state of 'becoming', continuously being worked on by itself and others.[158]

Findings of this nature are, intellectually, a stab to the heart of the intensely agentic, self-sufficient, fully formed leader self who, with their prescribed personal characteristics, skills and attributes, sits elevated, at centre-stage of the most influential theories in the field.[159] From this perspective, we are to understand the leadership stage as cluttered with other actors and their agendas, while the leader is one in continuous struggle with this and with 'pulling off' a leader identity.[160] The focus of this literature is primarily on talk-in-interaction, which orients it to examining the micro level of social relations.[161] The aim is typically to theorize the practices and processes deployed in the enactment of leadership relationships.

Amongst all this, some efforts particularly stand out as offering new ways of conceptualizing and theorizing leadership that draw inspiration from history and philosophy and not just psychology: something I have earlier suggested is much needed. Keith Grint, for example, has formulated a variety of different ways of understanding leadership. In *The Arts of Leadership*, he proposes that we understand leadership as a socially constructed and contested terrain which involves, most centrally, an ongoing engagement between leaders and followers over questions of identity (who we are), strategic vision (where we are going) and tactics (how will we get there), and which is reliant on the leader's ability to engage in persuasive communication 'to ensure followers actually follow'.[162] These matters, he argues, in turn give rise to the four arts which inform the practice of leadership, namely philosophy, the fine arts, the martial arts and the performing arts.[163] He elucidates the potency of this theorization through detailed case studies of historical events and of specific high-profile leaders.

In a later effort to further re-think leadership, Grint used historical case studies to develop and demonstrate a contextually sensitive heuristic model which acknowledges the common connection of 'leadership' with formal authority in organizations and hence with both 'management' and 'command'.[164] In this model, he proposes that choosing between 'leadership', 'management' and 'command' ought to be informed by an analysis as to whether the challenge at hand is understood as being 'wicked', 'tame' or 'critical' in nature, this understanding being itself a contested process. In yet another work, he proposed that leadership is an 'essentially contested concept' but that it typically involves ideas about leadership as to do with person, result, position and process.[165] In order to overcome these limited frameworks for understanding, Grint foregrounds the paradoxes involved in leadership, its hybrid nature as it connects people, processes and technologies and the difficulties in assessing cause and effect when it comes to leadership. He advocates that the ethical assessment of leaders relies both on the results achieved and on followers, from whom leaders learn how to lead. He also proposes that leadership is a function of what goes on in the interaction between leaders and followers, this now being the focus of relational theories of leadership.[166] In all these accounts, what Grint offers is a less grandiose and anti-essentialist account of leadership. What he provides are broad frameworks for guiding our understanding, an approach which is in sharp contrast to the tightly defined and parsimonious propositions that constitute the social scientist's conventional way of theorizing. Rather than technical precision, the aim is to offer a richer yet less prescriptive mode of knowing.

Ladkin also offers a non-conventional account of both how we might come to understand leadership and how it might most usefully be practiced.[167] Drawing on Husserl's phenomenological framework, Ladkin argues that leadership is a phenomenon which involves multiple dimensions in which the perception of the perceiver is of central significance. She also foregrounds a focus on purpose, wisdom and the leader–follower relationship in her account, which she frames as an attempt to offer new answers to old questions. For Ladkin, like Grint, there is no one correct approach to leadership, nor a precise manner in which it may be defined or observed, although there are ethical boundaries within which leadership should function. These perspectives, then, fly in the face of mainstream thinking which constantly seeks precision in its analysis of leadership.

Sinclair has also sought to move beyond conventional analyses to offer a new way of understanding leadership that is grounded in humanistic concerns and values.[168] She argues for the importance of psychoanalytic factors as a source of our fears and desires in respect of leadership. In addressing the problematic of power, Sinclair offers a framework of options involving advocacy of change, covert subversion, activism, critique, collaboration and experimentation as productive ways of working with power. In drawing attention to the embodied nature of leadership practice, Sinclair draws on her experience as a yoga practitioner and her study of various Eastern philosophies, connecting leadership to issues of breath, mindfulness, spirituality and the letting go of the ego which such perspectives offer. Infused throughout Sinclair's efforts to re-conceptualize leadership is a concern to overcome the gendered assumptions which are embedded in conventional understandings while also grounding our understanding of leadership in a focus on the purposes or ends that it serves.

What Grint, Ladkin and Sinclair offer, then, are in-depth attempts to reconceptualize leadership in ways that overcome or move away from the problematic assumptions and effects they see as dominating current understandings. These examples serve as inspiration for this study, albeit that my analysis focuses principally on how we may think about leadership, our discourse, as the foundation from which practice emerges. In their most recent assessment of the state of critically informed leadership research, Alvesson and Sveningsson note that inquiry into the 'culture- and discourse-driven nature of leadership is neglected in most of the literature'.[169] My aim here is to go some way towards redressing this neglect.

THE HISTORY OF LEADERSHIP THOUGHT

There are many historical texts which consider leadership. Notable philosophers such as Plato, Aristotle, Lao Tzu, Sun Tzu, Seneca, Cicero, Machiavelli, Montesquieu, Locke and Hobbes are all known to have addressed different aspects of what we today call leadership. Added to these is the vast number of written histories from Herodotus (ca. 484–425 BC) and Plutarch (ca. 46–120 AD) onwards, which focus on the character and deeds of monarchs, politicians and military leaders.[170] Collectively, these works can be understood as constituting a widely diffused and inchoate 'history of ideas' about leadership, for in these texts we find something of what has been thought about leadership. For the purposes of this study, however, texts of this nature actually constitute data, rather than literature, for these texts typically analyze leadership rather than the history of *thinking* about leadership.

Remarkably little effort has been made over the last century to analyze the history of thinking about leadership.[171] This may be due to a perception that leadership ideas from times past are now irrelevant or of dubious credibility, not having been produced in accordance with modern scientific methods. Ideas from the past have at times been used as inspiration for contemporary work, and it is not unheard of for scholars to imply that their thinking connects in some ways with the 'great minds' of the past.[172] However, the focus over the last century in social science-based studies of leadership has been to produce 'new knowledge' and new theories.[173]

While scholars frequently chart developments in social scientific studies of leadership, the aim is typically to identify the gap which their own study or theory will address, or to provide a descriptive account of major developments within the field.[174] Work of this nature does not generally seek to trouble the assumptions contained within the literature in order to subject it to fresh analysis, nor does it seek to situate leadership within its wider social context.[175] Instead, such accounts typically produce a progressivist narrative of increasing enlightenment in our understanding of leadership, portraying today's knowledge as superior to that of the past.[176] Consequently, there is a need to find some way of disrupting this progressivist narrative and offering an alternative interpretation of developments in the field.

Only rarely have modern leadership scholars sought to critically analyze the history of thinking about leadership and the analysis which has been done to date is quite limited in its scope. Knights and Morgan address the 'strategic leadership' discourse since the mid-1980s.[177] Trethewey and Goodall Jnr focus on changes in leadership theories in post-World War II USA, identifying social and political factors which, they argue, were important in rendering those theories relevant.[178] Western considered theoretical paradigm shifts in leadership knowledge over the course of the 20th century, linking these to changing production methods, the workings of capitalism and theoretical shifts in the human sciences.[179] However, the scope and focus of these analyses are, as is unavoidably the case, limited. Here, I offer an alternative scope and focus of analysis which ventures into times and issues not previously addressed.

CONCLUSION

While there traditionally existed a strong moral and political philosophy base to the Western study of leadership, today it is the psychology-based study of organizational leadership which dominates our understanding. Most leadership research today is being produced via positivist and quantitative methods of inquiry which are poorly designed to cope with dynamic, complex contexts and hence we see the widespread use of reductionist techniques, isolating tightly specified aspects of social reality for interrogation. Utilizing these methods of inquiry and knowledge accumulation, 'new leadership' theories have matured to such a degree that their key claims are now widely accepted amongst scholars and dominate the field. Consequently, a state of 'normal science' currently prevails in mainstream leadership studies: the field is predominantly focused on a small number of key ideas and relies on a limited set of ontological and epistemological assumptions and methodologies. Despite the extensive nature of this literature, the knowledge it produces is, thus, profoundly narrow in nature and, as my analysis has shown, it rests on some problematic assumptions.

The key 'new leadership' ideas about leaders who are 'visionary', 'charismatic' and 'transformational' have been widely promulgated and have come to constitute the disciplinary norm for many practitioners. 'New leadership' has also come to be understood as a highly valued and potent force for good, with little questioning going on as to why this is so and what problematic effects may arise from this. Given all these factors, it has become increasingly difficult to conceive of alternatives to our current dependence on leaders as offering the answer to every problem. Critically informed examination of the form and formation of this way of thinking is therefore necessary.

Critically oriented studies reveal leadership as a site of ambiguity, struggle and tension where 'new leadership' models incite narcissistic and irresponsible leadership. Meanwhile, alternatives to the leader-centric notions which dominate the field are also developing, highlighting the relational, emergent co-production of meaning and results as a different way of understanding leadership. Some important connections between developments in leadership thought and the wider social context have been identified, but much more can yet be done to enrich our understanding of how and why we understand leadership in the way we now do. While the critical literature is limited in its scope, the findings to date are provocative, for they indicate that the conventional narrative of leadership science as a progressive, humanistic endeavour is a profoundly problematic account.

The concerns I have raised throughout this chapter, with respect to our existing understanding of leadership, motivate and inform the question which shapes and guides this book, namely: why has our understanding of leadership come to take the form it now does? What I explore here is the back-story which has led us to our current situation, demonstrating why we must and how we can focus our efforts on thinking differently about leadership. The scope of analysis is broad in terms of the time horizon covered and, simultaneously, detailed in respect of the particular dimensions I focus attention on. I put leadership thought in context, looking at the 'problems' which leadership scholars have sought to address. I address the key themes and assumptions we find in the history of leadership thought, the subjectivities and relationships incited and produced by this thought, its social function, and look at which aspects of it have changed or remained the same over time. For those wanting to understand in more depth the Foucauldian framework which informs these analytic moves, the Method Notes at the end of the book will assist in this and should be your next step. Otherwise, in the next chapter I turn to my first case study of leadership discourse which looks at the leadership thought of the Classical Greeks. What we find in the era of Athenian democracy is a truth about leadership which seeks to undermine the validity of democratic rule.

NOTES

1.　Sandberg and Alvesson, 2010
2.　Adair, 2002; Avery, 2004; Bass, 2008
3.　Bass, 2008; Hargrove, 2004; Schruijer and Vansina, 2002
4.　Annas and Waterfield, 1995; Jardine, 2010
5.　Hargrove, 2004; Schruijer and Vansina, 2002
6.　Guthey, Clark and Jackson, 2009
7.　Jackson and Parry, 2011
8.　Alvesson, 1996
9.　Bryman, 2004; Hunter, Bedell-Avers and Mumford, 2007; Schruijer and Vansina, 2002
10.　Atwater et al., 2014, p. 1174
11.　Gardner et al., 2010
12.　Avery, 2004; Bass, 2008; Northouse, 2004
13.　Collinson, 2011; Schruijer and Vansina, 2002; Western, 2007
14.　Goethals and Sorenson, 2006
15.　Yukl, 1999
16.　Bass, 2008; Gardner et al., 2010; Lowe and Gardner, 2000
17.　Collinson, 2011; Schruijer and Vansina, 2002
18.　See, for example, Barber, 1992; Goodin and Klingeman, 1996; Roskin et al., 2000; Wolff, 2006
19.　Gardner et al., 2010; Lowe and Gardner, 2000
20.　Antonakis et al., 2004; Bryman, 2004; Gardner et al., 2010
21.　See, for example, Barber, 1992; Quatro and Sims, 2008; Wolff, 2006

22. Eisenstadt and Weber, 1968
23. See, for example, Conger, 1989; Conger and Kanungo, 1987; House, 1977
24. Alvesson, 1996; Sinclair, 2007; Western, 2007
25. Alvesson and Sveningsson, 2012; Bolden et al., 2011; Collinson, 2011
26. Avolio et al., 2009; Bass, 1985a; Bolden et al., 2011
27. Avolio et al., 2009; Bass, 2008; Yukl, 2012
28. Huczynski and Buchanan, 2006; Jackson and Parry, 2011; Northouse, 2004
29. See, for example, Wang and Howell, 2012; Zhang, Tsui and Wang, 2011; Zhu et al. 2011
30. Alvesson and Spicer, 2012; Hunter et al., 2007
31. Alvesson and Sveningsson, 2012; Gardner et al., 2010; Schruijer and Vansina, 2002
32. Bolden et al., 2011; Bryman, 2004; Gardner et al., 2010
33. See, for example, Gabriel, 1997; Kets de Vries, 2003, 2006
34. See, for example, Goleman, Boyatzis and McKee, 2002; Kotter, 1988
35. Osborn, Hunt and Jauch, 2002; Schuijer and Vansina, 2002
36. Antonakis et al., 2004; Avolio et al., 2009; Bass, 2008
37. Kuhn, 1996
38. Bass, 2008; Fletcher, 2004; Jackson and Parry, 2011
39. For an overview, see Yukl, 1989, 1999, 2012
40. See, for example, Bass and Riggio, 2006; Goleman et al., 2002; Kouzes and Posner, 2007
41. See, for example, Bass, 1985b; Bass and Riggio, 2006; Conger, 1989
42. See, for example, Bass and Riggio, 2006; Bennis and Nanus, 1985; Burns, 1978
43. See, for example, Bass, 1985a; Bass and Steidlmeier, 1999; Burns, 1978
44. Alvesson and Sveningsson, 2012; Bolden et al., 2011; Collinson, 2011
45. See, for example, Avolio and Gardner, 2005; Gardner, Avolio and Walumbwa, 2005
46. Bass, 2008; Bolden et al., 2011; Jackson and Parry, 2011; although, for a recent critique of the predominant instrument measurement used for studies of transformational leadership, see Van Knippenberg and Sitkin, 2013, and subsequent commentary by Alvesson and Kärreman, 2015
47. See, for example, Braun et al., 2013; Hu et al. 2012; Wang and Howell, 2012
48. See, for example, Avolio et al. 2004
49. Caza and Jackson, 2011; Jackson and Parry, 2011
50. Ford and Harding, 2011
51. See, for example, Antonakis, Cianciolo and Sternberg, 2004; Bass, 1985a; Hunt, 1999
52. Hunt, 1999; Jackson and Parry, 2011
53. See, for example, Antonakis, Cianciolo and Sternberg, 2004; Avery, 2004; Hunt, 1999
54. See, for example, Bass, 1985a; Bennis and Nanus, 1985; Kotter, 1988
55. See, for example, Bass and Riggio, 2006; Peters and Austin, 1985; Zaleznik, 1977
56. See, for example, Bennis and Nanus, 1985; Kotter, 1988; Peters and Austin, 1985
57. See, for example, Burns, 1978; Collins, 2001; Goleman et al., 2002
58. See, for example, Bass, 1985a; Bennis and Nanus, 1985; Burns, 1978
59. Bass, 2008; Jackson and Parry, 2011; Northouse, 2004
60. Antonakis, Cianciolo and Sternberg, 2004; Avery, 2004; Jackson and Parry, 2011
61. Jackson and Parry, 2011; Sinclair, 2007; Tourish, Craig and Amernic, 2010
62. See, for example, Bass, 1999; Kotter, 1996; Kouzes and Posner, 2007
63. 1996, p. 457
64. 1996, p. 457
65. 1996, p. 458
66. 2011, p. 7
67. 2015
68. Alvesson and Spicer, 2011a; Bolden et al., 2011; Collinson, 2011
69. Alvesson and Sveningsson, 2003a, 2003b; Ford et al., 2008; Grugulis, Bozkurt and Clegg, 2010
70. Alvesson and Sveningsson, 2003b, 2003c; Bolden et al., 2011; Jackson and Parry, 2011
71. See, for example, Bennis and Nanus, 1985; Goleman et al., 2002; Zaleznik, 1977
72. Bennis and Nanus, 1985

73. Conger, 1989; House, 1977
74. Bass, 1985a; Burns, 1978
75. Kouzes and Posner, 2007
76. Alvesson and Sveningsson, 2003a, 2003b, 2003c; Ford et al., 2008; Grugulis et al., 2010
77. Bolden et al., 2011; Ford et al., 2008; Jackson and Parry, 2011
78. Alvesson and Willmott, 1992; Collinson, 2012
79. Alvesson and Spicer, 2011a; Collinson, 2011; Ospina and Uhl-Bien, 2012
80. Foucault, 1977, 1978, 1980
81. Ford et al., 2008; Sinclair, 2007
82. Foucault, 1977, p. 192
83. See, for example, Alvesson and Sveningsson, 2003a, 2003b, 2003c; Ford et al., 2008;
     Nicholson and Carroll, 2013
84. Alvesson and Deetz, 2000; Alvesson and Willmott, 1992
85. See, for example, Filmer, 2004 [1648]; Plato, 2007. Original date of publication is noted
     in square brackets
86. Fletcher, 2004; Gemmill and Oakley, 1992; Western, 2007
87. See, for example, Bass and Riggio, 2006; George, 2003; Goleman et al., 2002
88. Alvesson and Spicer, 2011a; Tourish et al., 2010
89. See, for example, Adair, 2002; Burns, 1978; Wren, 2005
90. 2008, p. 25
91. Pfeffer, 1977; Porter and McLaughlin, 2006
92. Alvesson and Sveningsson, 2003a; Pfeffer, 1977; Schruijer and Vansina, 2002
93. See, for example, Bass, 1985a; Kotter, 1988; Peters and Austin, 1985
94. Calás, 1993; Collinson, 2005; Trethewey and Goodall Jnr, 2007
95. Collinson, 2011; Jackson and Parry, 2011; Sinclair, 2007
96. Alvesson and Sveningsson, 2012; Pfeffer, 1977; Porter and McLaughlin, 2006
97. Bass, 2008; Jackson and Parry, 2011; Rost, 1993
98. 1989
99. Alvesson, 1996; Alvesson and Sveningsson, 2003a, 2012; Ford et al., 2008
100. Alvesson and Deetz, 2000
101. Alvesson, 1996; Barker, 2001; Gemmill and Oakley, 1992
102. See Goethals and Sorenson, 2006
103. Alvesson and Spicer, 2011b; Ford et al., 2008; Schruijer and Vansina, 2002
104. See, for example, Adair, 2002; Bass, 2008; Bennis and Nanus, 1985; see also Alvesson,
     1996; Alvesson and Sveningsson, 2012
105. 1985, p. 3
106. 2008, p. 25
107. Alvesson, 1996; Alvesson and Deetz, 2000
108. See, for example, Adair, 2002; Bass, 2008; Northouse, 2004
109. Alvesson, 1996; Foucault, 1970, 1972
110. Alvesson, 1996; Alvesson and Deetz, 2000; Foucault, 1970, 1972
111. Alvesson and Deetz, 2000; Schruijer and Vansina, 2002
112. Foucault, 1970, 1972
113. Alvesson, 1996; Alvesson and Deetz, 2000; Foucault, 1970, 1972
114. 2000, p. 3
115. 2008
116. 1996
117. 2003a, 2003b, 2012
118. Alvesson, 1996; Alvesson and Sveningsson, 2003a, 2003b, 2012
119. Foucault, 1985, 1986
120. Alvesson and Spicer, 2011b; Bolden et al., 2011; Collinson, 2011
121. Alvesson and Deetz, 2000; Alvesson and Skoldberg, 2000
122. Alvesson and Deetz, 2000; Collinson, 2011
123. Meindl, Ehrlich and Dukerich, 1985; Meindl and Ehrlich, 1987
124. Meindl et al., 1985; Meindl and Ehrlich, 1987

125. Pfeffer, 1977; Salancik and Pfeffer, 1977
126. Meindl et al., 1985; Meindl and Ehrlich, 1987
127. Alvesson, 1996; Alvesson and Kärreman, 2015
128. Foucault, 1977, 1978
129. Calás and Smircich, 1991; Ford and Harding, 2007; Ford et al., 2008
130. Sinclair, 2009, p. 281
131. Collinson, 2005, 2006
132. Tourish, 2014
133. Alvesson and Sveningsson, 2003a; Ford et al., 2008
134. Alvesson and Sveningsson, 2003a
135. Ford et al., 2008
136. Alvesson and Sveningsson, 2003a; Ford and Harding, 2007
137. Sinclair, 1998, p. 173
138. Ford and Harding, 2011
139. Ford and Harding, 2011
140. Calás and Smirchich, 1991; Meindl et al., 1985; Meindl and Ehlich, 1987
141. Calás and Smirchich, 1991; Sinclair, 2009
142. Tourish, 2014
143. Alvesson and Sveningsson, 2003a; Ford et al., 2008; Sinclair, 1998
144. See, for example, Knights and Morgan, 1992; Trethewey and Goodall Jnr, 2007; Sinclair, 2007; Western, 2007
145. 2007
146. 1992
147. 2007, p. 28
148. 2007, p. 457
149. See, for example, Alvesson and Sveningsson, 2003a, 2003b, 2003c; Ford et al., 2008; Sinclair, 2007; Tourish, 2014
150. See, for example, Knights and Morgan, 1992; Sinclair, 2007; Trethewey and Goodall Jnr, 2007; Western, 2007
151. Grint, 2005a
152. Fairhurst, 2007; Ospina and Sorensen, 2007; Uhl-Bien and Ospina, 2012; Uhl-Bien, Russ and McKelvey, 2007
153. Fairhurst, 2007, 2009; Fairhurst and Grant, 2010; Sutherland, Land and Böhm, 2014; Shamir, 2007; Tourish, 2014; Uhl-Bien and Pillai, 2007
154. Alvesson and Kärreman, 2000; Fairhurst and Putnam, 2004
155. Collinson, 2011; Fairhurst, 2007; Kelly, 2008; Ospina and Sorensen, 2007
156. Ospina and Sorensen, 2007; Smircich and Morgan, 1982; Tourish, 2014; Uhl-Bien and Ospina, 2012
157. Grint, 2000; Ladkin, 2010; Wodak, Kwon and Clarke, 2011
158. Ford et al., 2008; Hosking, 2007; Ospina and Uhl-Bien, 2012
159. Bass, 2008; Northouse, 2010; Sinclair, 2008
160. Ford and Harding, 2011; Kelly, 2008
161. Alvesson and Deetz, 2000; Alvesson and Willmott, 2012
162. 2000, p. 27
163. Grint, 2000
164. 2005a
165. Grint, 2005b, p. 1
166. Uhl-Bien and Ospina, 2012
167. 2010
168. 2008
169. 2012, p. 209
170. See also, for example, Carlyle, 1993 [1840]; Hook, 1945; Olechnowicz, 2007
171. Schruijer and Vansina, 2002
172. See, for example, Adair, 2002; Burns, 1978
173. Antonakis et al., 2004; Bass, 2008; Northouse, 2004

174. See, for example, Conger, 1999; House and Aditya, 1997; Hunt, 1999
175. Schruijer and Vansina, 2002; Sinclair, 2007
176. See, for example, Antonakis et al., 2004; Bass, 2008; Northouse, 2004
177. 1992
178. 2007
179. 2007

3 The Classical Greek truth about leadership

> The society we have described can never grow into a reality or see the light of day, and there will be no end to the troubles of states, or indeed . . . of humanity itself, till philosophers become kings in this world, or till those we now call kings and rulers really and truly become philosophers, and political power and philosophy thus come into the same hands, while the many natures now content to follow either to the exclusion of the other are forcibly debarred from doing so. This is what I have hesitated to say for so long, knowing what a paradox it would sound; for it is not easy to see that there is no other road to real happiness either for society or the individual. (Socrates, in Plato, *The Republic*, 473d)

INTRODUCTION

According to the above, it is only when a leader with great wisdom and unlimited authority is in charge that the well-being of humanity can be achieved. Effective leadership here rests on the leader's 'capacity to grasp the eternal and immutable' truth, entails the right to exercise absolute authority and is fundamental to the happiness of followers.[1] The leader, *he*[2] who knows best, is consequently said to be entitled not simply to respect but also to deference to all his decisions, without dialogue and without dissent: followers are to submit their will to that of the leader, to silence their voices, to do his bidding. A totalitarian model of leadership which produces transformational effects for followers is, thus, the proposition. Complete submission and total obedience to the leader are said to be critical to securing happiness. In what follows I show how this understanding of leadership came to be.

This chapter examines the form and formation of the Classical Greek scholarly understanding of leadership, a body of knowledge deeply informed by the social context in which it developed. I begin by considering the issues deemed problematic which inform this discourse before turning to examine its key features. Four key themes are identified and examined: the characteristics of leaders and followers; the responsibilities of leaders; the definition and purpose of leadership; and the scope of leader authority. I then turn to examine the processes of formation which helped to give rise to this discourse, before considering the underpinning epistemic foundations and rules which rendered these ideas sensible, viable and truthful to their proponents. Finally, I examine the social function and subjectivity effects of this discourse before offering some concluding comments.

Primary sources for this case study[3] are Aristotle's *The Politics*[4] (*Pols*); Plato's *The Republic*[5] (*Rep*) and *Statesman*[6] (*St*); and Xenophon's *Agesilaus*[7] (*Ag*), *Hiero the Tyrant*[8] (*HT*), *Oeconimicus*[9] (*Oec*) and *Memorabilia*[10] (*Mem*). These primary sources, partially excepting those by Xenophon, have been the subject of extensive ongoing commentary and are, thus, widely acknowledged as being important texts from this time.[11] In the modern era, Xenophon's status has waned but he, like Plato, was a pupil of Socrates and there seems little doubt that he was influential in his day.[12] It is known that his work was studied by Roman thinkers and practitioners and in the medieval period.[13] More recently, Adair[14] credits Xenophon as a key thinker on strategic leadership. For these reasons, the inclusion of Xenophon's works in this study seemed clearly warranted. Secondary sources comprise a variety of texts which consider various aspects of Classical Greek history and culture; these are deployed to assist in situating the discourse within the context in which it arose.

PROBLEMS

Classical-era Greece, despite its many great achievements, was a society marked by disorder, class conflict and frequent wars.[15] Athens, the base of the scholars considered here, endured constant political upheaval as it struggled to establish laws, practices and ways of governing that were acceptable to the competing classes and interests within it.[16] Beginning in around 550 BC, Athenian democracy posed a particular challenge to traditional norms and values, providing, as it did, a system of governance which replaced the rule of the aristocracy.[17] By the end of the 4th century BC, the extended and damaging Peloponnesian War with Sparta (431–404), along with various other controversial decisions made by the Athenian democracy, meant that there was an intense concern in some circles with this approach to governing and with the state of society more generally.[18]

Over this same period, the emerging standard for speaking the truth for scholars became the deployment of reason, in which conclusions were derived logically from the preceding propositions.[19] Laying arguments out for debate and scrutiny was now proclaimed as the philosopher's duty, following the lead offered by Socrates.[20] Reference to the gods and tradition alone was no longer an adequate basis for sustaining one's position as correct and truthful: new propositions and analyses were now needed.[21]

Striving to uphold morality and social order was also claimed as part of the philosopher's duty.[22] But the Athenian democracy posed a serious threat to these aims, in the view of these scholars.[23] A frontal attack on the ideas underpinning the Athenian democracy was dangerous, however, when exile or execution were its favoured means of dealing with dissenting views.[24] Socrates' conviction for sedition by the Athenian democracy, which led to his suicide in 399 BC, had likely sheeted this reality home to his students. As an attempt to address what was thus perceived as problematic, then, we find the invention of the perfect leader with absolute authority as the recommended means of securing morality and order. This account of the truth about leadership had, however, the simultaneous effect of 'proving' that democracy is contrary to what is natural and good.

KEY FEATURES OF THE DISCOURSE

So what is the understanding of leadership that was developed all those centuries ago? To understand the precise character of 'leadership' in this discursive formation, I examine the personal characteristics ascribed to leaders and followers, the responsibilities to which it is said leaders should attend, the definition and purpose of leadership and the scope of authority advocated for leaders, these being issues of central focus to those articulating this new truth about leadership. Recall that I am not interested here in whether these ideas are true in an empirical sense, as such questions are irrelevant to an analysis of this nature. Instead, what is of interest here is the character of *what is said to be true* and how this functions to incite particular ways of being a leader or follower and particular ways of doing leadership.

The Characteristics of Leaders and Followers

[W]hen god fashioned you, he added gold in the composition of those of you who are qualified to be Rulers (which is why their prestige is greatest). (Plato, *Rep*, 415a)

Imbued with this golden quality, a leader is said here to be 'second only to the Gods'.[25] Yet while the gods were immortal, they were also typically seen as flawed, somewhat unpredictable and prone to spiteful or foolish acts.[26] In contrast to these flaws the leader is said to be unwavering in his wisdom and morality, incapable of wrongdoing: he lacks only the gift of immortality.[27] The truth about leadership is knowledge which only the true leader can possess, and this knowledge is itself held to be morally virtuous and without fault.[28] As a result, mistakes by leaders are rendered impossible because, it is claimed, to possess knowledge of leadership enables and causes one to act without error.[29] However, while perfection is seen as having arrived on earth, the leader is not omnipotent, for both the gods and other people are said to be capable of impeding the achievement of a leader's goals.[30]

The domain of leadership here is largely restricted to those who are head of state, although military generals, senior government officials and businessmen are sometimes thought to require similar attributes and to have duties that are a subset of those expected of leaders.[31] The leader, as head of state, is said to be a person concerned only with the well-being of the state and its people. He is said to be totally devoted to the betterment of those he leads.[32] The existence of a true leader is regarded as a rare occurrence:[33] extensive discussion of various substitutes for the ideal of a single leader form a key feature of the wider discourse within which debate about leadership occurs.[34] Seen as being equipped with a divine capacity, then, leaders are regarded as rare individuals who stand for civilized society and against chaos and degeneracy.[35]

Personality and behaviour, adherence to moral and religious values and beliefs, and what we would understand as the public *and* private realms of life are regarded as important here: to understand leadership, indeed to determine if a man is a true leader, every aspect of the leader's life is, thus, subject to scrutiny.[36] A leader's eating and sleeping habits, his capacity to restrain his sexual desire for other men, his attitudes toward, and treatment of, both friends and enemies, and his willingness to use his personal wealth to benefit others are all part of this inquiry into the truth about leadership.[37] The sincerity of a leader's reverence for the gods, his refusal to allow paintings or sculptures of his likeness to be made, the plainness of his own clothing compared with that of the soldiers whose uniforms he supplies, and his loathing of malicious gossip are further examples of the matters that are treated as relevant to understanding leadership.[38] To understand leadership here, then, meant knowing every thought and action of the leader. Even the smallest of things could reveal the purity of the leader's wisdom and knowledge. Similarly, such details could also be used to separate out the 'shams' who are said to pretend to love virtue and wisdom but whose true goal is to serve their own interests.[39]

Nature and nurture are both treated as important influences by the Classical Greeks.[40] A man's leadership potential is said to be a birthright because 'from the hour of their birth, some are marked out for subjection, others for rule'.[41] The vast majority of people are, however, regarded as inherently incapable of leadership.[42] A proper education, which includes 'choral performances, hunting and field sports, athletic competitions and horse-races', is also considered influential in leader development.[43] Developing a love of honour and virtue, reverence for the gods, courage, knowledge and wisdom are seen as vital for a leader.[44]

A leader's actions throughout his childhood are said to be an important testing ground in both establishing his status as a true leader and in learning the many requirements of leadership.[45] The advice given is that a young leader should be constantly observed and continuously challenged to see if he can remain true to the pursuit of wisdom and virtue. Plato argues that 'a close watch must be kept on them, then, at all ages, to see if they stick to this principle, and do not forget or jettison, under the influence of force or witchcraft, the conviction that they must always do what is best for the community'.[46] The young leader is to be placed in frightening situations to test his courage, and tempted with various pleasures to test his capacity for self-restraint.[47]

What is produced in this discourse, then, is the most perfect of men, the one who is equipped to lead.[48] He exhibits all and only that which is honourable, virtuous and admirable in every action: it is this exacting completeness, this fulfilment of human potential, which distinguishes the true leader from the fake. The true leader here exemplifies a masculine ideal in the very prime of life, comprising a well-honed, mature strength of body, mind and soul.[49] There is no weakness, no flaw, not even the merest hint of the feminine, the elderly, the weak, the vulnerable or the damaged in this account of the true leader. Here, the leader is a superior being, yet it is vital too that he is sincerely humble, modest and understands the limitations of other people, for it is they who are said to be in such great need of his guidance.[50]

The leader's perfection is understood as being achieved through a combination of calculated and determined self-restraint, ebullient and free-flowing self-expression and a focused intense desire to excel.[51] It is portrayed as an act of will, the product of knowledge and as destined by nature into being.[52] Here, each and every moment of the leader's life is both an achievement and an expression of the multi-faceted, all-encompassing nature of leadership.

Looking *up* at the leader, the follower is portrayed as their very opposite: ignorant of what is true, what is right and what is proper.[53] Said to suffer from an excess of courage or self-restraint, followers are presented as having fundamental, unavoidable and irremediable flaws.[54] However, they are not held to be completely without merit: with careful education and through exercising complete obedience to the leader, it is claimed that followers may achieve a greater degree of knowledge and virtue, although never to such a degree as that possessed by the leader.[55]

Leader Responsibilities

> [T]he legislator must mould to his will the bodies of newly-born children.
> (Aristotle, *Pols*, 1335a: 5)

Here, the range of issues to which it is said a leader must attend is very extensive; this is no mere processual or behavioural formulation of leadership. Leaders are expected to focus on certain specified issues and to achieve certain specified outcomes. Leadership is understood as something which entails particular actions in respect of particular matters. There is extensive detail about what the leader should actually *do*, not simply behaviourally, but substantively. Leadership is said to have a critical role to play in the achievement of the desired social outcomes, and what that role entails is expounded at length.

The leader is expected, for example, to make decisions about the 'number and character of the citizens, and then what should be the size and character of the country'.[56] He is to determine how to grow the state's revenue, reduce excessive expenditure, plan for food production to meet the population's requirements, identify the state's strategic strengths and weaknesses, as well as those of the enemy, and deploy troops accordingly.[57] Knowledge of the art of war is expected of a leader.[58] Deciding on the location of the city-state is said to be part of the leader's duties, requiring consideration of such matters as effective defence, access to farmland and perhaps also to the sea, depending on the leader's view about foreign trade and the presence of foreigners in his state.[59]

Using his knowledge and wisdom, a leader is to decide the age at which people may marry and who shall marry whom, because, it is claimed, by ensuring that the right mix of character types is joined in marriage the leader can secure the future well-being of the state.[60] The leader is said to need to monitor and, when necessary, punish people's use of indecent language and to ensure that inappropriate visual images are not distributed amongst the population.[61] The exercise undertaken by pregnant women, the number of children a couple may have, child-rearing practices and oversight of those responsible for children's education are also issues for which a leader is seen as having direct responsibility.[62]

A leader is held to be responsible for actively maintaining legal, moral and religious standards and traditions.[63] This includes such matters as issuing laws for general application, making case-by-case decisions, ensuring religious festivals are properly conducted,[64] as well as punishing or exiling those who are 'driven to violate religion, justice and morality'.[65] The leader's whole attention is expected to be given over to ensuring the physical, moral and spiritual well-being of the people, attending to threats from both within and external to the state.[66] Instilling discipline and obedience amongst the citizens is treated as a key concern for leaders; it is claimed that only through obeying the leader's directives will good order and good outcomes be achieved.[67]

Ultimately, it is the achievement of an orderly society which the leader is expected to create, this being one in which people stick to their allocated class and role, obey the leader without question, comply with legal, moral and religious conventions and where 'consensus and loyalty' prevail.[68] This is what the Classical Greek scholars claim leadership demands. This is what they said people should expect of leaders and what they claim to be the truth in respect of leadership. Here, then, leadership is not so much about means, but about a specified set of ends held to be of great importance.

Definition and Purpose of Leadership

[T]o introduce order into the unlimited is the work of a divine power – of such a power as holds together the universe. (Aristotle, *Pols*, 1626b: 30)

A third characteristic of this discourse is the attention given to defining what leadership is and its purpose. Here, 'leadership' is who the leader is,[69] what might be called their individual character, temperament or what we today understand as personality.[70] It is also what the leader does, incorporating every moment of every day and every action.[71] It is about the outcomes which leadership is said (and called on) to produce, such as order and obedience.[72] Finally, it is about the underpinning knowledge and virtue which guide the leader in their being and doing.[73] This holistic notion thus incorporates the intellectual, moral and personal attributes of a leader, the full suite of activities in which a leader engages, and the outcomes of those activities: for the leader constructed here, nothing about who he is, what he does and the consequences thereof is to be beyond the reach of this definition.

Leadership is generally treated as a capacity exclusive to the person who is head of state or to those rare few who have the capacity to hold that position.[74] It is portrayed in such a way that it does not include anyone else, even though it is upon other people that leadership is enacted. Limited attention is paid to the nature of the interactions between a leader and their followers, nor is leadership understood as being something that is co-created between them.[75] Leadership here is not about a style or a process or a selected list of key behaviours. Instead, it is portrayed as including anything and everything in the leader's life. Here, leadership resides in the leader: it is not something which exists simply by virtue of his formal position, rather it is in him, it is of him, the whole of him, not just particular parts.[76] It is said to be about his every action as well as the specific actions he must take as he attends to the complex suite of issues which threaten or sustain the well-being of the state and its people.[77]

Leadership is thus claimed to incorporate every facet of the leader's character, every facet of their life, every action, everything they know and are and do.[78] This diffuse and all-encompassing notion, however, is intensely centred on what was seen as the purpose of leadership: to secure the well-being of the state and its people.[79] Everything comes back to that duty, that purpose, and anything and everything about who the leader is and what he does is expected to contribute to that purpose. Thus, while leadership is said to be exclusively about the person of the leader, with no role for other people, it is also said to be exclusively about service to the people, with no scope for the private interests of the leader.[80] In this discourse, the leader can be seen as both master and slave of the people, ruling over them but permitted to act only in their best interests, denied any capacity to act in his own interest.

Scope of Leader Authority

> [I]t is the business of the ruler to give orders and of the ruled to obey. (Socrates, in Xenophon, *Mem*, 3.9.11)

> Although from one point of view legislation and kingship do certainly go together, the ideal is for authority to be invested not in a legal code but in an individual who combines kingship with wisdom. (Plato, *St*, 294a)

To carry out the extensive range of duties discussed above, a leader is said to require complete and absolute authority on any matter to which he directs his attention.[81] The consent of the people is claimed to be irrelevant and there is no mechanism of independent review or appeal envisaged, meaning that the scope of the leader's authority is effectively unlimited.[82] A true and wise leader is said to defer to those who possess specific expertise, such as a doctor in respect of health care, a farmer in terms of farming practices or a ship's captain in terms of sailing.[83] However, the 'branch of knowledge' which is leadership is claimed to possess a broader, higher and deeper wisdom than any specialist area and so ultimately prevails over all others.[84]

Obedience to the leader is positioned as both an expectation and a moral virtue in this discourse and the use of coercive force is said to be justified if, in the leader's view, the situation makes this necessary.[85] Laws are said to have their place in terms of codifying the will of the ruler and in enabling justice to be dealt with administratively.[86] However, laws are also said to be insufficiently flexible to account for specific circumstances, leading to the claim that the leader should always retain the ability to make the final decision.[87]

It is claimed that granting such unlimited authority to a true leader will produce a system of government that is 'as far apart from all the rest as God is from humankind'.[88] Because a true leader is said to be not only wise but also completely moral, it is argued that there is no need for concern about the potential for abuse of the unrestricted authority a leader is to have over all others:

> People doubt that anyone could ever live up to this ideal rulership; they doubt the possibility of a moral and knowledgeable ruler who would dispense justice and deal fairly with everyone in the matter of their rights; and if such a ruler were possible, they doubt he would be prepared to rule in that way, rather than injuring and killing and harming any of us whenever he felt like it. And yet, if they were faced with the kind of ruler we're describing, people would feel perfectly comfortable; he'd take sole command of the only system of government which, if we were speaking strictly, we would call authentic, and he'd govern in a way which guaranteed their happiness.[89]

Here, then, what is claimed is that leadership creates happiness for all. The proposition is that only through ceding complete and absolute authority to the leader can this be achieved.[90] The difficulty, so clearly signalled, is to overcome the doubts borne of bitter experience about the plausibility of the all-perfect, all-powerful leader.

To sum up this discourse, then, what was advanced as being correct and truthful in respect of leadership is set out in Table 3.1.

Table 3.1   Key features of leadership in the Classical Greek discourse

- leaders are perfect, divine, knowledgeable and moral and this is part of the natural order
- leaders act only in the interests of the people; their purpose is to create order, security and well-being
- leaders are rare
- every aspect of the leader's life is part of leadership
- followers are inherently flawed and require leaders to guide them
- leaders should attend to all and any issues which affect the well-being of the state
- leaders should use unfettered authority to make whatever decisions they deem necessary and should be obeyed without question
- if these matters are enacted then human happiness is guaranteed.

PROCESSES OF FORMATION

> That some should rule and others be ruled is a thing not only necessary, but expedient. (Aristotle, *Pols*, 1254a: 20)

Much of the Classical Greek account of the truth about leadership may seem offensive or bizarre to today's reader. That the so-called founding fathers of Western philosophy held such views requires some explaining. I turn now, therefore, to consider the processes of formation which shaped the development of this account of the truth about leadership. The aim is to foreground the wider social context which helped render these ideas plausible and attractive to their intended audience, as well as to examine how they emerged and developed.

Ancient (ca. 750–510 BC) and Classical (ca. 5th–4th centuries BC) Greek society is known to have been strongly affected by both inter-state warfare and intra-state conflict which occurred between its various class groupings.[91] The institution of the polis, or city-state, with a population of only several thousand, was the core social and political unit of these times.[92] However, while the city-state was a fairly stable form of social organization, the constitutional form of government which applied within city-states was not.[93] Athens, of particular relevance here, experienced monarchical, oligarchical, aristocratic, democratic and tyrannical forms of government and was also, for a brief period, subjected to direct foreign rule by Sparta during these times.[94] Movement between the social classes was generally restricted and the different classes had differentiated levels of wealth, prestige and legal and political rights.[95] These times, then, were marked by continuous political and military conflict and upheaval between and within small city-states whose population was divided into distinct social classes.

This social context profoundly informs the account of leadership examined here. A common concern connecting the multitude of issues to which it is said leaders should attend is ensuring order and stability.[96] The stated need for leaders to decide who shall marry whom, for example, can be seen to reflect a concern to preserve rather than challenge the class system. The small population base of the city-state in which a leader knows the people he leads is taken as a given. The requirement for leaders to attend to issues of food production, troop deployment, and the location of the city-state reflects an unstable security environment, with limited means of defending key assets and limited capacity to stock-pile essential items. The expectation that a leader be directly involved in moral and religious as well as political and military matters reflects both the limited administrative machinery of the city-states and a worldview which saw such matters as inherently connected.[97]

This account of leadership, despite being produced largely via the new method of philosophy, was also strongly influenced by pre-existing Ancient ideas: the preoccupation with striving for perfection which is an important feature of the Homeric genre[98] is an example of this. Now, perfection was tied to the person of the leader.[99] Viewed as a political move, the new person of the perfect leader and his deeply flawed follower function as a strong case against those who promoted democracy; *if* these ideas about the characteristics of leaders and followers are accepted, *then* democracy is rendered undesirable as a consequence.[100]

With this particular conception of leadership, any urge to distribute decision-making, to hold leaders to account for their actions, or even to question their choices can be readily positioned as contrary to both nature and wisdom. That Socrates was convicted of sedition by Athenian democracy, leading ultimately to his death, that Plato and Xenophon were his pupils, and that Aristotle in turn was a pupil of Plato are matters widely accepted as historical fact.[101] Plato, Xenophon and Aristotle had good reason, in other words, to have a dim view of democracy. Here, the case *against* democracy derives, indirectly but still powerfully, from the case built *for* this particular conception of leadership. Consequently, this 'truth' about leadership which they promoted is not innocent and pure but is rather one imbued with political intent and impact.

A key strategy used to establish this truth and cloak its political intent is to deploy the then new philosophical method. The method presents itself as above and beyond political motive and influence, as pure and impartial in its deployment of logic and reason, such that all that flows from it is to be regarded as the unvarnished honest truth, finally revealed. It implicitly promises a process of discovery in which 'The Truth', understood as being knowledge which is both universal and timeless, is revealed.[102]

Tactically, the deployment of this method typically begins with the assertion of an unquestioned (but highly questionable) assumption. It then moves rapidly through to a series of interim findings reliant on this assumption before, finally, moving to a major conclusion which, advanced in isolation, would generate immediate critique. Founded on assumptions about the inadequacy of most people and the possibility of there being a perfect leader, Plato, for example, draws his reader inexorably through to the conclusion that

> as long as these wise rulers have the single overriding concern of always using their intelligence and expertise to maximise the justice they dispense to the state's inhabitants there's no defect in what they do, is there. After all, they're not only capable of keeping their subjects safe, but they are also doing all they can to make them better people than they were before.[103]

Using this power/knowledge technique, the goal of making people 'better' is used to justify a totalitarian model of rule. That the organization of public affairs was of such interest to early philosophers perhaps indicates the potency of the philosophical method as a strategic device to cloak the influence of power in shaping knowledge.

The conception of leadership developed here also reflects certain intellectual preoccupations and habits of the Classical Greeks. Scholarly Greek thought prior to and during the Classical period tended to place a heavy emphasis on attributing social events to individual human or divine causes, rather than, say, to systemic factors such as inter-class conflict or inter-state competition for access to strategic assets.[104] Both Herodotus[105] and Thucydides,[106] for example, typically attribute wars to individual or group actions and motives, rather than accounting for such events in economic, geo-political or sociological terms. Their preferred mode of thinking about causation in the social world tended to place the individual (male) human actor at the centre and to pay attention to both his motives and his actions.[107] It is this tendency to focus on individual motives and actions which informs the approach taken to formulating the truth about leadership. It results in the individual leader being placed centre stage, while the influence of followers, for example, or processual perspectives, remains beyond thought.

Ancient mythology and religious beliefs also shaped this account of the truth about leadership. By way of example, in *The Republic* Plato had a broad and ambitious agenda: to define what it would take to create the perfect society.[108] The question of what kind of person should rule was an important part of his design.[109] Establishing the truth about the perfect society was understood to be immensely challenging.[110] However, it was nonetheless seen to be an important, legitimate and worthy challenge, in which the philosopher's commitment to the use of rigorous logic and careful reasoning is contrasted favourably with traditional, conventional or sophistic modes of reasoning.[111] Indeed, those scholars whose work is examined here make considerable efforts to found their conception of leadership in logic and reasoning. The philosophic method was portrayed as the pre-eminent route to the truth.[112]

However, Plato (or at least his mouthpiece Socrates) does at times simply abandon philosophy and turn to the power of the mythic and poetic traditions. In seeking to promote his philosopher-king as the best and most truthful approach to leadership, he asks, 'I wonder if we could contrive one of those convenient stories ... some magnificent myth that would in itself carry conviction to our whole community'.[113] This story is to be 'nothing new – a fairy story like those the poets tell and have persuaded people to believe about the sort of thing that often happened "once upon a time", but never does now and is not likely to: indeed it would need a lot of persuasion to get people to believe it'.[114] In fact, the estimate is made that this story would not be believed 'in the first generation ... but you might succeed with the second and later generations'.[115] Despite this challenge, it appears that the story is worth telling, for 'it should serve to increase their loyalty to the state and to each other'.[116] Pure fantasy is thus deployed in pursuit of order and unity, which in turn rest on the leader.

This is not the only example where recourse to traditional, mythic or conventional knowledge can be seen within the then newly emerging philosophical paradigm. Aristotle makes appeal to the conventional knowledge of his time,[117] to the poetic knowledge of earlier times[118] and to the gods.[119] For Xenophon, the gods are especially important: no leader is regarded of worthy of endorsement as such unless he proves his love of the gods.[120] Accordingly, to ignore the influence still granted here to the gods in human affairs, for example, or to ignore the occasional recourse to mythology is to overlook an important continuity that connects the Ancient and Classical eras. Despite the efforts made, thought itself did not begin anew with the advent of philosophy.

A specific concern of relevance to these scholars was the abuse of power and authority, this being something they had experienced in their own lifetime.[121] In Classical Greek society, there was no 'free press' to challenge those in positions of authority.[122] The majority of the population comprised slaves or women denied any political rights.[123] The appropriate constitutional form of government was repeatedly under challenge and the institutions of government were typically small and fragile in their operations.[124]

All these factors gave leaders quite considerable scope to act as they saw fit, something which clearly concerned the scholars whose work we are examining here. Accordingly, the heavy emphasis given to the claim that true leadership requires the leader to serve the people, to attend only to their welfare and never to his own interests, is informed by the context in which this idea arose. The morally righteous leader we find in the papyrus scrolls which record this discourse serves as a pointed critique of the self-serving leaders who actually lived and breathed.

Plato, for example, describes the political leaders of his time as a 'motley band',[125] a 'gang',[126] as 'practitioners of sectarian politics' and 'agents of a massive sham ... supreme imposters and illusionists'.[127] A strong theme in *Statesman* is Plato's concern to 'distinguish a king with his wisdom from those who merely pretend to be a statesman, but in fact aren't in the slightest, however widely their claim may be believed'.[128] It is generally accepted that Plato spent time in Syracuse trying to educate the tyrant Dionysius II to change his approach to leadership.[129] In *Hiero the Tyrant*, Xenophon's aim is to persuade the character of Hiero away from self-serving tyrannical rule and toward ruling in the interests of the people. There was, then, a clear intent to change practice through the statements being made here about what constituted the truth about leadership.

To centre truth claims about the purpose of leadership so strongly around the idea of 'serving the interests of the people' can, thus, be seen as a strategic response founded on these scholars' concerns and values. The goal appears to be to produce an intellectual and moral basis for constraining leaders. However, coupled with the idea of service to the people as the purpose of leadership is the perfect person of the leader and the expectation of complete obedience to him. Liberation from tyrannical abuse may, therefore, have been a strategic goal of this discourse, but liberation from authority most certainly was not.

As a consequence of these many and various connections between what was said about leadership and the social context in which it was said, the discourse is not best understood as an abstract theoretical or philosophical inquiry. Rather, it is more usefully understood as a comprehensive manifesto formed to deal with the problems of the time: leadership, wisdom, virtue and order are the solutions it offers. What can be seen when this discourse is placed in its social context is that what it entails is an exercise in invention, not discovery. This is not 'The Truth', but a strategic response to a set of problems. This is not knowledge which is innocent or pure, but is instead knowledge which has been shaped to address certain values, concerns and interests. This is, therefore, knowledge which serves the interests of power. These findings are summarized below:

- the discourse draws on the mythic and poetic traditions as well as the philosophic method
- the discourse arises as a response to a social context of conflict and (perceived) degeneracy
- the account given of 'leadership' enables the covert de-legitimation of the idea of 'democracy'
- the discourse acts as a counter to the (perceived) abuse of power by contemporary leaders, providing an alternative conception which claims to be grounded in both nature and reason.

UNDERPINNING ASSUMPTIONS

Digging deeper, I turn now to examine the underpinning 'epistemic' foundations which I propose rendered this discourse sayable and sensible to its intended audience, recalling Foucault's understanding of an episteme as something like a basic 'structure of thought' which prevails at any given point in time.[130] I then demonstrate how these foundations informed the intellectual 'moves' which allow the discourse to cohere. I then present what I suggest are the unwritten rules governing the discourse.

Firstly, a marked preference for philosophical reflection and reasoning rather than empirical observation as the route to the truth is central to this episteme.[131] This orients thought to consider itself, but in so doing it need not consider the world that exists beyond thought. Secondly, belief in a stark and natural inequality between persons is a pivotal assumption and this, in turn, shapes the Greek concept of leadership. It is through recourse to 'natural' inequality that the 'excellence of character in perfection' which belongs to the leader alone is both established and sustained.[132] Others may have their own 'special attributes', such as the 'silence' that is 'a woman's glory'.[133] However, none shall compare in wisdom, honour and morality with that of the leader: a special, unique and intentionally superior space in the social fabric is consequently carved out for the leader from this core assumption.

This 'natural' inequality is called on to advance the case for leaders in other ways. The inherently flawed nature of most people, prone as they are said to be toward disorder and degeneracy, makes leaders, superior beings without such flaws, both necessary and desirable. It also requires the leader to constantly deflect people away from wrongdoing or error, and hence functions to legitimate the absolute authority to be granted to leaders. An assumption of natural inequality between persons, then, is so critical here that without it the discourse would lose its internal coherency.

This binary and hierarchical division of reality between leaders (perfect) and non-leaders (flawed) is, thirdly, typical of a more general feature of Classical Greek thought which other scholars have identified.[134] This division can also be found in their conceptions of male/female, gods/humans, natural/unnatural, good/bad, Greeks/barbarians and order/chaos.[135] This approach to the ordering of the universe assumed a dialectical dynamic exists between pairings, resulting in the perception of an inherently unstable universe riven by conflicting forces.[136] As we have seen, 'leadership' is positioned to play a key role in addressing social and moral instability, acting as a counter-veiling force to achieve morality and order. A key implication of this general structure of thought is that ambiguous or contradictory aspects of a phenomenon cannot be contemplated; accordingly, the possibility of conceiving of (true) leadership as having both positive and problematic aspects is effectively rendered unthinkable by the norms of the Classical Greek episteme.

The fourth epistemic feature of relevance is the Classical Greek notion of 'truth'. Here, the influence of Socrates on Plato, Xenophon and Aristotle is especially strong because, as noted earlier, for all these thinkers whatever is 'true' is also morally 'good'.[137] The equating of truth with moral goodness, opposed to what is false and therefore morally wrong, is an important element of the leadership discourse. It helps explain why, for example, Plato and Xenophon place such a great emphasis on seeking to define and describe what constitutes true leadership, distinguishing this from fake and therefore morally bad leadership.

Fifth, a particular understanding of nature also plays an important role in Classical Greek thought: nature functions as the exemplar for the social world.[138] Consequently, analogous reasoning from the physical universe to the human realm is a key method here for understanding ourselves. Thus, for example, herding animals provides an analogy for leadership in the early stages of Plato's *Statesman*.[139] This conception of nature also provides the template for what is good and true, 'for nothing which is contrary to nature is good'.[140] Consistent with this understanding of nature, then, the leadership discourse seeks to define leadership as something that is a natural phenomenon in order to secure its status as something that is 'good' and 'true'.

Sixth, the notion of the self is a further feature in the Classical Greek episteme which can be seen reflected in the leadership discourse. Here, the self is one that is to work on improving itself, but this pertains specifically to taking wise and honourable actions and engaging in proper conduct which others can see.[141] There is no assumption of an interior self which governs action; rather, to be seen is to exist and it is what others see that matters.[142] Here, it is one's deeds that warrant attention and are the means by which we may judge another's 'true' character. Thus, for example, Xenophon speaks approvingly of Agesilaus' habitual observance of religious rituals even in battle, of his treatment of friends and enemies, his clothing and his eating and sleeping habits.[143] Not only does this exemplify the importance of the connectedness of all things for the Classical Greeks, it also demonstrates that it is that which can be seen which matters, which warrants comment, which reveals one's true character.

Finally, in the Classical Greek episteme all things were thought to be connected in some way.[144] Consequently, the leadership discourse is connected to talk on such matters as the nature of reality, how we should live, both individually and as a social group, educational policy, military strategy, diplomatic theory, town planning, food production, and questions about how we ensure justice, order, cohesion and good behaviour in society and about the role of government and the rights and obligations of citizens. This connectedness of thought about what we would today conceive of as a set of separate topics or disciplines is not simply a crucial aspect of the leadership discourse itself; rather, it provides the substantive issues to which talk of leadership is and must be directed. This could hardly be further from the decontextualized and behaviourist orientation of leadership discourse today, but it is this very difference which allows us to see so clearly that, in contrast with our present focus on the 'how to' of leadership, the Classical Greek interest is on the purpose, the ends, the results which leadership was expected to deliver.

To demonstrate how these various epistemic norms play themselves out in the leadership discourse, consider the following examples:

> [T]o acquire these powers a man needs education; he must be possessed of great natural gifts; above all, he must be a genius. For I reckon this gift is not altogether human, but divine – this power to win willing obedience: it is manifestly a gift of the gods to the true votaries of prudence.[145]

Here, the equation is: leadership = proper education + 'nature' + 'genius' + a 'divine gift' = prudence. What is clearly implied as a consequence is 'morality' and 'good outcomes'. The order is not critical; for example, 'genius' implies 'prudence' but also implies 'leadership'.

> As long as these wise rulers have the single overriding concern of always using their intelligence and expertise to maximise the justice they dispense to the state's inhabitants there's no defect in what they do, is there? After all, they're not only capable of keeping their subjects safe, but they are also doing all they can to make them better people than they were before.[146]

Here, the equation is: leadership = intelligence + expertise, which = justice, leader perfection, morally good outcomes for the people and changing the people. The order is not essential to the logic: 'intelligence' is inextricably tied to 'the leader' whose perfection in turn leads to 'justice'.

Another example:

> to introduce order into the unlimited is the work of a divine power – of such a power as holds together the universe.[147]

Here, the equation is: leadership = the production of order = a divine power, which implies infallibility + a pure morality + the desirability of order. Here too the order is irrelevant: the production of order requires infallibility, for example, while pure morality equates with leadership.

With this discourse, then, what is produced is a multi-faceted and mutually reinforcing defence of totalitarian rule, founded in specific understandings of 'nature', 'reason', 'morality' and 'truth', with additional support coming from 'genius' and 'the gods'. The chain of reasoning may begin or end with any element, for in this discourse 'morality', 'truth', 'nature', 'knowledge', 'reason', 'wisdom', 'experience', 'genius' and 'divinity' are deeply connected and imply each other. So long as the premises are accepted, the conclusions follow. This is an elaborately interwoven intellectual construct.

These claims to speak the truth about the perfect leader, however, also stand in opposition to the empirical examples most frequently cited of self-serving, far-from-perfect leaders, examples which may also be true.[148] Consequently, these truths about leadership can, therefore, be understood as having been constructed out of a fiction which cannot be acknowledged: the fiction of the perfect leader. This (fictional) truth is built upon another truth whose existence is repeatedly acknowledged: the truth of the imperfect leader. This truth of the perfect leader is, therefore, surely more invention than discovery, for it directs itself away from the evidence of the imperfect leader, it dismisses it, it seeks instead to establish the truth of a perfect leader and present him as a discovery.

Viewed as a 'game of truth',[149] this discourse is hyperactive, product-ive and unrelenting. The persuasive strategies deployed here are mutually reinforcing and comprehensive: so long as one follows the chain of reasoning on its own terms, then the conclusions reached are rendered unavoidable and inescapable. However, what is put before us is a discourse which asserts the truth of the existence of the perfect leader while, simultaneously, referencing a contradictory empirical reality, namely the existence of the far-from-perfect leader. Consequently, the Classical Greek truth about leadership is founded on fictions, assertions and myths but presents itself as a rigorous search for the truth grounded in reason. What can be seen in Foucauldian terms as a strategic attempt to define what can be known and said about leadership, to carve out who shall rule, the terms of that rule and who shall be subjected to that rule, is no less than an uncompromising game of power which presents itself as the impartial search for the truth.

From the foregoing analysis, I propose that there are several implicit rules which govern this discourse. To be successful in this discursive regime, these norms are followed in order to be understood by others and to render what is said as credible. Firstly, 'good' things contain only goodness. That which is held to be 'good', which leadership is, is held to be unambiguously 'good' as well as being 'true', 'natural' and 'divine'. Correspondingly, whatever is held to be 'bad' is held to be completely bad, as well as 'fake' and 'unnatural'.

Secondly, to succeed within the confines of the discourse one may 'discover' only those truths which do not threaten the existing social order. The aim here is never to challenge the elite but rather to sustain their interests and status, to ensure that the 'truth' provides confirmation and support for the class and gender system then operant. Consequently, what is produced is an account of leadership which satisfies the interests of the aristocratic audiences to whom these scholars spoke: this 'truth' is saturated with political intent and effect while portraying itself as a neutral, open-minded enquiry.

Thirdly, the tenor of the discourse, despite the variety of narrative techniques that are deployed, is one that produces confidence about what is and what is known. This is a reassuring discourse. It seeks to simplify, not complicate matters. It does not seek to disturb or critique what is already thought to be so, which exists prior to its undertaking its own ritual, which is primarily one of form not substance. It does not critique its own assumptions but affirms them. The goal is not a discovery of new truths but rather a sophisticated rendering of pre-existing ideas into truths and from which the truth about leadership is invented before our very eyes.

SOCIAL FUNCTION AND SUBJECTIVITY EFFECTS

The macro-level function served by this conception of leadership is to warrant a benign dictatorship where there are no limitations placed on what the leader may do beyond those derived from his own morality and wisdom. As we have seen, laws can be overridden as the leader sees fit, and there is to be no right of appeal.[150] The small city-state as the best social form is taken as a given.[151] Obedience to leaders is presented as both a virtue and a necessity.[152] Extensive leader involvement in what we would today understand as matters in the personal and private domains of life is warranted here because those matters are deemed to be of collective interest.[153]

This account of leadership functions to bolster anti-democratic and anti-egalitarian ideas through its strong emphasis on the naturalness of inequality between persons. It simultaneously functions to reinforce the class, slavery and gender divisions of the time. Ultimately, follower interests are served here through complete subservience to the leader and rest on the assurance that true leaders will act only in their followers' best interests.[154] As a power/knowledge formation aiming to secure social cohesion, albeit at the expense of liberty and democracy, this conception of leadership is highly productive.

The subjectivity of the leader constructed here is, as we have seen, that of one driven to do that which is truthful, just, moral, honourable and in the best interests of others.[155] Here, no sacrifice is too great, no hardship too much to bear and no task too onerous, provided it serves the well-being of the people and the state.[156] There is to be nothing followers cannot ask of this leader; there is nothing this leader may deny them, provided only that what is sought is in their best interest. If it is not, then his right to deny it is said to be beyond question. Every moment of every day is to be dedicated to the precious cause of the well-being of the people and the state.

It is also, however, an unending experience of duty, of scrutiny, of denial of the leader's own interests and passions which has been proposed.[157] The leader, while master, is simultaneously servant and even slave. While all others must obey the leader, they are not to serve him; they do not exist to meet his needs. They may be subject to his rule and his authority but he is to serve them; his power over them is rendered legitimate only because it is said to serve them. Like a slave, he is permitted no private interests. He must serve the state and the people only, and never himself. In all that he does and all that he is, the leader here is a creature of and for the people. Simultaneously, however, the leader is positioned here as akin to a slave owner: the people may continue to exist only if he so decides. Their lives are to be in his hands, for he is to have complete unquestionable authority even in matters of life and death.[158] Whatever he seeks from them they must give.

Consequently, in this account the leader has absolute power yet at the same time he has none that may be exercised in his own interest. In this discourse, moreover, power suppresses and denies its existence through the language of 'service', 'nature' and 'morality' at the same time as it expresses and justifies its overwhelming presence and reach in the language of 'obedience to authority'. Despite these many tensions, what is clear, at least, is that the people are never to exercise power. Followers are deemed incapable of knowing or expressing even their own best interests; the leader will determine for them what they are.

The leader self which is constructed here admits of no flaw and denies any potential for error;[159] a supreme arrogance is simultaneously created and suppressed or, at least, directed toward serving others rather than serving itself. This self must convince itself and others of its perfection. It must remain distant and disconnected from normal human limitations and human pleasures. This complete outward focus of attention is derived from an 'inside' which is filled only with honour, reverence for the gods, courage, wisdom and virtue. What is to be 'top of mind' is the perpetual issue of how the leader may best act to ensure he makes the people 'better people than they were before'.[160] In doing so, his task is to make them more like himself, for he is the epitome of all that is good and wise and truthful. This exercise in transformation, then, is intended to result in followers who resemble as much as is possible the leader himself. This transformation is akin to reproduction by way of cloning. The enactment of leadership here seeks the endless production of imitations of the leader himself and the elimination of all alternative subjectivities.

The leader's belief in his superior capability, coupled with a devoted concern for the well-being of the people, seems also strongly akin to what a parent is expected to feel in relation to their infant child. Followers are perpetually infantilized in this discourse, presumed to be incapable of ever growing up.[161] The leader is to be as devoted as a loving parent, as powerful as an adult is compared with an infant, and as prepared to sacrifice their own needs in pursuit of the welfare of the people as a parent is expected to be for their child. Here, there is no more scope for meaningful dialogue and debate between a leader and their followers than there is between a parent and an infant who has yet to learn to speak.

The inherently deficient follower self which is created here seems induced to being awestruck by the leader's capacity for truth, virtue and wisdom and directed toward passivity, deference, subservience and obedience:[162] who are they, after all, to question or challenge the leader? The follower, then, is one who implies a childlike dependency and frailty that is exquisitely matched to the all-powerful, moral and wise parental figure of the leader.

The relations of power that are established between leader and follower are full of contradictions, simultaneously empowering the leader and denying him any scope to act outside of the comprehensive script of leadership that is laid out for him to adopt; simultaneously productive of a life-affirming nurturing attitude toward followers and productive of an intense need to deny them any scope to develop their own subjectivity. The leader is perhaps as much dominated and subjugated in this discourse as the follower, for neither is granted any meaningful freedom to choose; each has a prescribed role to play and there is to be no negotiation on this point.

The knowledge produced in this discourse provides a theoretical, conceptual and moral foundation to 'leadership' as a natural, empirical reality. This knowledge presents itself as having revealed something essential and enduring about the nature of the world. It constructs leadership as something that is knowable and describable but also as fundamentally difficult to replicate, because of its divine and rare ontological basis. Leadership is rendered both desirable and legitimate via the variety of persuasive techniques used in the discourse and not just through arbitrary force or tradition. The discourse sets a standard for leaders in terms of their conduct, the issues to which they should direct their attention, the scope of their authority and the kinds of outcomes they should seek to achieve. Leader power is made natural, desirable and without limitations, for the true leader is said to act only in the interests of the people.

Equally, though, this knowledge is disempowering to all others. Followers become raw material for the leader to 'mould to his will',[163] not active participants, and they are granted no valid wishes or rights of their own. Follower freedom and authority is rendered a nonsensical idea by the action of this discourse. Ideas of accountability or participation in decision-making are crowded out, silenced before they can be given a voice.

There is a totalizing gaze in the Classical Greek quest to know the truth about leadership. This gaze attends to both regularities, to common characteristics of leaders, as well as to the unique attributes of each leader: these are treated as exemplars from which other aspiring leaders may draw inspiration, as well as evidence relevant to determining whether that particular leader was a true leader or merely a 'sham'.[164]

This knowledge presents itself as pure, impartial reason, and cloaks many of its power effects in talk of nature, divinity, morality and service to others. This knowledge presents itself as having solved real problems, but it also suggests it has no limitations, no imperfections, no potential for adverse consequences. This knowledge cannot critique itself.

The overall effects produced by this discourse are manifold. A leader self is produced who is without flaw, is dedicated to serving the people and who is to be subjected to an unrelenting, all-encompassing gaze. A follower self who is to accept its inherent limitations, obey the leader and seek to become more like the leader emerges as the leader's dialectical opposite. Their relationship is to have parent–child dimensions to it, yet the leader is also akin to a master, a servant and a slave to the people. Leaders and followers are inextricably linked: neither is to be able to survive without the other.

A coherent body of knowledge is produced which presents itself as a pure, impartial truth, removed from concerns about power. Yet power saturates this knowledge, enabling it to warrant a system of government which is totalitarian in its reach and unlimited in the exercise of its powers. A social order wherein order, unity, obedience and the well-being of the whole are key priorities is enunciated and rendered natural and desirable.

The overall function that the Classical Greek concept of leadership serves is as a device for securing social cohesion. Complete obedience to those in positions of authority is rendered a necessity, a natural behaviour and a moral good. This conception of leadership provides a mechanism for suppressing conflict between persons and reassures us that someone does have the answers and will take care of us. Leaders provide an example of the divine and unlimited nature of human potential. Combined with a presumption that such potential is a rare quality, beyond the reach of most people, followers are left only to admire and obey those who do rise so high.

CONCLUSION

The Classical Greek leadership discourse offered a comprehensive solution to the problems which were perceived to plague Greek, particularly Athenian, society at the time the discourse emerged. Its emergence was, thus, no random event. The philosophical method offered a means for speaking old truths in new ways, while the perceived state of decline in Athenian society provided the motive to speak. The solution the discourse offers is leadership, conceived as something which pertains to both means and ends, conceived as something which both draws on traditional knowledge and which is also new.

'Leadership' here offers a new solution to old problems. At the same time, it functions to uphold the traditions, norms, values and interests of the Classical Greek aristocracy, for whom these scholars cared most. The knowledge produced is expressed as a genuine inquiry into the truth of things in which power is simultaneously exposed and hidden. Nature, morality and power are inextricably entwined in this conception of leadership. Ultimately, leadership emerges here as a mechanism for securing a totalitarian social order intended to benefit existing social elites while proclaiming to serve the interests of all.

NOTES

1. Plato, *Rep* 484
2. While Plato in *The Republic* envisages women playing an equal role in his Guardian class, on balance I favour the interpretation that he later rejects the possibility of female leaders in *The Statesman*. In the case of the other primary sources, it is unequivocally clear that leaders are thought of as exclusively male
3. For the purposes of this case, I adopt the Stephanus pagination regime for citation of specific elements of work by Plato and the Bekker numbers system for Aristotle. For specific elements of work by Xenophon, citation follows the book-chapter-section or chapter-section method as used in both Oxford Classical Texts and Loeb Classical Library publications of Xenophon's works. In selecting which of the various editions of these texts to draw from, recent translations have been preferred due to their usage of modern English, however earlier translations (see, for example, Jowett's translations of Plato and Aristotle) have been used to cross-check the interpretations
4. Aristotle, 2009
5. Plato, 2007
6. Plato, 1995
7. Xenophon, 2006
8. Xenophon, 1997
9. Xenophon, 1997
10. Xenophon, 1997
11. Grant, 1991; Russell, 1984; Tarnas, 1991
12. Cartledge, 2006; Gray, 2007
13. Gray, 2007
14. 2002
15. Grant, 1991; Morris and Powell, 2006; Russell, 1984
16. Finley, 1963; Irwin, 1989; McNeill and Sedlar, 1969
17. McNeill and Sedlar, 1969
18. Cartledge, 1993; Grant, 1991; Russell, 1984
19. Finley, 1963; Irwin, 1989; McNeill and Sedlar, 1969
20. Annas, 2009; Lane, 2001; Morris and Powell, 2006
21. McNeill and Sedlar, 1969; Russell, 1984; Vernant, 1995, 2006
22. Aristotle, 2009; Plato, 1995, 2007; Xenophon, 1997, 2006
23. Xenophon, 1997, 2006
24. Cartledge, 2006; Grant, 1991; Lane, 2007
25. Xenophon, *Ag* 11.13
26. Vernant, 1995, 2006

27. See, for example, Aristotle, *Pols* 1260a: 15
28. See, for example, Plato, *St* 297a
29. See, for example, Xenophon, *Mem* 3.9.5; Wilson, 2013a
30. See, for example, Xenophon, *Ag* 11.1
31. See, for example, Xenophon, *Mem* 3.4.12, *Oec* 21.2
32. See, for example, Aristotle, *Pols* 1265a, 1333b: 35
33. See, for example, Plato, *Rep* 503d
34. See, for example, Plato, *Rep* Part 4, *St* 297a
35. See, for example, Xenophon, *Oec* 21.11–12
36. See, for example, Plato, *Rep* 484–487
37. See, for example, Xenophon, *Ag* 3.2, 4.3, 5.1–5.7
38. See Xenophon, *Ag*
39. Plato, *St* 303c
40. See, for example, Xenophon, *Ag* 1.5
41. Aristotle, *Pols* 1254a: 20
42. See, for example, Aristotle, *Pols* 1279a: 35
43. Plato, *Rep* 412b
44. See, for example, Plato, *Rep* 503a
45. See, for example, Aristotle, *Pols* 1332b: 35
46. Plato, *Rep* 412e
47. Plato, *Rep* 413d–e
48. Aristotle argues at one point that 'kings have no marked superiority over their subjects' (*Pols* 1332b: 20), but he has in mind here only those with citizen status: slaves, then the vast majority of people and women were certainly not regarded as equal. Elsewhere, the tenor of his comments in respect of rulers who are deserving of praise makes it clear he sees them as the best of men (see, for example, Aristotle, *Pols* 1260a: 15, 1279a: 35)
49. See, for example, Xenophon, *Ag* 6.1, 11.6
50. See, for example, Plato, *St* 309a–b, d
51. See, for example, Plato, *Rep* 475b, 485e
52. See, for example, Aristotle, *Pols* 1325b: 1–10
53. See, for example, Plato, *Rep* 372e–374e
54. Plato, *St* 309
55. See, for example, Aristotle, *Pols* 1325b: 1–10, 1337a: 10
56. Aristotle, *Pols* 1326a: 5
57. See, for example, Xenophon, *Mem* 3.6.4–14
58. See, for example, Plato, *St* 303e
59. Aristotle, *Pols* 1327a–1327b
60. See, for example, Aristotle, *Pols* 1334b: 30; Plato, *St* 309c
61. Aristotle, *Pols* 1336b: 1–20
62. See, for example, Plato, *St* 308d, 310e
63. See, for example, Xenophon, *Ag* 1.27
64. See, for example, Plato, *Rep* 425, *St* 305d
65. Plato, *St* 309a
66. See, for example, Xenophon, *Ag* 7.1
67. See, for example, Aristotle, *Pols* 1326a: 30
68. Plato, *St* 311b
69. See, for example, Aristotle, *Pols* 1326b: 1–10
70. Plato dismisses contemporary commentators for their 'unphilosophic preoccupation with personalities' (*Rep* 500b) so 'character' and 'temperament' are terms more consistent with Plato's account of ideal leaders
71. See, for example, Xenophon, *Ag* 11.1–11.16
72. See, for example, Plato, *St* 301a, 309d
73. See, for example, Aristotle, *Pols* 1325b: 1–10
74. See, for example, Plato, *St* 297b; Xenophon, *Mem* 3.4.10
75. See, for example, Xenophon, *Ag* 8.2

76. See, for example, Aristotle, *Pols* 1260a: 15, 1333a: 30–4
77. See, for example, Plato, *Rep* Parts 7–8
78. See, for example, Xenophon, *Ag* 11.1–11.16
79. See, for example, Xenophon, *Mem* 3.1.2–4
80. See, for example, Aristotle, *Pols* 1259b: 35, 1265a: 15
81. See, for example, Plato, *St* 293d
82. See, for example, Aristotle, *Pols* 1326b: 1–10
83. See, for example, Xenophon, *Mem* 3.9.11–12
84. Plato, *St* 305e
85. See, for example, Plato, *St* 309a
86. See, for example, Aristotle, *Pols* 1269
87. Plato, *St* 297a
88. Plato, *St* 303b
89. Plato, *St* 301d
90. See also Xenophon, *Mem* 3.2.4
91. Grant, 1991; Morris and Powell, 2006; Thucydides, 2006
92. Finley, 1963; Grant, 1991; Morris and Powell, 2006
93. Finley, 1963; Grant, 1991; Herodotus, 1998
94. Grant, 1991; Morris and Powell, 2006; Russell, 1984
95. Finley, 1963; Grant, 1991; Morris and Powell, 2006
96. See, for example, Aristotle, *Pols* 1326a: 30; Plato, *St* 301a, 309d; Xenophon, *Mem* 3.9.11
97. Cartledge, 1993; Finley, 1963; Irwin, 1989
98. Finley, 1963; Vernant, 1995, 2006
99. See, for example, Plato, *St* 297b
100. See, for example, Plato, *St* 294a, 296e
101. See, for example, Grant, 1991; Russell, 1984; Tarnas, 1991
102. See, for example, Plato, *Rep* 500c–e
103. Plato, *St* 297a–b
104. Grant, 1991; Morris and Powell, 2006; Vernant, 2006
105. 1998
106. 2006
107. Cartledge, 1993; Vernant, 2006
108. Lane, 2007
109. Plato, *Rep* Part 4, 7
110. Plato, *Rep* 374e
111. See, for example, Plato, *Rep* 475b, 493, 521c
112. See, for example, Xenophon, *Mem* 3.1–3
113. Plato, *Rep* 414b
114. Plato, *Rep* 414c
115. Plato, *Rep* 415d
116. Plato, *Rep* 415d
117. See, for example, *Pols* 1259a: 1–35, 1273b: 25
118. See, for example, Aristotle, *Pols* 1260a: 30, 1267a: 1
119. See, for example, Aristotle, *Pols* 1259b: 10, 1325b: 25
120. See, for example, Xenophon, *Ag* 11.1
121. Finley, 1963; Grant, 1991; Morris and Powell, 2006
122. Morris and Powell, 2006
123. Morris and Powell, 2006
124. Morris and Powell, 2006
125. Plato, *St* 291b
126. Plato, *St* 291c
127. Plato, *St* 303c
128. Plato, *St* 292d
129. Finley, 1963; Grant, 1991; Russell, 1984
130. Foucault, 1972, p. 191

131. Cartledge, 1993; Russell, 1984; Vernant, 2006
132. Aristotle, *Pols* 1260a: 15
133. Aristotle, *Pols* 1260a: 30
134. See, for example, Cartledge, 1993; Vernant, 2006
135. Vernant, 2006
136. Vernant, 2006
137. Cartledge, 1993; Russell, 1984; Vernant, 2006
138. Cartledge, 1993; Irwin, 1989; Vernant, 2006
139. Plato, 267
140. Aristotle, *Pols* 1326b: 5
141. Cartledge, 1993; Vernant, 2006
142. Vernant, 2006
143. Xenophon, *Ag*
144. Cartledge, 1991; Finley, 1963; Vernant, 2006
145. Xenophon, *Oec* 21.12
146. Plato, *St* 297a
147. Aristotle, *Pols* 1320a: 30
148. See, for example, Plato, *Rep* 545a–576b, *St* 303c
149. Foucault, 1985, p. 6
150. See, for example, Plato, *St* 294a
151. See, for example, Aristotle, *Pols* 1326a
152. See, for example, Xenophon, *Mem* 3.9.11
153. See, for example, Aristotle, *Pols* 1326a
154. See, for example, Plato, *St* 297a, 301d
155. See, for example, Aristotle, *Pols* 1324a: 30
156. See, for example, Xenophon, *Ag*
157. See, for example, Aristotle, *Pols* 1331: 30–40
158. See, for example, Plato, *St* 309a
159. See, for example, Xenophon, *Mem* 3.9.5
160. Plato, *St* 297b
161. See, for example, Aristotle, *Pols* 1254b: 20
162. See, for example, Plato, *St* 308d
163. Aristotle, *Pols* 1335a: 5
164. Plato, *St* 303c

4 The 16th-century European truth about leadership

> [A] prudent prince has been a rare bird in the world since the beginning of time, and a just prince an even rarer one. As a rule, princes are the greatest fools or the worst criminals on earth, and the worst is always to be expected, and little good hoped for, from them ... (God) will have them receive riches, honour and fear from everyone in heaped measure. It is his divine will and pleasure that we should call his hangmen 'gracious lords', fall at their feet and be subject to them in all humility. (Luther, 2010 [1523], p. 30)

INTRODUCTION

The focus turns now to examine a very different episteme, in which the truth about leadership was proclaimed by reference to medieval Europe's standards, values and concerns. Specifically, I trace here the final stages of the medieval discourse on leadership and the emergence of an alternative based on Enlightenment thought. This case study, therefore, offers further evidence of the contingent, constructed and ultimately fragile nature of the truth about leadership and its processes of invention.

Over the course of around 900 years, medieval Europe developed a comprehensive body of leadership knowledge which sought to prescribe how princes ought best to carry out their responsibilities. A specific genre of texts known as 'mirrors for princes' set out this knowledge, and princes themselves were its intended audience.[1] Gilbert estimated that around 1000 such texts were written between 800 and 1700.[2] These texts were so popular 'throughout Western Europe for centuries that it is difficult to imagine a renaissance library wholly without them'.[3]

This chapter examines the form, formation and demise of this medieval truth about leadership, with a particular focus on texts from the 16th century. This body of knowledge is predicated on the fact of inherited, monarchical rule which was, at the time, the most dominant form of government and was understood as being both natural and desirable.[4] Talk of leadership at this time thus pertains exclusively to the person of the prince and his activities.

I begin by considering the issues deemed problematic which inform this discourse before turning to examine its key features. Recent research has shown that there was some diversity of opinion within earlier medieval thinking about leadership.[5] However, for the later texts, on which I focus, the major themes I have identified are: determining the appropriate set of leadership virtues a prince should possess or apply; policy and practical advice on substantive issues; debate on the basis and limits of princely authority; and advice on enacting the state of majesty that was held to be that of the princely leader.[6] Each of these four themes is considered in detail, leading to my conceptualization of how the late medieval model of leadership may be summarized.

I then turn to examine the processes of formation which gave rise to this discourse, before considering the epistemic foundations and rules which rendered these ideas sensible, viable and truthful to their proponents. After that, I examine the social function and subjectivity effects of this account of the truth about leadership. Finally, I look at the demise of this discourse and its replacement by an alternative conception of leadership informed by Enlightenment ideas.

The decision to focus primarily on 16th-century texts arose because there was a particular intensity to the debate about the truth of leadership at that time.[7] Craigie specifically contends that the 16th century was 'the most prolific period' for the 'mirrors for princes' genre.[8] At this time, the diffuse and complex developments we call the Reformation and the Renaissance certainly intensified old tensions, as well as creating new ones and new possibilities.[9] These developments helped unleash a process of change which, in terms of the discourse about leadership and associated practices, resulted initially in both 'absolutist' and 'enlightened' variants of monarchical rule in the 17th century and, later, in the emergence of 'social contract' theory and other Enlightenment ideas in the late 17th and early 18th centuries.[10] These Enlightenment ideas posed profound challenges to those truths about leadership which had been developed and largely accepted over the previous millennium.

This chapter, then, covers the final stage of the discursive regime which had developed over the course of the medieval era and considers the key elements of what came to supersede it. Today, only medieval political theorists and latinists show any interest in this body of work.[11] Indeed, 'when ... kings ceased to control the destinies of Europe, such works became rarer and rarer and their readers fewer and fewer'.[12] However, despite its now obsolete status, this knowledge constitutes an important but neglected chapter in the history of Western thinking about leadership. It has, moreover, helped to shape current understandings in ways not normally understood, a matter I will return to in Chapter 7.

For this study, I have focused on a selection of 'mirrors for princes' texts for which there exist credible, albeit not unanimous, references as to their importance and for which there is a (preferably modern) English translation available.[13] The scholarly efforts of Calvin, Erasmus, Luther, James VI, Machiavelli and Lipsius will be well known to students of late medieval/early modern European history. Other key texts, while not strictly part of the 'mirrors for princes' genre, nonetheless deal with the basis and limits of princely authority which are a feature of the 'mirrors for princes' literature.[14] Finally, emblematic of the ideas which contributed to the demise of the medieval truth about leadership is John Locke's *Two Treatises on Government*.[15]

PROBLEMS

Sixteenth-century Europe was a difficult and dangerous place, especially for leaders and those vulnerable to suffering the consequences of leaders' decisions.[16] Long-standing tensions between Church and State were intensified during this period, while the Church itself was riven by the turmoil generated by the Reformation.[17] Religious disagreement generated conflict within and between states, adding a further layer of complexity to pre-existing dynastic tensions and territorial disputes.[18] European society generally remained highly vulnerable to crop failure and disease at this time, meaning life was tenuous for the vast majority of the population.[19] However, literacy rates were rising and advancements in science and technology were beginning to emerge.[20] Meanwhile, the intellectual movement known as the Renaissance stimulated 16th-century scholars to re-examine many long-held ideas and practices, as their medieval worldview was increasingly exposed to Ancient Greek and Roman thought.[21]

In this context, a challenge of the moment to 16th-century leadership scholars was how best to educate a young prince-leader for the diverse and demanding duties that lay ahead of him.[22] Of concern was how best to persuade princely leaders, who claimed status as an instrument of God's will, that though they might start a war 'on impulse', their personal lack of military experience in the proper conduct of war could result in 'a vast tide of misfortune'.[23] Further, because 'the common man is becoming more knowledgeable and a mighty plague is spreading',[24] this trend was understood to threaten the stability of monarchical rule.

Promoting the word of God was understood as vital to sustaining society.[25] Securing peace, ensuring adherence to Christian values and making the advice handed down from the ancient Greeks and Romans available to leaders, to support their betterment, were understood as matters of great importance.[26] However, as a matter of some delicacy, 'for some reason (it is the truth, though not spoken here without proper respect) either by age, education, or nature, those in the palace do not attain to the very first degree of mental and intellectual capacities'.[27] Consequently, the dilemma was how to speak 'truth' to 'power' when that power claimed it came directly from God, yet it was, potentially, rather limited in its intellectual prowess. Such were the problems facing 16th-century scholars of leadership. In response, they continued to develop the earlier medieval invention of a rich, multi-dimensional account of leadership that sought to guide leaders from the cradle to the grave.

KEY FEATURES OF THE DISCOURSE

I focus here on four key themes of the 16th-century leadership discourse identified through my examination of the archive. I look first at the virtues said to be of importance for princes.

The Virtues of Leaders; Leadership as Virtue

> Let the teacher therefore depict a sort of celestial creature, more like a divinity than a mortal, complete with every single virtue; born for the common good, sent indeed by the powers to alleviate the human condition by looking out and caring for everyone ... Let the happiness of the whole people depend upon the moral qualities of this one man; let the tutor point this out as the picture of a true prince. (Erasmus, 2010 [1516], pp. 26–27)

Defining the virtues required by leaders is the most central pre-occupation of the 'mirrors for princes' discourse. The unique contribution of different authors is to proffer their own recommendations on the most important virtues. For Calvin, 'integrity, prudence, clemency, moderation and innocence' feature as his favoured virtues.[28] Erasmus argues for 'wisdom, a sense of justice, personal restraint, foresight, and concern for the public well-being'.[29] Lipsius offers us a highly formalized and hierarchical depiction of the core virtues required for civil, communal life,[30] which I have summarized in Model 4.1. Reading from left to right, the two most important virtues of prudence and virtue are conceptualized by Lipsius as being underpinned by, or made up of, a subset of other virtues.

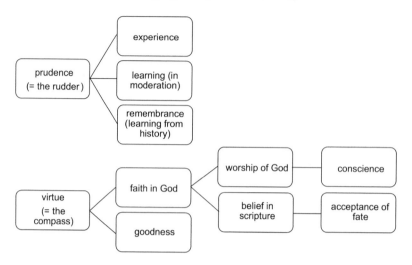

Source: developed from Lipsius, 2004 [1589].

Model 4.1   Justus Lipsius' basic model of core civil virtues

A more detailed and precise account of *leadership* virtues is also offered by Lipsius later in this text, speaking more specifically to the challenges he saw as facing princes in sustaining orderly rule.

A striking feature of the virtues set out in Model 4.2 is the sheer breadth of knowledge they entail. Leadership here requires a depth of military knowledge from the strategic through to the operational level.[31] It requires knowledge of Christian doctrine, of judicial processes, of the characteristics and skills needed in senior government officials and of ways to dress, speak and move that will evoke both fear and love from others.[32] The 'virtues' of leaders here comprise personal characteristics, behaviour, attitudes, habits, lifestyle choices, knowledge, skills or practices deemed desirable.[33] Here, the virtues relevant to leadership comprise substantive, moral/ethical, procedural, lifestyle, physical, behavioural and presentational components. The concept is rendered sufficiently elastic to include both that which is seen as 'necessary' and that which is more conventionally 'virtuous' in a moral sense.[34]

While royal status, and hence the right to lead, is conceived as being an inherited and divine gift from God, the development of the virtues required to lead well is held as being the result of learning combined with faith in God.[35] Erasmus advocates the inculcation of leadership virtues 'from the very cradle',[36] with the selection of the young leader's tutor being a critical decision that affects the future well-being of the

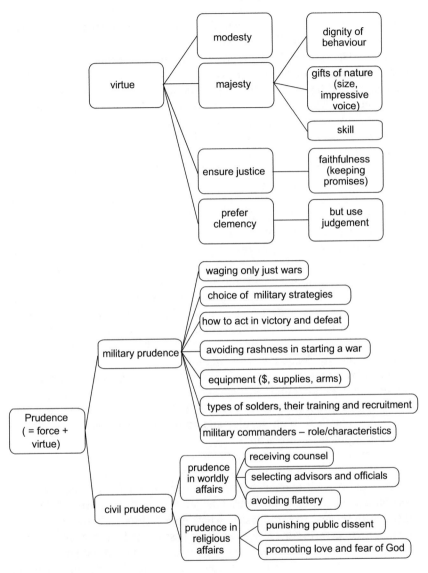

Source: developed from Lipsius, 2004 [1589].

Model 4.2   Justus Lipsius' model of core princely virtues

state, for 'a country owes everything to a good prince; but it owes the prince himself to the one whose right counsel has made him what he is'.[37] The young leader's nurses are to be 'women of blameless character', his companions are to be 'boys of good and respectable character', and he cautions that it is important to 'keep at a distance from his sight and hearing the usual crowd of pleasure-seeking youngsters, drunkard, foul-mouthed people, and especially the flatterers, as long as his moral development is not yet firmly established'.[38]

A central aspect of the leader's virtues is ensuring he has 'the best possible understanding of Christ', because 'what Christ teaches applies to no one more than to the prince'.[39] James VI articulated a similar view, claiming that leaders have a 'double obligation' to God: 'first, for that he made you a man; and next, for that he made you a little God to sitte [sit] on his throne, and rule ouer [over] other men'.[40] Leadership is thus said to necessitate knowledge of both secular and spiritual affairs. This focus on virtues, and the particular virtues which various writers proposed, typically accord strongly with the Christian morality of the time.[41]

However, we also find here repeated efforts made to contend practically with what was understood as being the realities of rule.[42] There is variability in the extent to which faith in God and the use of scriptural sources is emphasized. However, even Machiavelli, whose focus is primarily on how leaders can maintain their position and their state, and who proposes that it is acceptable if conditions so demand to act against religion, argues nonetheless that 'it is useful to seem ... religious'.[43] Fundamentally then, the virtues required of leaders, as articulated in this discourse, comprise both secular and spiritual dimensions, both ethical/moral and practical dimensions.

The texts vary in whether what is held to be desirable for leaders to do is strictly paired with the moral, ethical and religious norms of the day: at times, what is positioned as being 'necessary' or having practical value is recommended rather than a strict adherence to these norms.[44] Despite these differences in emphasis, what nonetheless coheres here is a common concern to advise leaders how best to lead, taking into account contextual factors that were broadly similar in nature: a monarchical and theocratic basis of authority; a feudal class system; competing dynastic interests; limited machinery of government; and religious dissent.[45] Importantly, none of these writers saw fit to offer an account of leadership which avoided completely issues of *realpolitik*.

The 'necessary virtues' are many and various and attract a good deal of attention. They include, for example, the calculated and prescribed use of deceit;[46] adopting a taxation policy that is not too onerous;[47] techniques for dealing with conspiracies, contempt and hatred;[48] and the best approach to take to censorship.[49] Ensuring the character of the government is stern, limiting the enactment of new laws, understanding both the character of the people and having knowledge of the land from a military perspective are promoted as important elements of leadership.[50] Being generous and mild while also instilling a fear and respect of princely authority, and not delegating matters which could undermine princely esteem or authority, also feature as relevant virtues for leaders.[51] Machiavelli's perspective on these matters of 'necessity' is of course well known: 'it is necessary for a prince, if he wishes to maintain himself, to learn to be able to be not good, and to use this faculty and not to use it according to necessity'.[52]

Foundations and Purpose of Leadership

[S]uch as light or darkness from the sun are to the world below, so too are most good or bad things from the Prince to his subjects. (Lipsius, 2004 [1589], p. 229)

I turn now to consider a second theme in the discourse which speaks of the foundation on which leaders' authority rests and the purpose of leadership. The truth about leadership as presented here is typically predicated on the understanding that hereditary monarchy is the best, most natural and/or divinely ordained form of government.[53] Reference to God's will, combined with the example of history, is used to establish both the legitimacy and desirability of monarchic rule, of inherited rule and of the scope of leader authority.[54] These key assumptions provide the platform on which the balance of the advice about how best to lead rests.

These assumptions profoundly inform the understanding of both leaders and leadership expressed here. Leaders, as God's representatives on earth, are expected here to uphold God's laws and to live according to God's commandments.[55] The expressed intention is that these laws and commandments constrain leaders' scope of action, positioning them as instruments of God's will rather than as independent, self-determining agents.

This means that leaders are, here, persons of both great and humble standing; great because they have been gifted with the authority to enact God's will, and humble because they are God's servants, only serving his will. Their greatness is also not without a price: the consequential responsibilities it creates results in leaders being especially vulnerable to failing God and thus losing their chance of achieving eternal life in God's heaven, while their humble standing renders them no more worthy of God's love and redemption than any other sinner.[56] Leaders are warned that 'the judgement after death is not the same for all: none are treated more sternly ... than those who were powerful. No other achievement will better enable you to win God's favour than if you show yourself to be a beneficial prince to your people'.[57]

The secular and spiritual scope of leadership, as proposed here, is also consistent with these key underpinning assumptions. Leadership here comprises responsibility for acting in a manner which supports the sustenance of both mortal and immortal life; both bodies and souls fall within the purview of leadership.[58] The intellectual achievement is a conception of leadership wholly consistent with the assumptions on which it rests, deeply connected with the social milieu in which it arose and which seeks to address the critical social problems of the day as understood by those who articulated these truths about leadership.

The purpose of leadership here is to maintain the public well-being, understood as comprising the promotion of religious adherence and civil order, as well as contending with all affairs of state. Leaders here are expected to be 'protectors and vindicators of public innocence, propriety, decency and tranquillity ... their own endeavour must be to provide for the common peace and well-being'.[59] Leaders are held up as 'God's jailers and hangmen' so that 'his divine wrath makes use of them to punish the wicked and maintain outward peace'.[60]

The centrality of princely leadership to social and spiritual well-being expressed here positions leaders as God's agents on earth. This view both reflected and reinforced the long-standing tension between Church and State which was such a central political issue throughout medieval times.[61] However, putting that tension aside for a moment and taking the discourse at face value, the purpose of leadership in this discourse is to be no less than God's deputy in a milieu whose prevailing worldview was to understand God as the source and centre of all things. The exalted status of God thus flowed directly and barely diluted into the exalted status of leaders.

The Substantive Requirements of Leadership

> [D]raw(e) all your law(e)s and processes to be as short and plain(e) as ye can. (James VI, 1950 [1599], p. 147)

Within this discursive regime, to purport to have knowledge of leadership necessitates speaking of the substantive issues to which leaders are expected to attend.[62] Similarly, for princes to be credible leaders they are expected here to acquire knowledge of a diverse range of what we today call public policy issues. This includes, for example, matters of diplomacy and state security, trade policy, the administration of justice, taxation policy, the control of public conduct, the selection of government officials and a strategic view of legislative change.[63] The advice that is given in respect of these matters includes how to think about these issues, identifying the kind of results leaders should seek to achieve, as well as advice on the 'how to' – techniques, tactics, strategies and methods.[64] The essential technical knowledge the leader must possess was also addressed.

In respect of state security, for example, Machiavelli recommends active and constant preparation. This hands-on process by the leader goes 'beyond keeping his men ordered and trained'. Rather, 'he must be frequently on hunts, and through these accustom his body to hardships, and meanwhile learn the nature of terrains'. This knowledge is said to be critical because it develops the skills needed to 'find the enemy, select encampments, conduct armies, order battlefields and besiege towns to your advantage'.[65]

When it comes to change, Erasmus recommends that 'the prince should avoid all innovation as far as proves possible: for even if something is changed for the better, a novel situation is still disturbing in itself. Neither the structure of the state, the customary public business of the city, nor long established laws may be changed without upheaval'.[66] Erasmus advocates incremental, subtle and gradual change if the status quo is intolerable, but argues that if the current situation is tolerable then change is not needed and should be avoided.

To uphold the standards of moral conduct, Lipsius recommends that leaders act to curb greed by limiting interest rates and profits and constraining excessive spending.[67] Associated with this, he argues that leaders must act to limit the pride people take in buildings, statues and tapestries, 'condemn ingenious and exotic' food and ensure that the manner in which people dress maintains a clear distinction between the sexes and the different social classes.[68] Lipsius recognizes that achieving these results will not be easy and so recommends the gradual application of fines and rewards, public shame and praise, and role modelling of the desired standards by the leader as necessary techniques and tactics for the leader to deploy.[69]

In respect of issues of law and order, James VI provides advice on the range of crimes which leaders cannot forgive: 'witchcraft, murder, incest, sodomy, poisoning and forging money'.[70] However, because he regards treason as possibly arising from the leader's own failures, he recommends each case be considered 'according to the circumstances ... and the quality of the committer'.[71] Maintaining law and order via the prompt exercise of coercive powers, balanced with clemency where such will enhance the leader's standing amongst the people, constitutes the prevailing recommendation in this discourse.

The attention given over to substantive issues, of which I have here addressed only a few by way of illustration, is a central feature of the 16th-century conception of leadership. Here, to speak of leadership is also to speak of any matter that falls within the public domain, as then conceived, as well as matters affecting the saving of souls and the sustenance of Christian values. The broad scope of this discursive regime serves to both reflect and reinforce the broad scope of leader authority entailed by the system of monarchical rule.

'Majesty'

> And because every city is divided into guilds or wards, he should take account of these collectivities, meet with them sometimes, and offer himself as an example of humanity and munificence, while nonetheless always keeping firm his dignity's majesty, for he does not want this ever to be lacking in anything. (Machiavelli, 2005 [ca. 1516], p. 111)

A further aspect of this account of the truth about leadership which I propose warrants attention is the special but rather tenuous qualities of the leader which are captured by the term 'majesty'. This is something which leaders are held to possess by virtue of their divine status, but equally it is something leaders must actively work at to develop and sustain.[72] The state of 'majesty' is something akin to an aura of the divine as well as of the earthly power which circulates about the person of the leader. 'Majesty' is an embodied skill or practice which includes the tone, content and extent of what leaders may say.[73] It can be diminished if leaders are seen too frequently by the common people,[74] suggesting that it is something which can be gazed upon but which will fade from view if seen too often by too many. 'Majesty' is enhanced by the clothing with which leaders cover their bodies, but can also be undermined if this clothing is unduly immodest: 'majesty' is grand but never garish.[75] 'Majesty' is exerted via the leader's bodily movement, which should imply dignity, power and authority.[76]

To maintain the aura of their earthly power, 'majesty' requires leaders to ignore matters beneath their dignity and to act decisively in response to dissent:[77] anything that could be understood as impinging on or denting their earthly power risks a diminution of their 'majesty', and hence becomes personal. This in turn means that attacks on the state are understood here as constituting attacks on the 'majesty' of the leader; not only does the prince embody the state, but also the security of the state in turn underpins and reinforces the 'majesty' of the leader.[78] This interdependence between, on the one hand, the person of the leader and their 'majesty', and the security of the state on the other, has the effect of strongly incentivizing the leader's focus on the well-being of the state, for his very 'majesty' is inextricably tied to that. This concept of 'majesty' thus constitutes a mechanism for promoting a sense of responsibility and accountability by leaders for the well-being of the state they lead. Equally, however, it creates an incentive for leaders to expand their state, via marriage, alliance or war, as doing so is understood to enhance their 'majesty'.

'Majesty', however, also functions to place all non-leaders in a subservient position vis-à-vis the leader, for it is an attribute available only to him. While courtiers and advisors may, through the careful exercise of their skills, be permitted to spend more time gazing upon the leader's 'majesty' than the average person, this quality nonetheless remains exclusive only to the leader.[79] There is no sense here that 'majesty' may 'rub off' in small quantities on those on whom the leader relies most closely.

The concept of 'majesty' thus functions to direct leaders' bodily expression, to inculcate a sense of responsibility and accountability by leaders toward their followers, and to exclude and render lacking all others. Its emphasis on bodily and verbal expression and clothing reflects the focus of the elite of early modern European society on courtly manners and the use of clothing as an expression of wealth and power.[80]

Overall Model

In this account, then, leadership is unavoidably about the administration of the state on behalf of God. It is about passing judgement and determining the appropriate punishment for those who have transgressed. Determining the appropriate laws under which society should operate, upholding the faith and making strategic choices about matters of state security are core requirements here. Leadership is also about the embodied display of 'majesty' by the leader so as to induce awe, obedience, fear, loyalty and love in followers. It is about choices made in terms of lifestyle by the leader: the time and effort dedicated to conducting official duties rather than engaging in leisure; the quality and quantity of food and drink consumed by the leader and his entourage; and the quality of clothing with which the leader dresses. It is about the ways and frequency with which the leader makes himself visible to the led, for an excess of visibility is said to undermine the desired level of mystique in which leaders should be shrouded in order to maintain their majesty.

The clear sense conveyed in this discourse is that leadership is a precarious and often dangerous matter for leaders. Followers are portrayed as typically unreliable in their loyalty, prone to 'judge and speake rashlie of their Prince',[81] while fate may also intervene at any time to undermine the leader.[82] Moreover, 'God ever looketh to your inward intention in all your actions',[83] and 'he is present with them, and indeed presides over them, when they make laws and pronounce equitable judgements',[84] so the leader's soul and afterlife are here continuously at risk.

The compound effect of these various themes is a conception of leadership which can be visually depicted as given in Model 4.3.

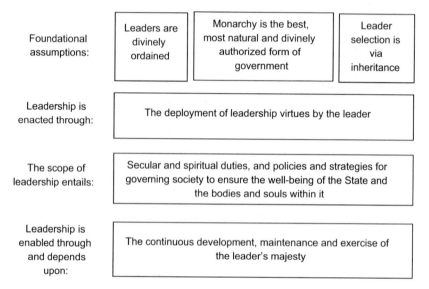

Foundational assumptions:	Leaders are divinely ordained	Monarchy is the best, most natural and divinely authorized form of government	Leader selection is via inheritance
Leadership is enacted through:	The deployment of leadership virtues by the leader		
The scope of leadership entails:	Secular and spiritual duties, and policies and strategies for governing society to ensure the well-being of the State and the bodies and souls within it		
Leadership is enabled through and depends upon:	The continuous development, maintenance and exercise of the leader's majesty		

Model 4.3   16th-century European leadership model

PROCESSES OF FORMATION

> The state is being undermined by party rivalries and afflicted by wars, robbery is everywhere, the common people are reduced to starvation and the gallows by rampant extortion, the weak are oppressed by the injustice of those in high places, and corrupt magistrates do what they please instead of what the law says: and in the middle of this, is the prince playing dice as if he were on holiday? (Erasmus, 2010 [1516], p. 47)

This account of the truth about leadership developed over the course of hundreds of years.[85] There is evidence to indicate that the discourse was repeatedly sensitive to developments in religious, legal and political theory throughout this time, adapting itself to maintain currency and credibility. Verway, for example, in his examination of the 13th-century work of William Peraldus, notes the specific ordering that leaders love God first, then themselves and then others as consistent with the then prevailing medieval worldview.[86] In his analysis of a range of 15th-century German texts, Strack reports on advice covering what leaders should do at various points during a church service, the specific religious knowledge they should possess and the qualities they should bring to their own confessional practices.[87] Yet in the 16th-century texts I have examined, these specific features have disappeared, replaced by others deemed more relevant to their contemporary context, even while the discourse still depends on other ideas which had accumulated over time. This sedimentation of knowledge, the sheer longevity of the key elements of this discursive regime and the practical reality that political and social arrangements were typically consistent with the ideas expressed in the discourse likely rendered these truths as self-evident, compelling and 'natural' in the eyes of those who lived in this time.

The production and dissemination of this discourse followed the then existing conventions for the production and dissemination of scholarly work: pamphlets and letters, both attributed and anonymous, were circulated amongst the intelligentsia, who themselves were to be found in the church, in universities and in royal courts.[88] The development of the printing press substantially increased the readership of such texts, but typically these texts were written by elites, for elites.[89]

The 16th-century texts examined here reflect a strong interest in current events and repeatedly expressed grave concern about the practical and moral state of affairs, such as shown in the quote from Erasmus at the beginning of this section. One of the most marked features of the 16th century was the extensive conflict which arose out of the schism in the Christian church known as the Reformation.[90] This intra-faith conflict of Christian against Christian was profoundly disturbing to conservative thinkers such as Erasmus and Lipsius,[91] while Luther, a leading reform thinker,[92] can be seen to have supported his goal of religious reform in his writing on secular authority by way of his generally disparaging account of leaders as poor adherents to God's commands.[93]

The issues raised in these texts can also be understood as a response to the rather more tenuous hold on power which 16th-century monarchs faced when compared with those of prior centuries.[94] This arose for a variety of reasons, such as more vociferous claims by the aristocracy for a greater influence in law-making as occurred in England and France, or popular unrest arising from the harsh conditions faced by the vast majority of the people, as seen in the German peasant revolts of 1524–1526.[95]

What came later, in the 17th and 18th centuries, were ideas (and actions) that directly threatened the foundations of monarchical rule.[96] However, in the 16th century it is not so much alternative ideas that threaten the sustenance of this discourse as the practical risk of armed conflict.[97] Consequently, the likes of Erasmus, Lipsius and Machiavelli do not actively address fundamental issues about the legitimacy of monarchical leaders because such issues were not those of the day. Rather, their efforts were more focused on the practical problems of achieving and maintaining oneself in power.

These 16th-century texts functioned, then, to sustain a system of practice and thought whose intellectual foundations were not perceived as being under serious threat at the time. The nature of the 16th-century challenge was practical rather than intellectual. Consequently, what occurred in the 16th century was a strong interlocking of scholarly discourse and social practice as each served to reinforce the validity of the other: the practice of engaging tutors for princes was reinforced by the focus placed on childhood development in leadership texts, for example. Leadership texts assume the validity of monarchical rule and, thus, addressed themselves to monarchs as their intended audience. The interweaving of Church and State is reflected in the texts, as is the practice of direct princely involvement in affairs of state, leading in turn to the need to speak of such matters when speaking of leadership. What we see in these 'mirrors for princes', then, is a mirror between discourse and practice, a mutually reinforcing dynamic which functions to legitimize, stabilize and normalize the status quo.

The Reformation affected the stability of this regime of truth because it resulted in a conflict which greatly intensified long-standing tensions between Church and State about issues of whose authority was to prevail on various issues, and between State and individual subject on issues of religious freedom.[98] However, in arguing that all Christians should directly access the word of God, unmediated by the interpretation and authority of the Church, protestant reformers (perhaps unwittingly) also unleashed a shift in understanding about how persons might access the truth which was later to have more enduring and radical impacts.[99]

In the medieval era, the word of God was understood to be the truth; the challenge was how best to understand what that word meant.[100] This in turn gave rise to the large body of medieval scholasticism as scholars, mostly clergy, debated the best interpretation of God's word.[101] Renaissance humanism began to erode this focus on biblical and patristic sources by treating Ancient Greek and Roman knowledge as having, despite its paganism, relevance, legitimacy and authority.[102] Sixteenth-century reformists such as Luther and Calvin sought to refocus attention on the bible but also posed the radical proposition that it was up to each individual to make their own interpretation and to form their own judgement.[103] This proposition, along with the notion of the natural equality of all and the revolutionary movements which committed themselves to these ideas, came in the 18th century to pose an unanswerable challenge to the discourse examined here, resulting in its demise.[104]

The constructive intent of this 16th-century discourse to both challenge and find a way to overcome what was perceived as poor or bad leadership by specifying what good leadership entailed is clear. Machiavelli's *Prince*, for example, ends with a plea that Lorenzo de Medici the Younger, to whom it was addressed, act to reverse Italy's decline which, according to Machiavelli, 'all proceeds from the weakness of the leaders'.[105] As Calvin claims,

> it is very rare for kings to exercise such self-control that their will never differs from what is equitable and right. And it is equally rare for kings to be equipped with such prudence and acuity of judgement as to be able [always] to discern what is good and useful.[106]

This discourse was clearly political in intent, seeking to define and distinguish what constitutes right and wrong, effective and ineffective, for those who hold princely office. It constructs arguments by means of which leaders may be judged, found wanting, criticized or praised. It creates standards for assessment at the same time as it offers advice on how to achieve those standards. However, all of this it does within the confines of its accepted assumptions: its politics are, thus, inherently conservative, or at most reforming, rather than radical. It constitutes a disciplinary form of knowledge, seeking to shape what is permissible and desirable by leaders. Key players in this discourse are 'insiders' who have varying degrees of standing within the systems of government then extant: a prince's tutors, advisors, actual kings themselves, as well as theologians, all participated directly in the production of this discourse over many centuries. The texts in turn serve to both enhance and reflect their standing and reputation, for only those close to leaders can credibly claim leadership knowledge.

UNDERPINNING ASSUMPTIONS

I turn now to consider the underpinning epistemic foundations which I propose rendered this discourse sayable and sensible to those who participated in it, after which I identify the implicit rules governing this discursive formation.

The all-encompassing scope of the leadership discourse is character-istic of the broader medieval episteme within which it developed. Here, a key assumption guiding thought is that of the inter-connectedness of all things, as each is understood as being part of God's design.[107] This holistic and profoundly religious understanding of the nature of reality, of all that is both seen and unseen, is infused in all aspects of this conception of leadership. Here, one cannot talk of leadership without also talking of God and his divine gift to leaders which renders them as such.[108] One cannot talk of the practical or secular matters to which leaders attend without reference to issues of Christian teaching which are to inform how those practical matters are to be dealt with.[109]

Renaissance humanism, as an intellectual movement, also constitutes an important feature of the epistemic paradigm shaping this discourse.[110] Consequently, to establish the credibility of the recommendations made, to affirm their status as both truth and wisdom, the deployment of both scholastic and humanist norms of citing biblical, patristic and classical sources is de rigeur in these texts. Lipsius' work is perhaps the most masterful of all the texts I draw on for this study in terms of how he satisfies these Renaissance norms, for his work comprises a patchwork of '2669 quotes from 116 authors'.[111] The impression constructed by the use of this form is that Lipsius has compiled the best of ancient wisdom to put before the reader and that his account is, thus, authoritative; indeed, this work was widely circulated and continuously reprinted for over two centuries.[112]

The nature and influence of religious beliefs and the intellectual and cultural values and norms of the Renaissance, thus, strongly inform this discourse. Here, issues of ethics and morality cannot be separated in accounting for leadership, nor can the substantive issues of governance. Accordingly, issues of form and substance, of process and morality, of power and ethics, of public and private cannot be pulled apart one from the other as they all have a part to play in this all-encompassing conception of leadership. These 'requirements', which shape what is sayable and sensible in respect of leadership, reflect the underpinning epistemic conditions then prevailing.

The implicit rules governing this discursive regime of truth are as follows:

- talk of leadership is to pertain only to the person of the prince, as something unique and divinely gifted to him
- talk of leadership must be tied to talk of God's will and the upholding of Christian values

- God's will and God's wisdom must be treated as ultimately unknowable but always right, without error
- consequently, it must be assumed that in exercising God's will leaders can never err, so the key task for participants in this discourse is determining what advice will best help leaders understand and carry out God's will
- talk of leadership necessitates talk of the substantive issues to which leaders are expected to attend and requires expert knowledge of these matters
- posit only that which will maintain the monarchical form of leadership intact and beyond question
- identify that which will maintain the king in his estate and further enhance his majesty.

Machiavelli tended toward lip service in respect of the religious elements of these rules,[113] but apart from this there is a remarkable degree of consistency in the texts examined in their adherence to these rules.

SOCIAL FUNCTION AND SUBJECTIVITY EFFECTS

The social function of this discursive regime is multi-faceted. The aim is clearly to uphold monarchical rule through the claims it makes about the desirability and divinely ordained inevitability of such a system.[114] However, at the same time, the aim is to persuade monarchical leaders of the value of acting in a manner consistent with selected Christian values and focused on the well-being of the people; ethical and social concerns are absolutely central issues here.[115] The discourse challenges and seeks to advise leaders on how to be 'better', both morally and in terms of their effectiveness. It also enables and encourages the giving of direct and blunt advice to leaders by those who can claim credibility for the advice given, according to the standards of the time. Consequently, this is no mere hagiographic enterprise, nor can it be treated simply as offering an apologist account of monarchical leadership. This constitutional model is assumed and not questioned, but, within the constraints of that model, the aim here is to generate results that will better serve the interests of the many and not only the few.

The discourse seeks to sustain its own viability through claiming both the necessity and desirability of its own existence and that of which it speaks.[116] Through the claims made to possess privileged knowledge of what it takes to lead well, the discourse positions itself as being of great value not only to leaders, but also to others who would wish to better understand leaders or who are destined to become leaders in future.[117] To the extent that leadership is positioned as being difficult, problematic and yet vital to social well-being, the discourse in so speaking warrants its own relevance and importance.

In respect of substantive issues of government policy, multiple effects are sought. By way of example, a conservative attitude toward making legislative change is promoted, preferring established laws over new laws.[118] The discourse advocates a restrained approach to taxation policy, such that tax is not overly burdensome on the people and leads to dissent or even rebellion.[119] The attitude promoted toward religious freedom is variable but generally errs toward a cautiously liberal stance, provided that the exercise of religious freedom does not result in threats to the maintenance of social order.[120] A cautious and cautionary approach to war is offered.[121] At a time when monarchical leadership was the accepted norm, the truth about leadership as advanced here was, thus, one which sought to materially influence government policy. Leadership knowledge here required not just knowledge of leadership behaviours, attributes, characteristics and techniques, but also knowledge about a wide range of public policy issues. What we today call 'political science' was here conjoined seamlessly with 'leadership studies'.

In terms of power, this discourse seeks emancipatory and repressive effects, for its aim is to both empower and constrain leaders. It offers a disciplinary regime of truth which seeks to control every aspect of the leader's life from birth to death.[122] At the same time, it warrants the system of monarchical rule which provides to the leader enormous power subject to very limited constraints.[123] The relations of power constructed here are determinedly unequal, reflecting the unique, divine status which marks out the leader as inherently superior, making his will more legitimate and more powerful than others. A surfeit of agency is granted to the leader in this discourse and this is clearly at the expense of the agency deemed legitimate to all others bar God.[124] Here, seeking to impose one's will or one's agency in direct contradiction to the will or agency of the leader is positioned as a most serious crime, an offence not only against the leader but against God himself.[125] The case that is made for the validity and utility of controlling follower agency could hardly be more comprehensive or intimidating. It reflects the appreciation that followers, particularly en masse, possess the power to frustrate, undermine and potentially impede the leader's rightful exercise of his power. This threat which followers pose is ever present.

The social function of this discourse is not only multi-faceted but it also operates at multiple levels. It seeks to influence leader behaviour in terms of both personal conduct and in respect of a wide range of policy issues, by prescribing the standards and strategies leaders should strive to adopt. It seeks to influence those who work directly with leaders in official roles, by setting a standard for what constitutes good advice and defining the responsibilities of such advisors to offer frank advice. Although it does not address itself to the ordinary person, the discourse does function to reinforce the enormous distance between such persons and their leader in terms of power, responsibilities, knowledge and status in the eyes of God. In the attitude it evinces toward the 'common folk', it seeks to maintain their lowly status vis-à-vis leaders and offers both encouragement and threat to ensure the acceptance of this situation.

Because leadership is inextricably tied to the powers and responsibilities of princely rule, the concept of leadership as expressed here cannot, by definition, apply to anyone other than the person of the prince *qua* the prince. A key concern is for leaders to ensure that followers respect, love and fear them, for this is considered necessary to maintain the leader's position. Lipsius associates hatred with the nature of kings and kingship, claiming that 'god made hatred and kingship together'.[126] Accordingly, 'kings live in fear'.[127]

This balance of respect, love and fear is to be achieved through a multiplicity of means. The prudent balancing of the use of force and acts of generosity, virtue and cunning, punishment and clemency are all deemed aspects of effective leadership.[128] A reliance on laws and formal procedures combined with the use of personal judgement and intervention, according to the king's will, is expected.[129] Visible displays of 'majesty' balanced with a distancing of the leader from the led are demanded, because 'the prince should be removed as far as possible from the low concerns and sordid emotions of the common people'.[130] To further maintain this distance of the leader from the led, while it is accepted that 'we have all our faults which (privately betwixt you and God) should serve you for examples to meditate upon and mend in your person', these 'should not be a matter of discourse to others'.[131]

For leaders, this discourse produces a disciplinary regime which aims to govern the totality of life, 'from the very cradle' through to entry into heaven.[132] Here, there is no aspect of the leader's life which sits outside the scope of what is deemed relevant to leadership; no space is permitted for a private self or a self that extends beyond the duties of the leader.[133] The leader is expected to conceive of themselves as both master and servant, focused only on doing that which will protect and enhance the well-being of the people and the state.[134] The notion of 'majesty' serves both to sustain the leader's sense of their unique and superior status and to render matters of state as being of deep personal significance insofar as they may either enhance or diminish the leader's majesty.[135]

The leader subjectivity constructed here is one that is grandiose yet also humble, outwardly calm and dignified yet inwardly perpetually anxious due to the onerous burdens placed upon it and the tenuous access it has to God's grace.[136] The leader is also expected to function as a role model for all citizens in terms of how to live a good and moral life: 'teach your people by your example, for people are naturallie [naturally] inclined to counterfaite [copy] (like apes) their Princes maners [manners]'.[137] The advice that leaders limit their exposure to the view of the 'common' people and consider themselves immune to their more 'base' concerns and tendencies suggests that this role-modelling process occurs either via rare glimpses or via second-hand transmissions of accounts of the leader.

The accumulation of worldly knowledge and sound judgement on complex affairs of state is positioned in the discourse as a lifelong expectation, incentivizing leaders to understand themselves as perpetual learners.[138] As learning from history is treated by humanist thinkers as a key source of wisdom, the kind of knowledge leaders are expected to acquire is the capacity to compare and contrast between different situations in order to discern what may be relevant to the situation at hand. So, for example, Machiavelli counsels that 'the prince ought to read histories, and in them consider the actions of the excellent men. He should see how they governed themselves in war, and examine the causes of their victories and losses, so as to be able to avoid the latter and imitate the former'.[139] The emphasis placed on the value of being surrounded by wise counsellors also positions leaders to understand themselves as dependent on these others to assist them in carrying out their duties and to value expertise in others.[140] Cumulatively, these elements in the discourse result in a strong emphasis on the ongoing accumulation of knowledge as a key aspect of leader subjectivity.

For followers, the subjectivity effects are various, as some followers are marked out in the discourse as having specific responsibilities toward the prince: to educate him in his childhood; to nurse him; to provide prudent counsel to him; to not flatter him; and to execute his instructions and laws in accordance with his will and without corruption.[141] Most followers, however, are to understand themselves as not marked by God as especially deserving, but rather as prone to varying weaknesses or errors and thus needing the leader to guide, to judge and to punish if required to bring them back in line with God's and society's expectations.[142] Followers are to understand themselves as privileged if they are permitted to gaze upon the leader, yet also potentially dangerous to the leader should their own immorality or lack of grace somehow 'rub off' on the leader.[143]

The leader–follower relationship as expressed in this discourse is one that is wrought with tension and profoundly unstable. The leader is to serve, to love, to fear, to judge and to punish the people.[144] Followers for their part are expected to love, to fear, to obey and to hate leaders.[145] Little of this relationship is to occur via direct interaction between the leader and the led.[146] Mutual distrust and distance are central to the leader–follower relationship here, reflecting the perceived underlying tension that followers are conflicted in their desire and willingness to be led: while they may at times understand and accept that it is in their best interest to follow the leader, they also resent and fear the leader's power over them. That this way of viewing leader–follower dynamics was widespread is reflected in the focus the discourse places on leaders actively managing the *realpolitik* of achieving and maintaining office.

What is sought of leaders in this discourse is extremely demanding.[147] Morally, they are typically expected to be as unsullied and upright as Christ was understood to be according to Christian doctrine, yet unlike Christ they were also expected to contend with the complex requirements of governing society.[148] These demands are rendered especially onerous because of the view that most people were 'ungrateful, changeable, pretenders and dissemblers, avoiders of dangers, and desirous of gain, and while you do them good they are wholly yours, offering you their blood, their property, their life and their children ... when the need is far off, but when it comes close to you they revolt'.[149]

This rather dismal depiction of the type of relationship that is said to exist between leaders and followers is a central assumption which shapes the conception of leadership seen here. Because followers are understood as being prone to capricious, disorderly and immoral behaviour, leaders are consequently warranted to use force and to authorize punishment so as to bring the people to order.[150] Leaders must also deploy the aura of 'majesty' and invoke the backing of God for their actions, so as to persuade followers toward compliance. The deployment of both force and persuasion, of both reward and punishment, and of both a religious and secular authority are, thus, inherent in this account of leadership.

In this discourse, the account given of the leader–follower relationship thus evokes a sense of a battleground: on the one hand, there is the leader's prudence, restraint and good judgement and on the other, the impulsive, licentious and short-sighted actions to which followers are prone.[151] Leaders are a critical source of constraint on followers, cajoling and coercing them to act more prudently and morally.[152] However, follower compliance is also central to a leader maintaining their 'majesty', while their resistance threatens not only this but also the expectation that he will bring about social order and encourage the saving of their souls.[153] Thus, while leaders and followers are here joined into a relationship of mutual dependency, there appears to be a very restricted sense of common interest. In this relationship, the potential for a battle of all against one seems ever present: that leadership is dangerous and tenuous for leaders, that hatred of the leader by the led is inevitable, are central messages.

EPILOGUE: THE END OF THIS DISCURSIVE REGIME AND ITS REPLACEMENT

The 16th-century truth about leadership is no longer accepted as true today. In fact, by the end of the revolutionary age those truths had been largely discredited intellectually, morally and practically in many parts of Europe and even more so in the 'new world'.[154] A new episteme had arisen, one in which the 'problem' of leadership was now resolved by a focus on the rule of law as opposed to rule arising from a specific, special individual. The debate between Filmer[155] and Locke[156] captures the key intellectual elements of this shift.

Filmer, writing in 1648, put forward an emphatic and dogmatic assertion of princely authority as based on biblical authority and inheritance right back to Adam. This authority, he argued, is absolute in nature and cannot be shared or disobeyed as to do so is to go against God's will. The inequality between leaders and the led is held to be both natural and unchangeable. Absolute monarchical rule is consequently positioned by Filmer as the only form of leadership that is proper and leaders are accountable to God and God alone. What is so important about Filmer's work for our purposes here is the mere fact of its existence.

As seen from the foregoing examination of 16th-century works, Filmer's claims were not in any significant sense new. The proposition that kings held their position as a consequence of God's will was, as we have seen, a long-standing feature of the 'mirrors for princes' genre. However, in Filmer's text his *only* concern is to sustain the validity of this view from what he perceived as dangerous threats arising from the anti-royalist movement. The sheer intensity of the debate over the origins, nature and scope of royal authority was a critical factor giving rise to the English Civil War (1642–46, 1648–49, 1649–51).[157] Filmer was at one point jailed for his support of the royalist cause and his house was ransacked.[158] In the high stakes context posed by these events, Filmer chose to focus his efforts on defending the fundamental assumptions upon which the body of leadership knowledge examined here rested. His work effectively constitutes a defence of first principles and of last measures.

The eventual outcome of the English Civil War and the subsequent Revolution of 1688 was the establishment of a system of constitutional monarchy, wherein the monarch's role was largely symbolic, their powers formally constrained, and parliament claimed sovereignty in law-making and directly oversaw the administration of government activities.[159] In the case of England, these changes were wrought more by force of arms than force of ideas.[160] Yet writing in 1690, Locke treated Filmer's thesis on the divine right of kings to rule as still sufficiently credible and influential as a regime of truth to warrant a direct and in-depth rebuttal. That rebuttal constitutes the first of Locke's *Two Treatises on Government.*

Locke's work is widely regarded as having played a central role in the Enlightenment, informing various democratically inspired revolutions of the 18th and 19th centuries and materially shaping the American Declaration of Independence and the American Constitution.[161] Locke's key proposition is that the natural freedom of all people is both God's will and human nature, meaning, consequently, that leadership of the state can only legitimately arise through a process of consent for none has the inherent right to rule over others.[162] Here, Locke was building on the liberal potential of Hobbes' *Leviathan*[163] wherein the relationship between individuals and society was conceived as having arisen by way of agreement or social contract. Locke rejected Hobbes' defence of the consequential absolute authority of the sovereign that Hobbes claimed existed subsequent to the agreement to enter into society. Instead, Locke held that the consent of the majority constitutes the basis of legitimate leadership, meaning in turn that democracy is the best form of government. Consequently for Locke, only within the confines of a constitutionally governed democracy may leadership occur, and leaders are formally accountable to their fellow 'man'.

In Locke's hands, 'leadership' was re-invented as an institutionalized concept, embedded in constitutional arrangements and not reliant on individual will. Leadership is here de-personalized and infused into processes of election and legally prescribed rights and powers. Leadership in Lockean terms is disembodied, diffused and distributed into systems and processes of government. It is everywhere in the formal machinery of government, but also in no one person.

Today, we conceive of Locke's work as being the expression of a political theory. However, it emerged as a direct challenge to Filmer's assertion of the validity of monarchical rule, which in turn constituted a central element in the 16th-century (and earlier) European conception of leadership. Locke's intention was, thus, clearly to challenge the leadership model of his times, an ambition so dangerous that he continued to deny authorship of his work until his death.[164] Today, this disembodied, institutionalized and constitutionally expressed conception of leadership is barely recognizable to our eyes as such.

CONCLUSION

Late medieval scholars produced an account of leadership wholly consistent with the long-standing system of monarchical rule and the religious and intellectual norms of their time. In so doing, this discourse also had its challenges for it sought to speak 'truth' to those in positions of immense power, to guide their thought and actions in a certain direction. This multi-dimensional account provided knowledge deemed vital for leaders to acquire, beginning from early childhood and continuing through the whole of their adult life. It offered guidance for living a 'good' and 'proper' life as a leader, addressing itself to all aspects of the leader's duties and to the safety of his body and soul. It sought to promote an approach to leading that served the well-being of the people and the state at the same time as it preserved the leader's superiority, legitimacy and power.

When political, intellectual and religious understandings changed with the emergence of Enlightenment thinking, this medieval construction of the truth about leadership faltered and was undone by challenges to its most basic assumption of divine, natural inequality. Moreover, despite its centuries of development this account of the truth about leadership could not be sustained as valid separate from its institutional expression in hereditary monarchical government. As kings fell from the throne throughout the 17th, 18th and 19th centuries, so too was this body of knowledge consigned to the past, deemed false and irrelevant. Yet, in its demand that leaders must seek to secure the betterment of others, there remains the potential for responsible leadership from which we could yet benefit.

NOTES

1. Gilbert, 1938; Morrow, 2005; Skinner, 2002
2. 1938
3. Gilbert, 1938, p. 5
4. See, for example, Bodin, 2009 [1576]; Erasmus, 2010 [1516]; Lipsius, 2004 [1589]. Original dates of publication are noted in square brackets
5. See, for example, Bejczy and Nederman, 2007; Strack, 2007; Verway, 2007

6. See, for key examples, Bodin, 2009 [1576]; Calvin, 2010 [1559]; Erasmus, 2010 [1516]; Filmer, 2004 [1648]; James VI of Scotland (later James I of England), 1950 [1599]; Lipsius, 2004 [1589]; Machiavelli, 2005 [ca. 1516]
7. Allen, 1951; Gilbert, 1938
8. 1950, p. 74
9. Cameron, 2001; Hopfl, 2010; Skinner, 2002
10. Black, 2001; Craigie, 1950; Laslett, 2010; Tooley, 2009
11. See, for example, Bejczy and Nederman, 2007; Strack, 2007; Waszink, 2004
12. Craigie, 1950, p. 74
13. i.e. Calvin, 2010; Erasmus, 2010; James VI, 1950; Lipsius, 2004; Luther, 2010; Machiavelli, 2005
14. See Bodin, 2009; Filmer, 2004
15. 2010
16. Allen, 1951; Cameron, 2001; Skinner, 2002
17. Cameron, 2001; Gunn, 2001; Jardine, 2010
18. Allen, 1951; Gunn, 2001; Skinner, 2002
19. Cameron, 2001; Gunn, 2001
20. Cameron, 2001; Gunn, 2001
21. Allen, 1951; Cameron, 2001; Russell, 1984
22. Erasmus, 2010; James VI, 1950; Machiavelli, 2005
23. Erasmus, 2010, p. 20; see also Lipsius, 2004 and Machiavelli, 2005
24. Luther, 2010, p. 32
25. See, for example, James VI, 1950; Lipsius, 2004
26. See, for example, Erasmus, 2010; Luther, 2010
27. Lipsius, 2004, p. 351
28. 2010, p. 53
29. 2010, p. 5
30. 2004
31. See, for example, Machiavelli, 2005
32. See, for example, Erasmus, 2010
33. See, for example, James VI, 1950
34. See, for example, Lipsius, 2004
35. See, for example, James VI, 1950
36. 2010, p. 5
37. 2010, p. 6
38. 2010, p. 8
39. Erasmus, 2010, p. 13
40. 1950, p. 25, text in brackets added
41. Cameron, 2001; Gunn, 2001; Jardine, 2010
42. See, for example, Lipsius, 2004
43. 2005, p. 95
44. See, for example, the stance taken by Erasmus (2010), Lipsius (2004) and Machiavelli (2005) on these matters
45. Allen, 1951; Cameron, 2001; Gunn, 2001
46. See, for example, Lipsius, 2004
47. See, for example, James VI, 1950
48. See, for example, Machiavelli, 2005
49. See, for example, Erasmus, 2010
50. See, for example, Erasmus, 2010
51. See, for example, Lipsius, 2010
52. 2005, p. 87
53. See, for example, Calvin, 2010
54. See, for example, Lipsius, 2004
55. See, for example, Erasmus, 2010
56. See, for example, Luther, 2010

57. Erasmus, 2010
58. See, for example, James VI, 1950
59. Calvin, 2010, pp. 59–60
60. Luther, 2010, p. 30
61. Allen, 1951; Cameron, 2001; Hopfl, 2010
62. See, for example, Lipsius, 2004
63. See, for example, James VI, 1950; Machiavelli, 2005
64. See, for example, Erasmus, 2010
65. 2005, pp. 85–86
66. 2010, p. 71
67. 2004
68. 2004, p. 489
69. 2004, p. 493
70. 1950, p. 64
71. 1950, p. 64
72. See, for example, Machiavelli, 2005
73. See, for example, Lispsius, 2004
74. See, for example, Erasmus, 2010
75. See, for example, James VI, 1950
76. See, for example, Lipsius, 2004
77. See, for example, Luther, 2010
78. See, for example, Lipsius, 2004
79. See, for example, Erasmus, 2010
80. Allen, 1951; Skinner, 2002; Waszink, 2004
81. James VI, 1950, p. 93
82. See, for example, Lipsius, 2004
83. James VI, 1950, p. 63
84. Calvin, 2010, p. 52
85. Allen, 1951; Skinner, 2002; Waszink, 2004
86. 2007
87. 2007
88. Allen, 1951; Skinner, 2002; Waszink, 2004
89. Allen, 1951; Hopfl, 2010; Jardine, 2010
90. Allen, 1951; Cameron, 2001; Gunn, 2001
91. Jardine, 2010; Waszink, 2004
92. Cameron, 2001; Hopfl, 2010
93. See Luther, 2010
94. Allen, 1951; Skinner, 2002; Waszink, 2004
95. Allen, 1951; Gunn, 2001; Skinner, 2002
96. Black, 2001; Briggs, 2001; Hampson, 2001
97. Allen, 1951; Cameron, 2001; Gunn, 2001
98. Gunn, 2001
99. Cameron, 2001; Gunn, 2001; Hampson, 2001
100. Morrow, 2005; Russell, 1984; Skinner, 2002
101. Russell, 1984; Skinner, 2002
102. Jardine, 2010; Skinner, 2002; Waszink, 2004
103. Cameron, 2001; Hopfl, 2010; Russell, 1984
104. Black, 2001; Hampson, 2001; Russell, 1984
105. 2005, p. 121
106. 2010, p. 56–57
107. Russell, 1984; Skinner, 2002; Tarnas, 1991
108. See, for example, Erasmus, 2010
109. See, for example, Lipsius, 2004
110. Allen, 1951; Jardine, 2010; Waszink, 2004
111. Waszink, 2004, p. 5

112. Waszink, 2004
113. 2005
114. See, for example, James VI, 1950
115. See, for example, Erasmus, 2010
116. See, for example, Lipsius, 2004
117. See, for example, Machiavelli, 2005
118. See, for example, Erasmus, 2010
119. See, for example, James VI, 1950
120. See, for example, Lipsius, 2004; Machiavelli, 2005
121. See, for example, Erasmus, 2010
122. See, for example, Erasmus, 2010
123. See, for example, Lipsius, 2004
124. See, for example, James VI, 1950
125. See, for example, Lipsius, 2010
126. 2004, p. 411
127. Lipsius, 2004, p. 413
128. See, for example, Machiavelli, 2005
129. See, for example, Lipsius, 2004
130. Erasmus, 2010, p. 24
131. James VI, 1950, p. 66
132. Erasmus, 2010, p. 5
133. See, for example, James VI, 1950
134. See, for example, Lipsius, 2004
135. See, for example, Machiavelli, 2005
136. See, for example, Erasmus, 2010
137. James VI, 1950, p. 53, text in square brackets added
138. See, for example, Lipsius, 2004
139. 2005, p. 86
140. See, for example, Erasmus, 2010
141. See, for example, Erasmus, 2010; Machiavelli, 2005
142. See, for example, Lipsius, 2004
143. See, for example, Erasmus, 2010
144. See, for example, Machiavelli, 2005
145. See, for example, Lipsius, 2004
146. See, for example, Erasmus, 2010
147. See, for example, Lipsius, 2004
148. See, for example, James VI, 1950
149. Machiavelli, 2005, p. 91
150. See, for example, Lipsius, 2004
151. See, for example, Lipsius, 2004; Machiavelli, 2005
152. See, for example, Luther, 2010
153. See, for example, James VI, 1950
154. Allen, 1951; Briggs, 2001; Hampson, 2001; Skinner, 2002
155. 2004 [1648]
156. 2010 [1690]
157. Black, 2001; Russell, 1984; Somerville, 2004
158. Russell, 1984; Somerville, 2004
159. Miller, 1983; Russell, 1984
160. Russell, 1984
161. Laslett, 2010; Russell, 1984; Tarnas, 1991
162. 2010
163. 1996
164. Laslett, 2010

5 The foundations of leadership 'science': Carlyle and the trait theorists

> All things that we see standing accomplished in the world are properly the outer material result, the practical realisation and embodiment, of thoughts that dwelt in the Great Men sent into the world. (Carlyle, 1993 [1840], p. 3)

> The evidence is all around us. It is in our daily lives – in our schools, businesses, social groups, religious organizations, and public agencies. It is in our local community, in our more distant state government and national government, and on the international scene. Leadership makes the difference. (Bass, 2008, p. 3)

CHALLENGING LEADERSHIP SCIENCE

Today, leadership scholarship is generally understood as according with the standards, values and norms of modern social science.[1] Most crucially, this means it is understood as offering an objective assessment of independently verifiable evidence leading to findings that, while always provisional, can nonetheless be trusted as accurate, fair and reliable until proven otherwise.[2] Knowledge generated via scientific methods is expected to be continuously improved, authoritative and to serve all of humanity, not just partisan interests.[3] This and the next chapter will, however, challenge the normal confidence that what has been produced in the era of modern leadership studies is a reliable and progressive science.

To be clear, I am not assuming that a truly objective, 'scientific' account of leadership can, in fact, be established, nor am I assuming that leadership has a definitive essence or character which exists outside of, or prior to, how we conceive of it. However, those are the assumptions to which most leadership scholars today hold.[4] Accordingly, over the course of this and the next chapter I directly challenge the extent to which a credible science of leadership has been achieved *according to the standards and assumptions by which the field typically operates.* I offer an alternative account of developments in the field.

As the quotes above from Carlyle and, nearly 170 years later, from Bass exemplify, the central preoccupation and positioning of modern leadership discourse has been its highly optimistic stance as regards the nature, value and impact of leadership. According to conventional understanding, this confidence that leadership is the answer regardless of the question has been subjected to the rigours of modern science over this time.[5] Starting from the modern era's first theorization, developed by Carlyle in 1840, it is generally accepted that leadership knowledge has subsequently become broader, deeper, more sophisticated and more firmly grounded as an account of the truth through applying the standards expected of the scientific process.[6]

In the mainstream of leadership studies, the established form and methods of social science are indeed followed faithfully. The careful definition of constructs, the use of anonymous surveys and advanced statistical methods of data analysis are common practices now used in studies of leadership.[7] These studies predominantly rely on an 'established' leadership theory and seek to expand knowledge of its characteristics, effects and antecedents.[8] It is, therefore, now widely accepted that certain important 'facts' about leadership have been established to the level of social scientific proof.[9] Developments in the field are typically explained as emerging from the scientific process wherein error is weeded out, ignorance progressively overcome and reliable knowledge accumulated.[10] Against all this, my argument is that it is the periodic power/knowledge 'revolutions' in theoretical paradigms, themselves a response to shifting problems and epistemic conditions, which have provided both the foundations and driving force for 'leadership science' and that these are not scientific in nature or origin. I propose that what is revealed in the archive is the skilful deployment of the discursive norms of science, all the while relying on largely unquestioned yet problematic assumptions and aims which are profoundly political rather than scientific in nature. Moreover, the dominant 'truths' which have been produced in this discursive regime are ones that I contend produce troubling effects for 'leaders', 'followers' and their relationship. The 'truth' about leadership which now dominates contemporary thinking is one which I argue insidiously seeks to control leader subjectivity so as to bring about its complete conformity with organizational interests. Simultaneously, follower autonomy and self-responsibility are subjugated in the name of enhanced workplace productivity framed as personal development. Such is the freedom from ignorance now on offer.

My contention is that what has emerged is most usefully understood as a highly sophisticated, faith-based discursive regime, both driven by and adaptive to shifting political, economic and social concerns. My argument is that 'leadership science' is not scientific at its base, nor is the mainstream of knowledge produced via this 'science' progressive in any sense of the word. I argue that what is 'known' relies on what is ignored or denied, what is claimed as the truth rests on what cannot be objectively determined, and what is promoted derives from a faith that is largely unquestioned because it has become normalized.

FOCUS

The modern era of the leadership studies field is generally agreed to have been dominated by different theoretical paradigms at different times.[11] These developments are summarized in Table 5.1. In this chapter, we will look at the first two of these paradigms: Carlyle's 'great man' thesis and trait theory. Chapter 6 will address the others. The shifts from one paradigm to another are conventionally explained as being due to advancements in knowledge, resulting in the pursuit of a new research direction.[12] The arguments made here suggest that other, non-scientific, factors and forces are actually much more relevant in explaining these repeated changes in direction.

Table 5.1　Major theoretical paradigms in leadership science

Time period	Dominant theoretical paradigm
Ca. 1840–1890s	Carlyle's great man thesis
Ca. 1890s–late 1940s	trait theory
Ca. late 1940s–late 1960s	leader behaviour
Ca. late 1960s–1978	situational/contingency models
Ca. 1978–present day	'new leadership' (charismatic, visionary, transformational theories)

Sources:　Bass, 2008; Huczynski and Buchanan, 2006; Jackson and Parry, 2011.

For each of these paradigms, I begin my analysis by identifying the issues deemed problematic which I argue shaped that paradigm's emergence. I then examine the key features of that discourse, its processes of formation, social function and subjectivity effects. I will, however, defer my assessment of the underpinning assumptions informing leadership 'science' until Chapter 6 in order to consider these aspects of the whole modern period at one time.

PROBLEMS

> There can be no question of the fact of inequality ... Its significance depends upon the proportion of men with great capacity and high faculty to those of the lower and lowest orders of gifts. Obviously there are fewer of the former, more of the latter ... the human race (is divided) into a few clever individuals, many ordinary, some decidedly stupid. (Lehman, 1966 [1928], p. 7)

> The gene-and-genius theory of leadership is that the source of the special ability that accounts for leadership is to be found in the relationship of the genes. That is a biological theory of leadership which has a eugenic phase, namely, that a person can select for marriage a mate who has special ability and can thus predispose his offspring to superior achievement and leadership. (Bogardus, 1934, p. 41)

The established order of things was undergoing dramatic change in mid-19th-century England. Industrialization was bringing about dramatic changes to traditional forms and relations of production.[13] Greater social mobility and rapid developments in science and technology were occurring, while the influence of the church was waning.[14] The 1832 Reform Act resulted in a broadened political franchise and undermined traditional privileges,[15] while slavery was legally abolished in most British territories in 1833. A more egalitarian approach to the rights of persons was, thus, gaining momentum, a development which threatened the traditional social order. The French Revolution (1789) and the loss of America from the British Empire (1783) had already pointed to the potentially dramatic consequences of these ideas.

For Carlyle, many of these developments were seen not as progress but as social breakdown. His response was to advocate the worship of heroic leaders as the means to reinvigorate a society he saw as increasingly immoral, lacking in cohesion and damaged by many of the developments noted above.[16] Carlyle's solution called on both the 'human spirit', so central to the Romantic worldview he held, and the new science of psychology. In doing this, he sought to overcome what he problematized as the excessively rationalist accounts of human nature and life promoted by the Enlightenment and simultaneously separate his ideas about leadership from those of the medieval era.[17] Most important of all, the problem, as Carlyle saw it, was to reinvigorate admiration for individual boldness and respect for leaders, which he saw as being undermined by the increasingly rational, secular, egalitarian spirit of his age.[18] This politically conservative, Romanticist view of the emerging modern industrial democratic society as being deeply problematic thus shaped Carlyle's development of the first modern theorization of leadership, a view which he first presented by way of a series of lectures in 1840. Leadership science began here, with Carlyle's invention of the modern hero-leader to whom obedience and worship were due.

By the end of the 19th century, the problematics informing leadership scholars were different, and from this came a changed approach to speaking the truth about leadership. Social Darwinian thought had influentially positioned social ills as arising from a mismatch between a person's natural abilities and their social position.[19] The task of leadership studies was thus to determine how best to identify those naturally fit to lead, thereby avoiding the harm to society which could arise if those not properly suited to leadership were wrongly selected. Establishing credibility according to the standards demanded by modern science meant that the use of statistics was now needed, so as to proffer quantitative evidence of leadership.[20] For leadership scholars, these factors demanded a focus on statistically identifying leader traits. For political conservatives, what was needed was evidence that leaders were indeed born to rule, thereby 'proving' that the inequality in society now being so strongly challenged by liberal, progressive thinkers was in fact natural. In the first part of the 20th century, leadership science duly responded to these issues, inventing trait theory as the route to discovering the truth about leadership.

KEY FEATURES OF THE DISCOURSE

From around the middle of the 19th century through to about World War II, the scholarly discourse on leadership focused almost exclusively on the personal qualities of leaders.[21] While scholars varied as to whether they considered that leadership qualities were inherited, and there was debate over the extent to which environmental factors were also important,[22] there was a widespread consensus that leadership was a personal trait.[23]

Beginning from around the end of the 19th century, the key task was generally conceived as determining to a scientific standard of proof those traits that marked someone out as a leader.[24] Taking their lead at this point from the natural sciences, early leadership scientists set out to map the terrain of leader traits in much the same way a biologist of the time would seek to identify the distinguishing characteristics of a newly discovered species of moth. The primary aim of this project became the progressive accumulation of knowledge and the discovery of universal laws which were assumed to govern the nature, prevalence and distribution of leadership.[25]

The measuring and documenting of bodily, social and psychological 'traits' and the accumulation of biographic and demographic data about leaders' family backgrounds feature as the key components in this endeavour.[26] Physical factors marked out for attention included matters such as tone of voice, manner of speaking, height, weight, appearance, physical prowess and health.[27] Personal characteristics of interest included intelligence, talkativeness, originality, adaptability, self-confidence, dominance, mood control, courteousness and the tendency to depression, anger and fighting.[28] Biographic and demographic factors of interest included marital status, birthplace, father's occupation and education, and the age at which certain achievements occurred.[29] Followers existed here merely as the deficient, the non-leader, the counter-point, the great mediocrity from which the leader stands out as exceptional and superior.

For those adopting the 'inheritance' thesis, the potential for their findings to contribute to the efforts of the eugenics movement to 'improve' the human population through selective breeding practices, would have been evident. This strand of leadership research was informed by and connected with studies of 'superior men' more generally.[30] For those not focused on issues of inheritance, the effective selection of leaders into positions of authority was understood to constitute the key application of their findings.[31]

The definitional criteria which informed this latter strand of research on leadership of small groups was that 'it is primarily by participating in group activities and demonstrating a capacity for expediting the work of the group that a person becomes endowed as a leader'.[32] This meant that a key interest for these early leadership scientists was identifying the characteristics of those whose actions were seen as enabling a small group to function more effectively: those who engaged in such actions were defined as leaders. However, what is notably a very minor aspect of this early work is a connection between organizational authority and leadership; indeed, in the empirical settings often employed in this work no such formal authority relationship existed between research subjects.[33] The workplace was not at this time understood as being an important research site for building leadership knowledge.

In terms of methodology, the analysis of biographies, biographical data and biographical dictionaries was the focus of those exploring the inheritance thesis.[34] Those focused on leadership in a small group context favoured methods such as observation, time sampling, peer rating, surveys, psychometric testing and interviews.[35] Arising from the belief that leadership was something innate, a significant proportion of studies in the first half of the 20th century used children, teenagers or young adults as their research subjects.[36] Irrespective of methodological differences and scholars' varying interest in the question of inheritance, whatever was understood as desirable, admirable or in some way exceptional was examined for its association with leadership, be it strength, beauty, intelligence, artistry, melancholy, wealth, aggression or athleticism.

As the field developed, a commitment to the compilation of statistical data became increasingly de rigeur, for the aim was to produce knowledge that could be held up as representative and generalizable.[37] Quantitative analysis was expected to render the workings of nature visible, removing mystery and overcoming ignorance. This means of establishing the truth about leadership came to be understood as being of such importance that extensive methodological explanations and defences are often to be found in these early texts, seeking to enhance the credibility of the conclusions reached in the reader's mind.[38]

In terms of power and power/knowledge, trait theory promoted the allocation of power and authority to an 'exceptional few'. It sought to render this state of affairs the result of nature and to confirm this by means of statistical evidence, drawing on the seemingly objective status of science for validation. It sought to directly counter the discourses of equality and democracy which, through the likes of the emerging women's, black and civil rights movements, sought to challenge existing gender-, race- and class-based distinctions in legal and political rights and to advance the Enlightenment ideal of natural rights. With trait theory, the question of who should lead was positioned as a matter beyond the purview of political contest: the 'right' to lead was to be a 'natural talent', legitimate and inalienable. While initially the pet project of Victorian gentleman scholars such as Carlyle and Galton, as it developed in the early 20th century, leadership science adopted in full the emerging norms of modern social science. Formal hypotheses were tested in structured studies, with scholars aiming for generalizable results and disseminating their findings via peer-reviewed journals. These moves sought to legitimate and establish the standing of leadership science as a scientific discourse.

PROCESSES OF FORMATION

Turning now to the processes of formation shaping this discourse, early leadership scientists understood themselves as entering unknown territory: the work of earlier times was from the outset rejected as untrustworthy, because it was not produced via what they held to be proper scientific methods.[39] However, the decision to focus on leader traits throughout the first four decades of the 20th century, why particular 'traits' were held to be of interest and the choice of statistical analysis as central to establishing the truth about leadership, was not random. Instead, these features of the discourse all derive from early influences, in particular the work of Thomas Carlyle,[40] who advocated the naturalness of inequality, the morality of obedience and the dangers of democracy, and Francis Galton,[41] who advocated the role of heredity factors in producing exceptional persons, the value of statistics and the importance of eugenic practices in shaping the future of humanity.[42] It is from these sources and the issues they deemed problematic that 20th-century leadership science first took inspiration.

Carlyle's influential 1840 lectures and their subsequent publication in book form, reprinted eight times in his lifetime, focused on the naturalness and desirability of 'heroes', great men of exceptional ability who, he argued, shaped the course of human history.[43] Carlyle advocated strongly for the value of worshipping such men as role models whose life and works should serve as the example for others to follow.[44] Further, for Carlyle the capacity and willingness to worship such heroes, to adopt the role of loyal follower, was itself deemed a mark of one's nobility and morality of character.[45] He positioned 'hero worship' as a natural and desirable phenomenon which produced the necessary degree of order and bonds of affection to hold society together.[46] For Carlyle, both leadership and loyal obedient followership were necessary, desirable, natural and moral.[47]

Carlyle identified six types of hero-leaders: gods, prophets, poets, priests, men of letters and kings, with the last being regarded as the most important. Linked with his notion of evolutionary progress in society, he saw men of letters and kings as the only two modern forms.[48] Carlyle's methodology for assessing the specific individual case studies he used to exemplify his argument included a biographical analysis of a leader's life and works, a physiognomic assessment (via portraits) of facial features to identify underlying character, an assessment of their style of speaking and a concern to determine the sincerity of their faith in God.[49]

Carlyle's thinking was profoundly influenced by the 19th-century English Romantic movement, this being a reaction to what was seen as the overly rationalist, mechanistic and atheistic focus of Enlightenment thought and the perceived negative impacts of industrialization on society and nature.[50] As a Romantic, Carlyle sought a return to a world more in love with nature than with machines, which valued passion rather than 'cold' reason, and which accepted and valued the 'natural inequality' between men because, he argued, 'there is no act more moral between men than that of rule and obedience'.[51] However, as Table 5.2 shows, the 'traits' later identified by leadership *scientists* in the early 20th century bear a strong resemblance to the characteristics of interest to Carlyle.

Table 5.2   *Similarities between Carlyle's Cromwell and 20th-century trait studies*

Carlyle's assessment of Oliver Cromwell as ideal modern leader	Some trait studies mentioned in Stogdill's literature review (1948)
'rugged stubborn strength' (p. 182) 'a clear determinate man's-energy' (p. 187) 'with his savage depth, with his wild sincerity . . . he looked so strange among the elegant . . . dainty . . . diplomatic' (p. 187)	physique energy/activity levels dominance ambition self-confidence
'did not speak with glib regularity' (p. 180) 'an impressive speaker . . . who, from the first, had weight' (p. 188) 'rude, passionate voice' (p. 188)	appearance and dress fluency tone of voice
'decisive, practical eye', 'has a genuine insight into what is fact' (p. 184)	practical ideas to solve problems sound judgement adaptability
'nervous melancholic temperament indicates seriousness' (p. 182) 'excitable, deep feeling nature' (p. 182) 'sorrow-stricken' 'almost semi-madness' (p. 187)	depressed unhappy excitable active restless
'sharp power of vision' (p. 187) 'a man with his whole soul *seeing* and struggling to see' (p. 187)	foresight insight intelligence originality
'courage and the faculty to do' (p. 187) 'grappled like a giant, face to face, with the naked truth of things' (p. 180)	persistence initiative fortitude

Sources: Carlyle, 1993 [1840]; Stogdill, 1948.

Stylistically, Carlyle offered romantic, gothic accounts of leaders which vividly and dramatically depicted the ideal to aspire to:[52] a rollicking good read if nothing else, intense, passionate and in no way disinterested, for so much was held to be at stake. However, later trait discourse deployed the credibility of science to coolly, dispassionately portray leadership as an innate quality of superior persons in statistical form.[53] Carlyle's too-passionate depiction of leadership did not survive the transition to a more formal 'scientific' discourse, even though his ideas provided influential clues for later studies to follow.

By the 1870s, Carlyle's methods were strongly criticized as lacking scientific rigour, most notably by Herbert Spencer, an influential early sociologist.[54] Subsequently, while Carlyle and, by association, the politically conservative concerns and interests of 19th-century English Romanticism provided one set of influences on early leadership scientists, Francis Galton, himself influenced by Spencer,[55] provided two others. Drawing on his cousin Charles Darwin's ideas, Galton focused on *inherited* traits as the source of what marks someone out as superior.[56] This focus formed the basis of a whole stream of subsequent research.[57] Galton's second point of influence was his use of statistics which has subsequently proved to be the core method of analysis still favoured by leadership scientists right down to the present day.[58] Galton initially studied 'hereditary genius', providing a statistical analysis of inherited traits.[59] Another major study examined English men of science.[60] Galton's broad concern was to identify patterns of inherited inferiority and superiority amongst the population, such that 'it would be quite practicable to produce a highly-gifted race of men by judicious marriage during several consecutive generations'.[61]

Carlyle's ideas about leader characteristics, along with Galton's claims about inherited traits and his use of statistics, thus provided the basis for leadership studies in the first part of the 20th century, a combination of thinking that was substantively both Romantic and eugenic and procedurally quantitative. While Carlyle and Galton offered radically different methods of analysis, both sought to promote the status and influence of 'exceptional men' at a time when proponents of democratic and egalitarian modes of governing were gaining greater influence. Both sought to promote the 'virtue' of obedience to 'superior men'. Their common aim was a social order which valued and enforced hierarchy and inequality, founded on what was held to be a naturally occurring biological–meritocratic order of inequality.

Galton was able to deploy his ideas about inherited traits in combination with statistical analysis to provide what was then understood as being an impressively scientific, modern and objective account of superiority and inferiority. He was a leading proponent in the eugenics movement[62] and his influence was of long standing in the field of leadership studies: Taussig and Joslyn's 1932 conclusion that 'natural inferiority' is the most likely cause of labourers' sons being under-represented amongst American business leaders and, moreover, that this under-representation cannot be due to environmental factors, is bolstered through explicit reference to Galton's work.

Galton's strong association with the later, much discredited eugenics movement, along with that of other leadership scholars such as James McKeen Cattell[63] and Havelock Ellis,[64] may well account for his absence in post-war accounts of developments in leadership studies;[65] his work is not referenced, for example, in Stogdill's influential 1948 review of the literature, although Galton, Cattell and Ellis are all cited in Smith and Krueger's 1933 review. Carlyle was also discredited from the 1920s onwards as a proponent of proto-fascist thought, a view later reinforced by Hitler's reputed enthusiasm for his work.[66] However, the methodological distance by then established between 'leadership scientists' and Carlyle's approach meant that this reassessment of Carlyle posed a less direct threat to the credibility of the field. The accepted history of leadership studies thus has it that trait theory was discarded because of inconsistent findings and a general lack of proof: Stogdill's 1948 review of the literature is often credited with having established this point.[67]

SOCIAL FUNCTION AND SUBJECTIVITY EFFECTS

Trait discourse positions 'leadership' as a 'good' and 'natural' quality, meaning that its advocacy of deference to leaders can similarly be positioned as 'good' and 'natural'.[68] The Galtonian perspective, with its particular focus on establishing the hereditary basis of leadership, forged a link to a broader agenda wherein science was to be deployed to support selective breeding policies and practices designed to improve the human race.[69] All in all, the social function of this discourse can be understood as providing a biological and scientifically warranted explanation not only for patterns of difference but also for patterns of inequality between persons and, through its association with eugenics thinking, a means for 'improving' the population. It was a discourse not only of discovery but also one with reforming ambitions: both Carlyle and Galton sought not merely to describe but also to change society with their work,[70] and subsequent participants in the discourse contributed to this project.

Trait discourse functioned, then, to reinforce attitudes and values of a more conservative orientation, countering competing discourses of a democratic or egalitarian orientation as well as discourses which emphasized 'nurture' rather than 'nature'. 'Superiority' here was not simply greater ability, responsibility or impact. It was also equated with morality, for it was claimed that 'persons of superior intellectual ability can be trusted to average high in decency, dependability, good will, and other social virtues'.[71] This capacity was said to be 'part and parcel of his original nature, based on the genes which co-operated with his environment in making him what he becomes'.[72] Victorian morality, the Romantic attachment to the exceptional and the natural in opposition to the norm and the manufactured, the eugenicists' interpretation of Darwin and the modern scientists' desire for precise measurement all found expression in this new science of leadership.

The subject of the leader constructed here is one predetermined by fate, biology or ancestry to be a superior being. Sketched initially as Carlyle's divinity, prophet, priest, poet, man of letters or king, rendered vivid through case studies of individual lives and works, facial characteristics, character and faith,[73] later depicted as a statistical outlier in Galton's work,[74] the image of the leader that first emerged in this discourse is of one who is consistently masculine, strong, capable and exceptional. The leader here, however, is also often troubled with melancholy, with the intensity of their passions and the isolation that comes from the basic fact of their inescapable difference from others.[75]

With the shift, around the turn of the century, to the use of structured scientific studies testing specific hypotheses, this rich and colourful gallery of leader portraits disappeared, leaving the subject of the leader to emerge incrementally, study by study, trait by trait. Leaders were now discursively constituted by way of the statistical compilation of attributes with 'proven' association.[76] However, the challenge of piecing together this mosaic was surely one of frustration, as while one study might confirm a particular attribute's association with leadership another would disconfirm it.[77]

By 1948, according to Stogdill's review, the leader could be confidently depicted as one who 'exceeds the average member of his group in the following respects: (1) intelligence, (2) scholarship, (3) dependability in exercising responsibilities, (4) activity and social participation, and (5) socio-economic status'.[78] Other 'traits' then claimed to have a high correlation with leadership included 'originality, popularity, sociability, judgement, aggressiveness, desire to excel, humor, cooperativeness, liveliness, and athletic ability, in approximate order of magnitude of average correlation coefficient'.[79] Taken as a whole, the leader thus emerges as an excellent chap, one who can be relied upon to do what is right, that is, to do that which will have sufficient alignment with dominant social norms and values as to not cause offence while also achieving to a high level. A self with no dark side, no anxieties and no frailties is the proposition.

While for Carlyle[80] followers' willingness to worship and obey a leader was an indication of *their* morality, by the time the discourse had moved into a formal scientific mode, followers provided the norm, the average, the unexceptional majority from which leaders stood out as both different and superior.[81] The leader–follower relationship itself was of interest to trait theorists only to the extent that followers might be asked by researchers to nominate the leader of their group.[82] Studying followers was relevant only to the extent that their 'averageness' helped distinguish them from the 'exception' who was the leader. Followers were constituted as the undifferentiated mass to which the leader-as-exceptional-man was to direct his attentions; effectively the follower had no specific subjectivity but was simply to be understood as inferior, as non-leader.

CONCLUSION

As with the Classical Greek and 16th-century European discourses, the new accounts of leadership developed by Carlyle and then the trait theorists carried considerable weight in their time. We see that with these accounts leaders are, yet again, constituted as exemplary individuals whose role it is to bring about order and morality, this notion being dependent on the claimed inability of most people to live a good life in the absence of a leader's guidance. The alignment of these propositions with elite interests, the deployment of methods of inquiry which were seen to be advanced and sophisticated, and the proclaimed ability to offer solutions to issues seen as being problematic, all these power/knowledge techniques served both to generate a field of study and to warrant a range of social practices through which, yet again, 'leadership' functioned as a counterweight to egalitarian forces. As we turn now to explore leadership thought in the post-war era through to the present day, the question to be considered is what, fundamentally, has changed in what is proclaimed as the truth about leadership?

NOTES

1. See, for example, Antonakis et al., 2004; Bass, 2008; Northouse, 2004
2. Blaikie, 2000, 2007; O'Leary, 2004
3. Cresswell, 2003; Hacking, 1999; O'Leary, 2004
4. Alvesson, 1996; Alvesson and Spicer, 2011a; Barker, 2001
5. See, for example, Schriesheim et al., 2004; Bass, 2008; Northouse, 2004
6. See, for example, Avery, 2004; Bass, 2008; Hunt, 1999
7. Bass, 2008; Gardner et al., 2010; Lowe and Gardner, 2000
8. Gardner et al., 2010; Lowe and Gardner, 2000
9. See, for example, Avolio et al., 2009; Bass, 1999, 2008; Gardner et al., 2010
10. See, for example, Bass, 1999; Hunt, 1999; Yukl, 2012
11. Bass, 2008; Huczynski and Buchanan, 2006; Jackson and Parry, 2011
12. See, for example, Bass, 2008; Hunt, 1999; Yukl, 2012
13. Daunton, 2011; Feldman and Lawrence, 2011; More, 2000
14. More, 2000
15. Brock, 1973
16. See Carlyle, 1993 [1840]. Original date of publication is noted in square brackets
17. Carlyle, 1993 [1840]
18. Carlyle, 1993 [1840]
19. Bannister, 1979; Gillham, 2001
20. Benjamin, 2007; Brush, 1988
21. Avery, 2004; Bass, 2008; Jackson and Parry, 2011
22. See, for example, Galton, 1970 [1875]; Gowin, 1919; Taussig and Joslyn, 1932
23. Shartle, 1979; Smith and Krueger, 1933; Stogdill, 1948
24. Smith and Krueger, 1933; Stogdill, 1948
25. Smith and Krueger, 1933; Stogdill, 1948
26. See, for example, Cattell, 1906; Clarke, 1916; Ellis, 1904; Galton, 1970 [1875]; Lehman, 1966 [1928]; Sorokin, 1925; Taussig and Joslyn, 1932; Thorndike, 1936; Visher, 1925
27. Smith and Krueger, 1933; Stogdill, 1948
28. Stogdill, 1948
29. See, for example, Galton, 1970; Taussig and Joslyn, 1932; Thorndike, 1936
30. See, for example, Cattell, 1906; Clarke, 1916; Ellis, 1904; Galton, 1970; Sorokin, 1925; Visher, 1925
31. See, for example, Bogardus, 1934; Gowin, 1915, 1918, 1919
32. Stogdill, 1948
33. Smith and Krueger, 1933; Stogdill, 1948
34. See, for example, Cattell, 1906; Ellis, 1904; Galton, 1970; Sorokin, 1925; Taussig and Joslyn, 1932
35. Smith and Krueger, 1933; Stogdill, 1948
36. Stogdill, 1948
37. See, for example, Clarke, 1916; Ellis, 1904; Sorokin, 1925
38. See, for example, the efforts of Galton, 1970; Taussig and Joslyn, 1932; Thorndike, 1936
39. Carlyle, 1993; Galton, 1970
40. Carlyle, 1993
41. Galton, 1970
42. Gillham, 2001; Godin, 2007
43. Carlyle, 1993; Goldberg, 1993 [1840]; Hook, 1945
44. Carlyle, 1993
45. Carlyle, 1993
46. Carlyle, 1993
47. Carlyle, 1993
48. Carlyle, 1993
49. Carlyle, 1993
50. Ferber, 2010; Goldberg, 1993

51. 1993, p. 171
52. See 1993
53. See, for example, Cattell, 1906; Clarke, 1916; Ellis, 1904; Galton, 1970
54. Goldberg, 1993
55. Gillham, 2001; Goldberg, 1993
56. Galton, 1970
57. See, for example, Cattell, 1906; Clarke, 1916; Ellis, 1904; Sorokin, 1925; Taussig and Joslyn, 1932; Thorndike, 1936; Visher, 1925
58. Alvesson, 1996; Gardner et al., 2010
59. See Galton, 1892 [1869]
60. Galton, 1970
61. Galton, 1892 [1869], p. 45
62. Gillham, 2001; Godin, 2007
63. Cattell, 1906
64. Ellis, 1904
65. Gillham, 2001; Godin, 2007
66. Goldberg, 1993; Grierson, 1977 [1933]
67. See, for example, Bass, 2008; Huczynski and Buchanan, 2006
68. See, for example, Cattell, 1906; Ellis, 1904; Thorndike, 1936; Visher, 1925
69. Gillham, 2001; Godin, 2007; Hasian Jnr, 1996
70. Gillham, 2001; Godin, 2007; Goldberg, 1993
71. Thorndike, 1936, p. 339
72. Thorndike, 1936
73. Goldberg, 1993
74. 1892, 1970
75. See Carlyle, 1993; Galton, 1970
76. See, for example, Cattell, 1906; Clarke, 1916; Ellis, 1904; Sorokin, 1925
77. Smith and Krueger, 1933; Stogdill, 1948
78. Stogdill, 1948, p. 63
79. Stogdill, 1948, p. 63
80. Carlyle, 1993
81. See, for example, Clarke, 1916; Ellis, 1904; Sorokin, 1925
82. Stogdill, 1948

6   Our modern era of leadership 'science'

INTRODUCTION

By this stage, it is quite evident that there are some common ideas about leadership in the discursive regimes of the Classical Greeks, 16th-century Europe, Carlyle and the trait theorists. The repeated positioning of leadership as something natural and, ergo, something good is just one continuity in thought. However, it may also be tempting, from the perspective of the early decades of the 21st century, to rationalize away the credibility of earlier scholars' efforts to speak the truth about leadership as not having been grounded in 'real' science, by which is likely meant positivist methods of inquiry. It may be tempting to dismiss these earlier efforts as founded in mythic, religious and pseudo-scientific forms of reasoning, limitations from which you may assume we are now freed. In this chapter, however, through analysis of the form and formation of the major paradigmatic developments which have dominated leadership studies in the post-World War II era, the proposition is advanced that faith-based reasoning constitutes a central feature of current thought, despite its proclaimed scientific rigour. For each of the paradigms explored here, I begin my analysis by identifying the issues deemed problematic which I argue shaped that paradigm's emergence. I then examine the key features of that discourse, its processes of formation, social function and subjectivity effects. In the latter part of the chapter I examine the underpinning assumptions shaping modern leadership science before turning to offer an overall assessment of the nature of that science.

THE DEMISE OF TRAIT THEORY AND THE RISE OF BEHAVIOURAL THEORIES

I can recall the excitement and stimulation ... the feeling of being in on an exciting new venture, breaking new ground. At that time, leadership was thought of as a personality trait ... the catch was that it was difficult to get hold of what the traits were. (Fleishman, 1973, p. 2)

Problems

At the end of World War II, America's newly established military, political and industrial dominance was a source of national pride.[1] It was also a state of affairs seen as by no means assured.[2] With the felt need to keep enhancing the productivity and technology gains achieved as part of the war effort, leadership in the workplace quickly became the critical domain of interest for leadership studies.[3]

Among management thinkers, a continued move away from a Taylorist orientation to workplace control[4] toward the 'harmony' offered by a human relations perspective[5] was being strongly advocated.[6] This shift was seen as vital to ensuring that poor labour–management relations did not impede the future development of American industry.[7] The perceived threat of communism, moreover, demanded that workplace control remain in managerial hands.[8]

Trait theory was, whether openly acknowledged or not, poisoned by way of its association with eugenics and hence Nazism. Advancing the notion that leaders were 'by nature' superior beings when the ashes of the Holocaust were still warm was unlikely to attract a positive response. However, the war had also reinforced to observers of leadership the idea that those in positions of authority varied greatly as regards their approach and the impact of that.[9] In an episteme committed to 'progress' as one of its most cherished ideals, in which the quest to know ourselves through the application of science constituted a major pre-occupation, better understanding of these differences called out for attention.

To respond to these various developments, a new approach to leadership science needed to be carved out in such a way that it could command the interest of those with authority to allocate research funds, secure managerial support and meet the norms of the wider field of the human sciences. A focus on leader behaviour rather than traits was the response to these problems. This invention came to provide the basis for the next few decades of research.

Key Features of the Discourse

A rapid and fundamental shift in the truth about leadership occurred, then, around the end of World War II. By the late 1940s, talk of leadership had been re-oriented to a focus on patterns of supervisory behaviour.[10] Trait theory, which had dominated the field for so long, was still advanced occasionally.[11] However, most leadership researchers were instead pursuing a different agenda, one now dedicated to enhancing workplace productivity and morale via supervisory behaviours conceived of as 'leadership'.[12] These behaviours were presumed learnable and teachable; the assumption of leadership as an innate quality of superior persons was specifically abandoned.[13]

Commitment to the perceived virtues of theoretical parsimony now shaped this discourse, in direct contrast with the never-ending list of leader traits previously collected.[14] By the early 1950s, leadership was held to be adequately described as comprising two patterns of supervisor behaviour, according to the influential Ohio State University studies.[15] The first of these was 'consideration', meaning a supervisor's inclination to 'behaviour indicating friendship, mutual trust, respect, a certain warmth and rapport between the supervisor and his group'.[16] The second was 'initiating structure', meaning 'acts which imply the leader organizes and defines the relationships in the group, tends to establish well defined patterns and channels of communication and ways of getting the job done'.[17]

Studies at Michigan State University developed similar constructs: production orientation and employee orientation.[18] Lewin, Lippitt and White's notion of leadership as ranging along a continuum from autocratic–laissez faire to democratic styles of supervisory behaviours also received some continuing attention.[19] However, their deployment of terms which carried with them overtly political connotations was not an approach adopted by most leadership scholars.

With this new means of accounting for leadership, the leader as a specified coherent subject possessing its own needs and will disappeared from view. This new conception of leadership could be more thoroughly dissected into what were claimed to be its component parts than trait theory had ever permitted. Now, precisely defined behaviours became the focus of attention, along with the promise that these could be attached to any person in a supervisory position.[20] It became the norm to conceive of leadership purely as a set of discrete behaviours, independent of considerations of 'character' or context.

With an accumulating body of evidence, it became viable to speak of the correlation of specified leader behaviours with issues of organizational concern such as morale, turnover, grievance rates and productivity.[21] 'Leadership' became a formula, a behavioural recipe of universal potential and utility.[22] It could, here, be considered separately from issues of politics, ethics and power, for the assumption of the legitimacy of supervisory authority rendered such matters redundant. Moreover, the recommended focus on both tasks and people positioned this new discourse as one that was humane and concerned with questions of employee well-being.

Subordinates were now automatically classified as followers and, drawing on human relations conceptions of the worker, presumed to be dependent on supervisors/leaders for both guidance ('initiating structure') and support ('consideration').[23] The effect of leaders' behaviour on followers' job satisfaction, morale and work performance was what was considered interesting and relevant, with the consequence that follower agency was positioned here as being of lesser importance and impact than leader agency.[24] The basic project of leadership research thus became one entirely dedicated to enhancing managerial influence and effectiveness, this being assumed as something good for the organization, the supervisor/leader and the follower/employee.[25]

With behavioural theory, the power to claim to speak the truth about leadership was derived from conducting large-scale formal studies and then proclaiming the results as proof of certain facts about the world.[26] That challengeable assumptions and the privileging of selected values and interests were unavoidably embedded in the design of these studies[27] was typically expunged from the discourse as a means of establishing credibility. That the use of survey methodology could not overcome the indeterminacy of language and that such data can be interpreted in more than one way[28] were ignored when asserting the value and validity of what was now on offer.

As an exercise in power, behavioural discourse relied on the communicative ease offered by its use of parsimonious models to help garner attention and pose ideas in a form that was readily digestible and memorable. It made use of accepted channels of scholarly discourse and drew on the credibility offered by its governmental and business backers.[29] It sought to produce supervisor-leaders who were both humane and effective, ensuring compliant, productive followers who would meet the needs of their employers while simultaneously being 'satisfied' with their work.[30] Behavioural theory also countered traditional notions of innate superiority, treating leadership as something teachable, learnable and open to all in supervisory roles, thereby positioning it as being consistent with the democratic ideal of equality of opportunity.

Processes of Formation

In accounting for the formative processes which shaped this move to behavioural theory, Stogdill's 1948 review of the trait literature is, as noted earlier, normally portrayed as the key turning point.[31] Yet by 1944 Hendry claimed that researchers interested in 'leadership for and in a democracy' had already established that 'leadership as a particular or unique combination of traits ... is a fabrication'.[32] Lewin claimed experiments had shown that

> in a precise manner ... the character and the abilities of the individual, his ideals, his goals, his motivation and his values, his perception and his productivity, his friendliness and objectivity, his tendencies to domination and submission ... can be changed to a large extent by changing the social atmosphere or the group belonging of this individual.[33]

It would seem, therefore, that history has incorrectly attributed the first major social science-based critique of trait theory to Stogdill[34] rather than to Lewin.[35]

Stogdill did, nonetheless, assess much of the previous four decades' worth of social science-based leadership research in a highly influential paper published in 1948. One of his often quoted conclusions was that the findings from this research demonstrated that 'an adequate analysis of leadership involves a study not only of leaders but also of situations'.[36] However, he also noted that a number of traits had been repeatedly identified as showing strong associations with leadership, a contradictory finding from those noted above by Hendry and Lewin. In light of a number of his findings it seems by no means inevitable that Stogdill's review should have been taken as sounding the death knell of trait-based research. Yet that is indeed how it has come to be understood and, moreover, by and large what subsequently happened.

At the time of publication, Stogdill was employed at Ohio State University and an active member of a substantial leadership research programme initiated at the end of World War II.[37] That programme had, *from its inception*, determined to focus on leader behaviour, not traits.[38] According to Shartle, who held the position of project director, this focus derived from his pre-war and war-time experience with the US Department of Labor where he had directed a research programme involving job, process and organizational analysis associated with planning for the war effort.[39] This lineage positions Shartle as a direct intellectual descendent of the scientific management paradigm.

Shartle later explained: 'my own interest was primarily leader behaviour. I felt that if we could get a handle on it, the program would be worthwhile'.[40] Bowers and Seashore report that *by 1945* the Ohio project had developed an instrument with 'nine dimensions or categories of leadership behaviour'.[41] What is noteworthy, then, is that the decision at Ohio State University to focus on leader behaviour pre-dates Stogdill's analysis of the limitations of the then predominantly trait-oriented research. Neither Shartle nor Stogdill make any mention of Hendry or Lewin's 1944 texts, so it is impossible to know if these influenced their thinking. However, what the archive indicates overall is that it was Shartle's personal determination for research to be focused on leader behaviour, and not the review of the trait-based evidence produced by Stogdill, which triggered the behavioural focus chosen by Ohio.

Fleishman also reports that the focus on behaviour was not without its sceptics:

> [I]n the late forties, some felt that leadership was almost entirely a function of the type of group led and that it might be impossible to predict whether a leader in one group would be successful in another. This, of course, is a pretty pessimistic view if we consider the problems of selecting and training for leadership. Subsequently, the pendulum swung toward the middle ground with assumptions made that the group situation is highly important, but there are some general principles about leadership which allow certain generalizations.[42]

Shartle's determination to change the direction of leadership research can be understood as an astute assessment of the wider social climate in the post-war period. By this time, Hitler's claims of racial superiority and inferiority could be seen as disconcertingly similar to claims of natural superiority in terms of leadership. Indeed, as early as 1933 Grierson[43] had identified links between Carlyle's 'great man' theory and Hitler's politics, while Galton's eugenics had also by this time been strongly rejected by most American social scientists.[44]

More broadly, amongst the many effects of the war were a heightened interest in the effective functioning of large-scale organizations, in issues of productivity, morale, absenteeism, the dangers of authoritarianism and an optimistic belief in the practical potential of science and technology to resolve such problems.[45] These concerns provided a fertile set of interests which rendered a focus on leader behaviour and its impact on workplace performance attractive to researchers and to funders of research such as the military, government and major corporations. That the field of psychology was also at this time strongly influenced by Skinner's behaviourist perspective is a further factor informing the choice to focus on leader behaviour.[46] The 'pessimism' which Fleishman[47] reports came from a strongly situationalist perspective on leadership may also have helped sway the focus toward leader behaviour for researchers seeking to advance the field.

Also immediately in the post-war period, Michigan State University established a leadership research programme.[48] The intellectual antecedents and predilections of this programme were informed by the 'human relations' perspective.[49] From this perspective, the relationship between supervisors and subordinates was understood as affecting productivity and workers were understood as having 'needs' and potentially destructive tendencies if those needs were not addressed by management.[50]

Advocates of the human relations perspective such as Mayo saw themselves as redressing the focus on rational planning, organizing and controlling which classical management theorists Taylor[51] and Fayol[52] had emphasized as being the key concern of managers. The aim of leadership scholars adopting this perspective was to position the 'leadership' dimensions of managerial work as warranting more attention, and the chosen method for demonstrating the value of this was by measuring the link between these dimensions and organizational results. In combination, the Ohio and Michigan State studies had by the early 1950s begun to produce a steady stream of behaviour-based studies and models which came to dominate the field through to the mid-1960s.[53] These models reflected their dual heritage of both scientific management and human relations.

There were dissenting voices which have subsequently been lost from the conventional narrative of progress in the field. A special issue in 1944 of the *Journal of Educational Sociology* focused on 'Leadership in Democracy' set forth an approach informed by quite different political and methodological perspectives from those informing the Ohio and Michigan studies. Notable amongst those contributing to this effort was the already influential social psychologist Kurt Lewin. Having fled Germany in 1933 because of the rising tide of anti-Semitism, and having then gone on to study discrimination and prejudice,[54] Lewin advocated for the contextually rich framework offered by field theory and the participatory nature of the action research method to inform leadership studies.[55] For him, the future of leadership research was also one that should be strongly informed by political and ethical concerns:

> [P]articularly in a democracy, the right of the common man is upheld. Vigilant criticism and a jealous watch over the limitation of the leader's power are considered basic virtues ... the success of the war should strengthen the belief in the superiority of the democratic form of leadership ... the danger that in politics, in education, and in industry after the war fascistic leadership forms will be propagandized in the name of democratic discipline is by no means past.[56]

Lewin's aspirations for the future direction of leadership research were not fulfilled: following his death in 1947, those who took on his work at the then newly established Research Centre for Group Dynamics at the

Massachusetts Institute of Technology (MIT) pursued a limited notion of workplace democracy with little radical intent or potential.[57] Instead, a small network of scholars centred on Ohio State and Michigan State universities provided the driving force to change the focus of leadership discourse away from traits to behaviour.[58] Their attentiveness to changing circumstances and mind-sets allowed them to propose a new approach of appeal to those with the money to fund major research programmes. The optimism which marked the early stages of this discourse was, however, fairly short-lived, as the utility of the crisp and clear leadership recipes on offer proved variable in different settings. By 1966, Korman's meta-review of studies using the Ohio State model found that 'there is as yet almost no evidence on the predictive validity of "Consideration" and "Initiating Structure"'.[59]

Social Function and Subjectivity Effects

In terms of its social function, the behavioural theory approach to conceptualizing leadership initially carried with it the then radical impact of undermining the pre-existing, long-standing essentialist notions of leadership, by separating 'leadership' from ideas about personhood and natural superiority. This move aligned leadership thought with broader notions about equality of opportunity and democracy which were then being strongly emphasized as central aspects underpinning America's success in the war, along with its scientific and industrial capability.[60] However, the more enduring historical impact has been the pairing of 'leadership' with managerial work, as this has provided the basis for all subsequent major developments.

In the selection of a recommended focus on both relationships and tasks as the desired leader behaviours, this approach sought to overcome what it saw as the limitations or dangers of an excessive or inadequate focus on only relationships or only tasks, thereby challenging both the Taylorist and human relations traditions.[61] Leader behaviour discourse implied that leadership required a balanced approach in which both people and production were of equal importance, positioning the leader-supervisor as guardian of the interests of both capital and labour and adjudicator of how those interests were to be reconciled.[62] Here, leader-supervisors were held to have a duty of care in respect of those they led, affirming the view that those persons were to be treated with respect and consideration for their opinions and needs.[63] Equally, the needs of the organization were also expected to be taken seriously: work was to be organized efficiently and effectively and standards of work were to meet the level demanded by the organization.[64] Conceptually at least, there was a radical potential in the idea of raising the status of human concerns to equal that of economic concerns in the running of organizations. However, by focusing on measures of *organizational performance* to demonstrate the value of 'leadership' this potential was lost and has yet to be reclaimed. 'Leadership' was captured by, rendered subservient to and put to work in the service of organizational goals.

By connecting 'leadership' with both supervisory positions and with task and relational outcomes seen as desirable, it came to be understood as an important source of managerial influence on firm performance. This in turn meant that 'leadership' could become a topic of legitimate concern and interest to management, rendering their opinions, expectations and aspirations of importance to researchers. By adopting the prescribed behaviours, leader-supervisors could be expected to improve workplace relations and performance,[65] meaning that the discourse functioned as a disciplinary regime in which supervisors were expected to behave in a certain fashion, irrespective of personal preference. The broader interests this regime of truth thus served were managerial and organizational.

With this particular approach to leadership, what is valued is both reason and reasonableness, the latter being understood as the skilful moderation of potentially conflicting interests, respectful interactions between persons and the achievement of a work output that can be met without undue pressure.[66] What is valued and promoted is the right of the organization to demand certain results and to expect those results to be achieved, *and*, simultaneously, what is valued and promoted is the right of followers to be heard and treated with care and respect.[67] These outcomes were understood as being both aspirational and entirely within reach, however, what is simply assumed is the validity of these particular ways of defining reason and reasonableness. The approach implies a limited notion of workplace democracy, absent of union influence, wherein followers may legitimately seek to influence leader decisions, but only within the parameters of production requirements set unilaterally by senior management acting reasonably. Politically, this was a highly loaded move, as union influence had grown significantly during the war.[68] Leadership discourse functioned to render this influence unnecessary, as reflective of a pathology which 'leadership' could remedy.

The discourse also functioned to reinforce broader attempts to build a post-war consensus that American business was fundamentally 'on track' with a managerial hierarchy as its key organizing model.[69] Supported by this new understanding of 'leadership', the discourse contributed to the wider aim of ensuring that America maintained its proven ability to outstrip every other nation in terms of productivity and standards of living. At the same time, a further social function of this approach to conceptualizing leadership was to reinforce an expectation of stability in the work environment. Leadership was understood here as an exercise in ongoing interaction between persons, with no particular emphasis given to issues of change and creativity.[70]

Behavioural discourse constitutes a unique scenario compared with all other discursive regimes examined in this study, for it neither produces nor relies on an account of the leader as a human subject. Here, there is no broader conception of leader interiority, of leader aims, values, needs or desires; it speaks only of those behaviours it defines as constituting leadership. These behaviours are attached to the position of the super-visor, but without any further interest in the characteristics of the person who holds that position. Here, the discourse claims to have discovered and defined leader behaviours so that these may be enacted by whomever it is that holds the position of supervisor. Consequently, it is as if leadership were a set of clothing which could be put on at the beginning of the work day and removed at the end, having no deeper impact, meaning or relation to the person of the supervisor, connecting only to their position. This intriguing possibility runs counter to the rest of the Western tradition examined in this study, wherein the exceptional and knowing agent appears time and again in various forms as the foundation and source of leadership.

Relatedly, behavioural discourse also offers no clear conception of followers as persons with particular characteristics which typify them and define them as such. Followers instead exist here as 'everyman' and 'everywoman'. They are credited only with having legitimate and reason-able needs to be treated with care, consideration and respect, and are presumed to be normally amenable to fulfilling reasonable requests made in a reasonable manner by a person with formal authority over them.[71] Consequently, what can be seen here is a basically egalitarian conception of 'leaders' and 'followers' as persons, with the only basic point of difference between them being the positional authority of the leader and the particular duties and responsibilities which come with that. Here, leaders and followers are potentially interchangeable, for it is the position one holds that renders one a leader, not a fundamental aspect of the self.

CONTINGENCY/SITUATIONAL THEORIES

Our theory provides a conceptual framework and a preliminary set of guidelines for determining how to match the leadership situation and the man. (Fiedler, 1967, p. 248)

The essence of the theory is the meta proposition that *leaders, to be effective, engage in behaviors that complement subordinates' environments and abilities in a manner that compensates for deficiencies and is instrumental to subordinate satisfaction and individual and work unit performance.* (House, 1996, p. 323, italics in original)

Problems

From around the mid-1960s, American society quite suddenly entered into a period of rapid and dramatic change. The so-called counter-culture which emerged at this time rejected many established norms, values and ways of doing things and, in particular, directly challenged traditional systems of authority.[72] Individual freedom of expression was increasingly valorized, and enacted in often dramatic fashion.[73] The personal became understood as political.[74] Established class, race and gender relations were all subjected to intense scrutiny, while social protest movements became extremely active and even, in some cases, violent.[75] Breaking the law became, in many instances, a deliberate act driven by political aims. Elements of the anti-war movement not only criticized the Vietnam War as bad foreign policy, but also more broadly promoted peaceful, harmonious modes of interacting, problematizing the use of force and coercion as morally untenable under any circumstances.[76] The actions of the masses now seemed more potent than had previously been understood.[77] Accordingly, at work, at home and in the world at large, American values and practices were suddenly seen as problematic. In amongst all this turmoil, the role, conduct and status of manager-leaders were not immune.[78]

The challenge for leadership scholars at this time was, thus, to craft an approach which recognized these changing social mores while still sustaining the status of leadership. They needed, moreover, to account for leadership in a manner which recognized the shift in organizational theory towards open systems thinking,[79] as well as broader shifts within psychology toward cognitive perspectives.[80] A growing concern with bureaucratic inflexibility and a growing interest in the influence of contextual factors on businesses were further elements demanding attention.[81] The inventive response to these factors was to conceive of leadership as situationally contingent.

Key Features of the Discourse

Contingency and situational theorists proposed that there was no one best way to lead and that attending to both leader behaviours and situational factors was necessary to understand and practice leadership.[82] The contextual matters now deemed to be of critical relevance were strictly delimited to those within the workplace setting, maintaining the separation of supervisory leadership from questions of politics which had developed with the advent of behavioural theory.

Proposals to account for situational factors in leadership theorizing had been made even when behavioural theory was dominant, but did not initially attract much attention or support.[83] However, in 1967 Fiedler developed a multi-faceted model in which he argued that leaders should be matched to situations which best suited their behavioural preferences. The novelty of his approach attracted immediate attention, offering as it did a potential solution to the dilemma posed by Korman's recent review.[84]

House,[85] Vroom and Yetton[86] and Hersey and Blanchard[87] quite quickly put forward their own contingency/situational models, all of which argued that different situations demanded different leadership approaches. Each proposed specific models for conceptualizing both the situation and the leader response. Regardless of these points of difference, having largely assumed for more than 20 years that there was one best way to lead, the field now switched assumptions, focusing on the discovery of multiple approaches to leadership, arguing that matching leader behaviour to situational factors was key. This shift was rhetorically presented as an advancement in knowledge, rather than as a sudden reversal in a core assumption.

For early advocates of this mode of conceptualizing leadership, Tannenbaum and Schmidt,[88] leadership required either a democratic, autocratic or laissez faire approach, depending on the nature of the work, the workplace and the workers: the choice to dictate, to abdicate or to share authority was assumed here as being the sole prerogative of supervisor-leaders. Fiedler's model advocated a matching between a leader's task or relationship preference, on the one hand, and the degree of structure in the work tasks, the leader's positional power and the state of the leader–follower relationship, on the other.[89] A careful assessment of these factors was intended to ensure that leaders were placed only in situations which would play to their preferences and not expose them to followers who might challenge their lead.

Vroom and Yetton, drawing on decision science methods, sought precisely to define the range of situations a leader might face and to prescribe for each the best approach to decision-making.[90] This model can be understood as a means of mitigating the uncertainty and risk which was now seen to be facing leaders in securing followers' willing compliance. House's path–goal model proposed that leaders assess a prescribed range of both environmental factors and follower characteristics: from that assessment, leaders were then to select their approach from a prescribed set of options.[91] Hersey and Blanchard proposed an approach in which the extent of latitude granted to followers depended on the leader's assessment of their ability and psychological 'maturity' (or docility?) to perform the task required of them.[92]

Factors such as the nature of work and the workplace were, thus, important aspects of situational/contingency models, while more attention also now went to the 'problem' of followers and the leader–follower relationship. With the development of these models, there was an increased concern to manage and mitigate the difficulties which followers and other contextual factors might pose for leaders.

Researchers moved away from offering a standardized 'one size fits all' recipe for leading based on the findings of large-scale empirical studies with this shift to contingency/situational thinking. Instead, what developed was a competing suite of 'set menus' based on smaller studies or 'lessons' drawn from consulting experience, with theorist A recommending for context B to use leader style C, while theorist D set forth what they considered to be a relevant contextual factor E and proposed leader behaviour response F.[93] The basic nature of contingency/situational thinking is such that it lends itself to the production of a proliferation of different models, and that is indeed what occurred.

In abandoning the shared search for the one best way to lead which behavioural theorists had largely adhered to, it became much more viable for scholars to advance their own favoured perspective largely irrespective of what others might propose. Now, so long as the contextual factors examined differed between theorists, each could claim to have produced findings relevant to those specific factors which need not be directly compared with other findings.[94] That these varying models could not be tied together to produce a coherent account of the truth about leadership[95] was hardly now a concern for most, given the assumption that there was no one right way to lead and given the commercial and professional success on offer for those able to develop and promote their own models.

The expectations placed on leaders were heightened with the move to contingency/situational theories: skilled diagnosis of follower 'needs' and, excepting Fiedler,[96] the tactical capacity to then shift one's approach became the new standard for leaders to meet.[97] Followers' state of mind toward their work and workplace became a focal point for leader attention, with leaders expected to assess and respond to that.[98] This was a rapid and dramatic change from behavioural theory where leaders were given a set formula to adopt, quite irrespective of any assessment of the situation or of followers.

With the shift to contingency/situational models, more attention was given over to followers, although the nature of this attention was one now increasingly focused on extracting optimal work performance and managing their problematic behaviour. Followers were now presented in varying forms and ascribed varying merits according to their actual performance, ability to perform and willingness to meet the leader's expectation.[99] Followers were understood as potentially being reluctant, hostile, suspicious, merely compliant or enthusiastic, diligent and committed.[100] Followers' tendency to enter into or remain in varying states of capacity and willingness to perform was understood as being a direct consequence of the approach taken by leaders. Followers' state of mind about their work and workplace was now of legitimate concern and of importance to leaders, demanding constant leader scrutiny.[101] The capacity of leaders to shift followers' state of mind was here both assumed and rendered more powerful than followers' own will.

Yet if followers were now understood as a problem, leadership was nonetheless heralded as the answer, producing a self-sustaining, self-fulfilling dynamic. The situation was, thus, that 'while disagreeing with one another in important respects, these theories and models share an implicit assumption that while the style of leadership likely to be effective may vary according to the situation, *some* leadership style will be effective *regardless* of the situation'.[102] That alternatives to leadership and the limits of leadership had been identified in a number of recent studies[103] did not constrain the confidence of the claims now made for the efficacy of leadership. That leadership might be understood as an attribution rather than a definite pattern of behaviour or personal characteristic[104] did not impede this new discourse.

Rather, a multi-faceted frame wherein the leader–follower relationship, the follower state of mind with regards to their work and workplace, and leader diagnosis and response to that, were now all positioned as central components of the truth about leadership.[105] The workplace focus and the expectation and legitimacy of leader authority over followers were matters entirely taken for granted. The assumption of the relative weakness of follower agency to determine their own state of mind about their work and workplace compared with that of leaders was so embedded that it demanded neither attention nor explanation. In this new account of the truth, leaders were authorized to reach much further into the minds of followers, to colonize their thinking more completely and to enhance their productivity and job satisfaction to a much greater extent. Stripped of its ostensible goal of achieving a balance of both human and production needs what was now on offer was a series of guidebooks on managerial manipulation.

Contingency/situational thinking, however, very quickly led to a proliferation of competing theories.[106] While advocates of different theories could claim that there was a steady building up of knowledge in respect of a given theory, the challenge of bringing together a coherent body of scientifically validated knowledge was increasingly seen as a serious concern. Consequently, a further key feature of the archive during this time was a growing sense of frustration that the product of scholarly efforts was deeply problematic.

As early as 1959, Bennis had claimed that 'of all the hazy and confounding areas in social psychology, leadership theory undoubtedly contends for top nomination. And, ironically, probably more has been written and less is known about leadership than about any other topic in the behavioural sciences'.[107] Miner went as far as proposing that 'the concept of leadership itself has out-lived its usefulness'.[108] Melcher argued that 'the study of leadership these last seventy years has resulted in little accumulated knowledge that permits one to understand or predict the effects of leadership approaches, or that provides a better understanding of how to be an effective leader'.[109] Soon after, Lombardo and McCall characterized the field as marked by a 'mindboggling' number of 'un-integrated models, theories, prescription and conceptual schemes'; they claimed that 'much of the literature is fragmentary, trivial, unrealistic and dull' and that 'the research results are characterised by Type III errors (solving the wrong problems precisely) and by contradictions'.[110] Thus, while proponents of contingency/situational theories continued to advocate their efficacy, others raised serious doubts about the state of leadership knowledge.

Processes of Formation

That the move to contingency/situational thinking arose at least in part as a consequence of the difficulties in establishing the validity of behavioural theory is not contested here. As noted earlier, Korman's 1966 meta-review of studies deploying the Ohio State behavioural model was damning. The inherent limitations of a static, two-factor model to sustain a whole field of research were likely also evident to scholars wanting to enhance the influence of their efforts. However, the extent to which behavioural theory was directly imported into the suite of contingency/situational models which came to prominence should not be overlooked.

Fiedler, for example, took for granted that leaders could be divided according to their task or relationship preference,[111] replicating the key conceptual componentry used in both the Ohio and Michigan behavioural models. House's model also included a not dissimilar notion of the key elements of leader behaviour.[112] Hersey and Blanchard explicitly built off the 'consideration' and 'structure' components of the Ohio State studies, complementing this with their concept of follower psychological maturity.[113]

Consequently, while contingency/situational theories constituted, on the one hand, a dramatic reversal in the prior assumption that there was one best way to lead, they simultaneously continued to assume that leader behaviours were central to explaining leadership, and that these could be adequately captured in a few key dimensions. This type of intellectual mutation is, of course, commonplace, but given the lack of evidence for behavioural theory, as established by Korman's meta-review, it meant that 'progress' in leadership 'science' was more rhetorical than substantive in nature.

Other factors were influential in facilitating the appeal of contingency/ situational models. The 1960s had seen an increasingly hostile attitude develop toward 'bureaucratic', impersonal or inflexible modes of functioning by those in positions of authority.[114] Social norms and expectations were shifting rapidly; Whyte's 'organization man'[115] was increasingly seen as a straightjacket which inhibited individual expression and fulfilment. An approach to theorizing leadership which offered choice was, thus, well suited to the broader cultural milieu of the time: acknowledging individual needs and differences, and acknowledging that specific conditions carried with them different opportunities and dilemmas, was in accordance with wider developments in thought.[116] Within the discipline of psychology, cognitive approaches were gaining ascendency as the critique of a strict behaviourist perspective gathered more support.[117] For leadership scholars to demonstrate the alignment of their work with this and with developments in the broader management literature[118] would also have facilitated the appeal of contingency/ situational models.

Social Function and Subjectivity Effects

In abandoning the earlier pursuit of a singular model of effective leadership, contingency/situational discourse functioned to open up new opportunities for leadership scholars: this approach to conceptualizing leadership facilitated publishing and consulting opportunities for entrepreneurial researchers able to develop a model that could be claimed as being uniquely tailored to situations or contingencies of interest to particular audiences. These entrepreneurial researchers could now establish status and credibility much more readily through the development of their own models than was possible when the field focused on coherence and accumulation of knowledge pertaining to a singular version of the truth about leadership. A milieu in which the existence of many truths about leadership was rendered both possible and desirable was, thus, also one wherein leadership scholars could readily compete for commercial gain and status.

The broader social function of contingency/situational discourse was to elevate the status of leadership as an activity which entails the skilful, considered and legitimate manipulation of others, resulting in improved organizational results. Leadership was now increasingly positioned as a solution to the problem of employees dissatisfied with inflexible or bureaucratic modes of interaction.[119] The heightened complexity this discourse ascribed to leadership serves to enhance the status of leaders, for they were now understood as persons in possession of sophisticated diagnostic and decision-making skills deployed responsively. Leadership was thus increasingly emphasized as being of critical importance with the advent of contingency/situational thinking; bolder claims were made as to its necessity, potency and complexity.

In contingency/situational thinking, the person of the ideal leader is portrayed as a skilful and considered diagnostician of worker/follower behaviours, whose aim is to secure willing compliance, satisfaction and productivity. Excepting Fiedler, who regards a leader's preference for a task or relationship focus as largely fixed, as with behavioural theory leaders are positioned as being persons concerned to satisfy the needs both of organizations and those who work within them. Leaders appear here as persons highly attentive to the human dynamics of the workgroup, able to carefully analyze and then flexibly (other than for Fiedler) respond to those dynamics. Here, the leader's behaviour may be directive, collaborative or passive, depending on their analysis of the situational requirements.

With this development, leaders were once again understood as knowing agents, via the assumption that leader cognition precedes leader behaviour. Fiedler's interest in the leader's interior life, for example, sought to determine the 'underlying need-structure of the individual which motivates his behaviour in various leadership situations'.[120] As with behavioural discourse, the primary issues of concern demanding leader attention continued to be workplace relationships and task performance. The overall effect of these developments constituted a raised expectation of leaders when compared with behavioural theory, as leadership was no longer a set recipe to follow but rather involved assessing and selecting from a set of ingredients to bring about the optimal approach and result.

Followers remained, as with behavioural discourse, persons with legitimate needs and concerns. However, they were now also understood as persons whose agency may be problematic, potentially even posing a threat to the leader's ability to exercise his/her rightful authority.[121] Followers' state of mind was thus something to which the leader must be alert and responsive, due to its potentially disruptive capacity. This in turn suggests a relationship between subjects who each seek to influence the other but where the expectation is that the leader, through skilful diagnosis, will bring the follower around to willing compliance and satisfaction.

The leader–follower relationship, as portrayed here, suggests a constant state of assessment on the part of the leader as to the follower's state of mind, technical capability and willingness to comply with the leader's wishes.[122] In what was seen as its ideal state, the relationship was said to entail mutually respectful and trusting connections between leader and followers. In what was understood as being an undesirable state, the relationship was said to be marked by follower mistrust, hostility and overt or covert resistance; here the pressure was on both leader and follower to change that dynamic. With Fiedler's model, follower power and opinion was explicitly positioned as a potential problem to be managed, and so carries with it the constant risk of leader failure. Overall, the leader–follower relationship in contingency/ situational discourse was understood as being potentially unstable, with the expectation always that where the relationship was other than trusting and respectful, it is the leader who can and should change this state of affairs.

'NEW LEADERSHIP'

> The crisis in leadership today is the mediocrity or irresponsibility of so many of the men and women in power, but leadership rarely rises to the full need for it ... We fail to grasp the essence of leadership that is relevant to the modern age ... No central concept of leadership has yet emerged. (Burns, 1978, pp. 1–3)

> [A] crucial contribution of transformational/charismatic leadership has been in terms of its rejuvenation of the leadership field, regardless of whatever content contributions it has made. This rejuvenation came about because of what most would consider a paradigm shift that has attracted numerous new scholars and moved the field as a whole out of its doldrums. (Hunt, 1999, p. 129)

Problems

By the late 1970s, claiming to an American audience that leadership was now in a state of crisis was quite easily done. The turmoil generated by Watergate, the failure of the Vietnam War, the OPEC oil crisis, stagflation and the competitive challenges now eroding America's industrial supremacy all added to the sense that America had somehow lost its way.[123] Simultaneously, positioning leadership as a vital force which could produce dramatic and widespread change was also readily done at this time, when the likes of Martin Luther King, John F. Kennedy, Malcolm X and Gloria Steinem had attracted such great attention, affection and regard for their efforts to bring about change.[124] Connecting this case for a new approach to leadership with an appealingly optimistic view of human potential[125] both demanded, and helped to create, a radical reconceptualization of the truth about leadership.

Coming from outside the workplace-focused leadership literature, political scientist James MacGregor Burns tackled this task largely without reference to that literature.[126] In so doing, he simultaneously created a means for those workplace-focused leadership scholars to simply step away from the troubles facing the field and to begin exploring 'new leadership'. Since then, this discourse has sustained itself by continuously problematizing modern society as being so complex, ever-changing and demanding that leadership is vital to the continued progress of human society. Followers' inability to realize their full potential in the absence of 'new leadership' has been continuously problematized over the course of this discourse. 'New leadership' was invented to address these concerns.

Key Features of the Discourse

James MacGregor Burns' *Leadership*, the key foundational text inform-ing the development of the 'new leadership' paradigm, was first pub-lished in 1978. By the mid-1980s, contingency/situational models were by and large eclipsed as 'new leadership' thinking came to dominate the field of leadership studies.[127]

The portrayal of the leader, as first proposed by Burns, is that of an agent of morally uplifting change who has a transformative effect on followers. In this account, a leader's relationship with followers is said to be one 'not only of power but of mutual needs, aspirations and values'.[128] It is claimed that 'leadership emerges from, and always returns to, the fundamental needs and wants, aspirations, and values of the followers . . . (it) produce(s) social change that will satisfy followers' authentic needs'.[129] A key assumption at this early stage is that 'followers have adequate knowledge of alternative leaders ... and the capacity to choose among those alternatives'.[130] An expectation that leaders and followers have common interests is thus an important feature of Burns' original thinking, as is the assumption that followers can choose their leader. These assumptions in turn provide a basis for expecting that the ethical conduct of leaders will accord with what followers would expect and deem acceptable. Should it not, follower support can and will be withdrawn.

The return of the leader as exceptional person pre-dates Burns via House's[131] theory of charismatic leadership. This theory was grounded in a psychological understanding of charisma as that which excites a devoted follower response,[132] rather than in Weber's sociological notion of charismatic leadership as an emotionally based form of authority relations.[133] While House's work led to a stream of further research,[134] its broader impact is its contribution to the process of positioning leadership as the work of exceptional individuals and for the emotional responses of followers to be seen as an important aspect of leadership.

Burns' account of 'transforming leadership' assumed mutuality between leaders and followers not only in terms of shared needs, wants, aspirations and values, but also in terms of psychological functioning.[135] Here, leaders are understood as persons driven to express themselves through leadership, while followers are understood as persons whose potential can only be released through the leader's influence: Maslow's hierarchy of needs was adapted through Burns' introduction of the leader as the motive force which impels followers toward self-actualization.[136] A psychological co-dependency is thus held to function between leader and follower wherein each needs the other to achieve their potential.

Burns' initial attempt at reforming the nature, scope and direction of leadership discourse constituted a strongly normative and qualitative plea for change.[137] Grounded in both a sustained critique of current thinking and practices and the careful selection of exemplars deemed indicative of what was desirable, undesirable and emergent, Burns' work evoked a sense of untapped potential to theorize about and practice leadership in a dramatically different way to that on offer via situational/contingency theories. Read in conjunction with House's initial work,[138] while narrower in scope, these developments provided a basis from which leadership could be radically reconceptualized.

Burns argued that a psychological universal underpinned the phenomenon of leadership, positioning leadership as something which arises from the natural workings of the human psyche.[139] He argued that the achievement of change was a central focus for leaders and spoke of 'transforming' leadership as constituting both an ideal and a necessity for the modern context. His model confidently assumed that adherence to the norms and values of American democracy were such as to place leaders who followed those norms and values on morally unquestionable ground.

A number of leadership theorists were quickly attracted to Burns' ideas and ideals. Peters and Waterman, for example, spoke of 'the search for excellence' as the defining characteristic of successful business leaders, arguing that pressing for change and bold goals was both a virtue and a necessity.[140] Bennis and Nanus focused on 'visionary' leadership, placing the emphasis on the ambitious goals effective leaders were held to advance, these visions being derived from the leader's creative capacities.[141] However, it was Bass'[142] reformulation which sought to substantiate the claims made by Burns by deploying social science norms of speaking the truth.

Bass developed a specific set of leadership processes which he claimed are the means by which what he renamed *transformational* leaders achieve the dramatic changes in performance now positioned as being the true value of leadership.[143] Developed through various iterations, Bass' model came to comprise four 'transformational' and two 'transactional' components and it is this which has come to be the most influential and extensively researched theory in 'new leadership' discourse.[144]

In this model, 'intellectual stimulation' refers to the leader's capacity to identify new ideas and opportunities which challenge followers' accepted ways of thinking and acting.[145] 'Individualized consideration' means the leader's treatment of followers as unique persons with their own hopes and fears in which the leader shows interest, always encouraging them to grow.[146] 'Inspirational motivation' is the leader's capacity to articulate a vision or goal which followers find highly appealing and which excites their support, while 'idealized influence' means the leader acts as a role model, with their standards of behaviour setting the bar for others.[147]

Burns had claimed that leadership took two different forms: transforming and transactional leadership.[148] For him, the latter was understood as lacking a higher purpose, as concerned only with instrumental exchange, while the former was positioned as being both necessary and desirable to bring about social change for the benefit of all. Bass, however, reconceptualized Burns' proposition, arguing that transformational and transactional approaches could and should be combined.[149] The driver for this reconceptualization was that Bass' model was intended for application to the workplace environment.

In paving the way for the ready integration into organizational life of these new ideas, Bass took it for granted that 'leadership' would be enacted by 'managers' who held positions of formal authority.[150] Consequently, Bass' model incorporated into his conception of 'leadership' the by-then standard expectation that managers could issue rewards and sanctions to workers depending on their performance.[151] This deliberate coalescing of the moral authority of leadership with the formal authority of managers provided the basis for both extending managerial influence and enhancing their social status. Burns' original assumption of follower choice in regard to who shall lead[152] was simply ignored when 'new leadership' discourse entered the workplace.

This combining of leadership with management, however, simultaneously enabled the discursive division of people deemed 'leaders' from those who were simply 'managers', positioning the former as superior to the latter. Building on Zaleznik's influential HBR article which argued that 'leaders' were psychologically different and achieved superior results to 'managers',[153] Bass' thinking[154] also aligned with Bennis and Nanus who claimed that 'managers are people who do things right while leaders are people who do the right thing'.[155]

This positioning has continued largely unchallenged through to the present day.[156] The effect is that while one might hold managerial authority, it is only through engaging in 'visionary change' which 'transforms' others that one's credentials as a leader can be firmly established. This effective takeover of 'management' by 'leadership' in terms of social status in turn positions leadership knowledge as highly desirable and generates demand for access to this knowledge. Those who know the secrets of leadership hold the keys to success and fame in this version of the world. Leadership texts and development programmes aimed at practitioners have become big business on the back of this repositioning of the status and nature of leadership.

With Bass' model, a ready-made leader identity, available for wider dispersion and intended for replication, was placed on offer.[157] The 'new leader' here is fully and formally specified as a charismatic individual with high levels of 'self-confidence and self-esteem', capable of defining priorities and meaning in a manner which others find persuasive.[158] Leaders are portrayed here as persons motivated to inspire others through emotional appeals and intellectual stimulation and concerned also with the needs, views and development of individual followers. The leader is expected (and warranted) to induce changes in thought and practice in regards to such diverse matters as 'who rules and by what means; the work-group norms, as well as ultimate beliefs about religion, ideology, morality, ethics, space, time, and human nature'.[159] To achieve these kinds of results, the leader 'invents, introduces, and advances the cultural forms', resulting in change to 'the social warp and woof of reality'.[160]

Because it is now assumed that the leader functions in a workplace setting with formal authority, withholding or granting rewards dependent on performance also becomes part of the leader's role.

Followers are portrayed in 'new leadership' discourse as persons with unmet needs and unrealized potential: to address these gaps in their lives consequently requires the intervention of the leader.[161] It is said that followers may not fully understand their own true needs and hence the leader is to be the one who can reveal these to them.[162] Matched to this, the follower is portrayed as someone in need of guidance, amenable to change, needing to be changed, requiring someone else to prompt this change, and benefiting from this change.[163] Followers are said to be naturally self-serving but amenable to becoming self-denying. Via the leader's intervention, followers are expected to 'transcend their own self-interest for the good of the group, organization, or country'.[164] This focus on followers' potential for good is markedly more positive than the distrust evident in contingency–situational accounts.

Processes of Formation

The emergence of the 'new leadership' discourse in the America of the late 1970s and 1980s can most usefully be understood as a strategic response to a range of social, political and economic factors and events. At this time, America had experienced for some years high-profile political leaders whose rhetorical flair, as well as the content of their ideas, had excited a strong emotional response from both supporters and opponents.[165] President Kennedy and Dr King are particularly noteworthy examples. These experiences rendered American culture especially receptive to a concept of leadership which was dramatic, bold and focused on the achievement of change. While charismatic leadership theory sought to account for the appeal of such individuals, transformational leadership theory offered a broader agenda with a greater focus on substantive change, and was perhaps also more palatable at a time when charismatic leaders such as Hitler and Mussolini remained etched in living memory.

While both the Vietnam War and Watergate provoked significant unease about the moral authority of leaders,[166] 'new leadership' theory seemed to offer a solution to such concerns via its (ostensible) focus on follower needs. The ongoing effects of the so-called counter-culture which questioned the established ways of doing things meant that it was increasingly difficult for those in positions of authority to secure willing obedience simply by reference to their authority.[167] 'New leadership' recommended persuasion by appeal to both facts and values and encouraged the development of each individual follower. Here too, then, the alignment between issues of interest in the broader cultural context and the specific form of 'new leadership' was strong, and helps to explain its appeal.

During the 1970s and 1980s, America's industrial sector had also been struggling to retain its competitiveness, with challenges such as the oil crisis and stagflation eroding confidence that American business and political leaders knew what to do.[168] 'New leadership', meanwhile, placed the achievement of change at its very heart. It claimed that leadership could overcome resistance to change, and positioned change as of inherent virtue.[169] It positioned leaders as beings with superior levels of insight, foresight and strength of character such that others could rely on their guidance and direction.[170]

The seductive appeal of these ideas[171] for a business audience contemplating the need for a radical overhaul of American industry can hardly be underestimated. The discourse of 'new leadership' spoke directly to an audience contemplating an environment which was seen as having dramatically changed and which appeared to require widespread reform and new ways of doing things to regain American dominance. 'New leadership' theories put themselves forward to offer 'new answers to new questions ... using a new paradigm or pattern of inquiry'.[172]

The bold claims made about leaders' ability and right to shape others' reality, values and beliefs were readily asserted and accepted in a cultural context already primed to see those in authority as fundamentally benevolent in intent and effect.[173] This context shapes what is sayable in respect of leadership as much as it shapes the silences and omissions we can see in this discourse. The appetite to so readily accept the claims made about leaders, to grab at them with such enthusiasm, serves as an endorsement of Meindl et al.'s contention that a romantic view of leadership colours contemporary perceptions,[174] generating a focus on the potentially positive aspects of leadership and a turning away from the potentially problematic aspects of a relationship based on inequality.

Proponents of 'new leadership' have sustained interest in its efficacy and truthfulness for over two decades by effectively deploying the full range of techniques for dispersing ideas which are at the disposal of the modern academy. Research programmes and degrees, conferences, executive education programmes and publishing combined have resulted in an active, credible discursive regime whose underpinning assumptions are now rarely questioned.[175] Key advocates such as Bass and Hunt have held editorial positions at what is now accepted as the leading journal in the field,[176] while emerging scholars have been encouraged by their mentors and supervisors to build on existing theory.[177]

'New leadership' approaches are now mature and widely accepted.[178] The successful dispersion of this account of the truth about leadership has rendered legitimate, even expected, the idea that manager-leaders are entitled to work on the psyche of employee-followers. Rather than being understood as a gross invasion of personal autonomy and an abuse of managerial authority, this is positioned as nurturing the follower's potential. Yet when these ideas are placed in the context of the longer-term development of 'leadership science', as examined here, what seems evident is that 'new leadership' is an alchemic mix of trait and behavioural modalities firmly attached to a conception of change as both necessary and desirable, a framing which happily coincides with the requirements of advanced capitalist economics.

Social Function and Subjectivity Effects

As we have seen, in this discourse 'leadership' and 'stability' are placed in opposing camps. 'Leadership' is here associated with change, reform and upheaval, with whatever is bigger, better, faster, stronger and newer, expected to conquer whatever is smaller, slower, weaker and older.[179] In the context in which it arose, then, 'new leadership' discourse can be understood to function as a strategic power/knowledge formulation which supports the requirements of capitalism to find new sources of profit by asserting the desirability and inevitability of constant change and improved performance.

The role granted to leaders positions them as facilitators of the requirements of capitalism, while followers function as consumers of leadership with the promise that such consumption will satisfy their 'authentic needs' for someone else to direct their work and re-shape their self.[180] The discourse functions to enhance the moral authority of managers and to extend the scope of managerial intervention;[181] with the development of 'new leadership' discourse, managerial intervention extends beyond merely motivating the employee to work harder to defining the employee's values, beliefs and reality.

This extension of leadership into new realms was a clear break from previous models. In claiming that leaders can and should change followers' reality, values and beliefs, individual autonomy and responsibility for such matters are pushed aside, yet we are told that this is really in followers' best interests. Instead, those in authority are tasked with addressing these concerns on followers' behalf. 'New leadership' has sought to colonize domains of existence not previously understood as the purview of managers; in so doing, it serves the interests of organizations desirous of securing the willing compliance and wholehearted enthusiasm of their employees. There seems to be no issue too challenging for the 'new leader' to take on, no problem beyond their capacity to solve. It is as if leadership is the answer, no matter what the question or problem, an essential force for good, and only good, in which leaders are imbued with special gifts. Here, their corner offices are akin to holy places while their utterances have become the source of truth and salvation.

With 'new leadership' came the full-blown return of the knowing, intentional, exceptional subject as both the central focus of leadership discourse and the source from which the desired effects and results emanate. As constructed here, the leader is someone who expresses themselves through and in others, who influences others to become more like the leader.[182] Leader success is thus here akin to reproduction by way of cloning. The new visionary, transformational, charismatic leader may take a male or female form and can be found in factories and offices everywhere, encouraging others to become like them, appealing to both reason and emotion.

Leaders, as depicted here, are persons who harbour no doubts as to their own capacity;[183] the only challenge may be to find followers whose 'authentic needs' match those of the leader. Leaders' ability and apparently fundamental need to change the beliefs, values and reality of others is said to be governed by a relationship of symbiosis that is to be formed between leaders and followers.[184] This apparently will suffice to ensure that leaders do not abuse their position. Leaders' capacity to imagine a different future, to engage others' enthusiasm for that, to enhance others' performance and to nurture their development means that leaders function here in creative, strategic, operational and interpersonal modes with equal ease. There is apparently nothing of which the new leader is incapable.

However, the self of the 'new leader' is also one which can never be satisfied with what exists outside itself, because change is rendered a compulsive requirement for the new leader.[185] There is always to be something in the 'new leader's' environment needing improvement or change. There is no scope for stability, for modest goals or merely adequate performance. In this conception of leadership, everything and everyone must shine, always. Nothing is ever quite good enough. There is a demand for constant movement: so long as something is changing the 'new leader' warrants their own existence, their very being. If nothing changes, it is as if the 'new leader' ceases to exist as such.

Complementing this conception of the leader, the follower exists in this discourse as a person whose potential can be achieved only through the actions of a leader.[186] Hence, the 'new leader' is one who frees followers from a life of unrealized potential to which they are otherwise condemned. Here, it is as if followers are perpetually in limbo in the absence of the leader, waiting for the leader's inspiration, advice, sanctioning or reward to guide their next move. Followers, as depicted here, offer a passivity which serves as a perfect counter-weight to the energy of leaders. While followers are credited with possessing values, goals and dreams of their own, these are simultaneously discredited as being self-serving and inauthentic in the absence of the leader's influence.[187]

The relationship between leader and follower in this discourse is full of (unexamined) paradoxes: leader self-expression is intended to bring about follower self-denial, yet this is simultaneously said to be in the follower's authentic interests, of which she/he may be unaware.[188] A follower's potential can here only be achieved by leader intervention, implying an inadequate or non-existent agency on the part of followers. However, the leader's very existence relies on followers being willing to change themselves (to become more like the leader), suggesting that the agency to resist resides in followers, posing a threat to the leader's success. Problematically, it seems that if followers become leaders, a proposition posed as the ultimate achievement of leadership,[189] this would result in both leader and follower losing their distinctive subjectivity and role as well as their raison d'être. As a potential identity script for actual persons to deploy,[190] the 'new leadership' discourse thus offers a precarious existence.

UNDERPINNING ASSUMPTIONS IN LEADERSHIP 'SCIENCE'

Having now examined each of the major theoretical paradigms which have dominated the era of leadership science in this and the preceding chapter, in the remainder of this chapter I move to consider the epistemic foundations and rules which have shaped leadership science, before offering an overall assessment of its characteristics.

Carlyle's epistemology comprised a mix of whiggish historiography, biography and physiognomy, the latter being the study of faces to determine underlying character.[191] When combined with the author's own determination to search for the 'truth of the matter', the result was an account which claimed to offer insight into the nature and character of the leaders whose lives he analyzed. However, this approach to establishing the truth about leadership would not survive the transition to the deployment of natural science techniques in leadership studies which Galton championed.

Galton's methods included the use of questionnaires which he then interpreted using both quantitative (counting of occurrences) and qualitative methods.[192] He drew on 'faculty psychology', in which various personal qualities were thought to be located in different parts of the brain and able to be detected through measuring the head or assessing behaviour,[193] along with his interpretation of Darwin's work on inheritance. This resulted in a focus on family characteristics, including race and place of birth, parental occupation, temperament and appearance relative to that of the leader.[194] Galton's analysis of the qualities of exceptional men included such factors as an assessment of their health, head size, perseverance, impulsiveness, memory and interest in religion. Other matters deemed of relevance included educational experiences and the self-assessed origins of their interests.[195]

From around the beginning of the 20th century, building on Galton's work, the mode of knowledge production became less exploratory and more focused on testing specific hypotheses.[196] Initially, not only great men but also small children were the objects of analysis: the task was to establish the markers which separated leaders from followers.[197] As the field developed, it came to rely almost exclusively on the methods, norms and ethics of positivist modern social science, aiming to produce research findings that were generalizable, quantifiable and repeatable.[198] Over the course of the 20th century, much effort went into testing hypotheses that aim to define and measure the components, antecedents and effects of leadership and to identify (statistically) the relationships between these variables: establishing the correlation of constructs has been the standard to which scholars have aspired.[199] Changes in theoretical paradigms have meanwhile provided the context for determining which variables and constructs are deemed most worthy of attention.

Consistent with the wider project of modern social science, leadership scholars have also been concerned to improve the human condition.[200] Since World War II, leadership discourse has strongly directed its attention to improving workplace performance, this being understood as something of benefit to everyone.[201] This focus has marked the outer limits of what has been rendered valuable and relevant, providing a rationale for the production of knowledge oriented to instrumental and commercial concerns. A focus on the bodies of leaders as demanding analysis has declined since the demise of trait theories: behavioural, contingency/situational theories and 'new leadership' theories have focused on behaviours and techniques from which the presence of leaders' and followers' bodies has been removed.

With the strong emphasis leadership discourse has placed on quantitative data as the gold standard for reliable evidence,[202] establishing the truth about leadership has seen a turning away from matters not amenable to ready quantification. Consequently, contextual and political concerns and the lived experience of leading and following, matters not easily confronted in surveys, have effectively been rendered marginal and indeed almost irrelevant in this epistemic milieu. Tracing the long-term impact of leadership has proved to be largely beyond the limits of the favoured epistemology.[203] Instead, the correlation of constructs, established by means of administering a one-time survey to a sample group, has been treated time and again as proof positive of the value and desirability of leadership.[204]

Modern scholars have by and large rejected as irrelevant or unreliable all previous leadership knowledge not produced via scientific method.[205] In adopting the model of the natural sciences as the standard which should inform 'rigorous' and 'reliable' leadership studies, the most basic assumption informing research efforts has been that the object of study, leadership, exists as an ontological fact, prior to or beyond discourse and subjective interpretation, possessing naturally occurring regularities and thus governed by 'universal laws'.[206] The aim of leadership research within this intellectual framework is, thus, one of discovering 'what really exists'.

However, with the shift by most scholars to the assumption that there is no one best way to lead following the failure of behavioural theories to sustain support, a subtle but profound move away from the norms of the physical sciences also occurred at the level of basic epistemology. The careful definition of constructs, the use of anonymous survey techniques and the subjection of data to complex statistical analyses all go to suggest that scientific rigour and discipline guide the production of authorized texts in this discourse. However, the acceptance by the field of a proliferation of competing models also clearly implies an acknowledgement that there is no one truth to be found in respect of leadership. This situation poses no great difficulties for those of an interpretivist or postmodern persuasion in matters of epistemology. However, most leadership scholars have remained decidedly positivist in the claims they make.[207] Consequently, a key epistemic feature of the field is its surface-level commitment to the establishment of a scientifically credible 'Truth' about leadership, combined with an underlying and unacknowledged assumption that many versions of the truth about leadership can be established and need not cohere. This in turn means that the discourse rests on norms that are simultaneously both scientific and not scientific. The result is an alchemic mix in which fact and faith, disciplined knowledge and pet theories combine to produce many versions of 'the Truth' about leadership whose inconsistencies need not be addressed.

As a result of these foregoing developments, the following implicit rules now govern the mainstream of leadership discourse:

- Position leadership as offering a powerful solution to the most pressing concerns of the day, so as to continuously reinforce its desirability, inevitability and value.
- Assume leadership is timeless and natural, on the one hand, and modern and amenable to change, on the other, and ignore the contradictions in these assumptions.
- Treat that which can be readily quantified according to accepted standards of statistical analysis as being most credible and worthy of attention and dismiss as irrelevant that which cannot be quantified.
- Assume social progress is inevitable and that humans, in particular leaders, are perfectible provided only that we strive for this goal.
- Assume there exists no conflict between the interests of leaders and followers, or between organizations and those who work for them.
- Assert one's commitment to the scientific endeavour, but make no effort to reconcile competing versions of the truth about leadership.

These rules function to sustain the mainstream of leadership scholarship as being apparently scientific in nature.

LEADERSHIP SCIENCE RECONSIDERED

The 'scientific' truth about leadership has repeatedly been subject to fundamental shifts in thinking. As we have seen, the key driver of these developments is not improved knowledge but power and power/ knowledge, expedient but skilful responses to changes in what is seen to be problematic. In this era of leadership science, initially leadership was thought to comprise innate, possibly inherited, qualities of superior persons. Then it became a pattern of supervisory behaviour, a recipe which all those holding such positions were expected to adopt. Next, leadership became a selection of supervisory behaviours deployed according to an assessment of the circumstances at hand. It was now a set of ingredients rather than a recipe, and was understood as requiring sophisticated skills whose value to organizations was increasingly emphasized. For the last quarter century, the charismatic leader as the agent of visionary, transformational change has dominated our understanding of leadership, an approach which supports, reinforces and normalizes the demands of advanced capitalism for constant change.

These often dramatic shifts in our basic conceptualization of leadership were not driven by the progressive accumulation of scientifically robust knowledge. Rather, what was deemed problematic and demanding of response changed; scholars skilfully deployed the mechanisms of knowledge production and distribution at their disposal, connected their ideas with widely accepted beliefs and values, and then repeatedly produced a new version of the truth aligned to these factors.

As part of these developments, an implicit acceptance that contradictory truths about leadership may exist has developed, relieving scholars of the need to reconcile their varying results and models. This fracturing of the field's epistemological standards enabled more opportunities for scholars to pursue their own favoured interpretation: producing the truth about leadership now requires obeisance to the methods of modern science but not to its most fundamental claim, namely that through science we can come to know 'the Truth'. Notably, the 'control group' study, an examination of follower behaviours and results in the absence of their managerial leader in order to fully test the impact of leadership, is not a feature in this discourse. This leaves the 'romance of leadership'[208] and 'attribution' theory[209] as equally plausible explanations for the effects claimed for leadership, for how can we know to the level of certainty normally expected of a science what the effect of 'x' (leadership) is on 'y' (followers), unless we study 'y' in both the presence and absence of 'x'?

At the level of core assumptions, the field has been one in a state of flux. Model 6.1 shows that the major theoretical developments examined here have relied on changing basic assumptions about the extent to which leadership is an innate or learned quality and in the degree to which they advocate a singular or flexible approach to how leaders ought to lead.

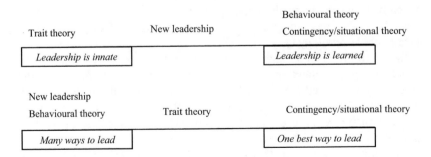

Model 6.1   Basic assumptions in leadership science

What this reveals is not a domain of knowledge where continuous progress has occurred, but rather one where core assumptions have been subject to rapid and fundamental change. Indeed, with 'new leadership' discourse we have moved to a position which is closer to that of the trait theorists. Were these shifts in thinking due to compelling evidence revealing the error of extant understandings, then this could be understood as an example of scientific progress. However, I contend that what my study reveals is that political, social and economic factors have been critical factors driving these changes, while 'evidence' has had a very limited role to play in 'advancing' leadership knowledge.

From the perspective of the current day, the critical shift which occurred mid-century was the combining of managerial authority with leadership such that it has now become normalized to speak of one in relation to the other. The radical potential of treating the human issues to which leaders were expected to attend as of equal importance to economic considerations in the running of organizations was lost when the value of leadership was measured in terms of organizational performance. This development has instead had the effect of rendering leadership a means of advancing managerial interests and a function enacted in pursuit of organizational goals. The initial fascination with leader traits offered no basis for these developments. Rather, post-war political sensibilities and concerns with productivity were the driving force, drawing on and adapting both human relations and scientific management.

Leadership 'science' has, by and large, produced knowledge which claims to be context free, aiming for findings that will be accepted as generalizable accounts of the truth about leadership. What has been constructed is a science of correlations derived largely from the administration of surveys to American managers and workers. The approach typically taken relies on the expectation that universal and discoverable laws shape the phenomenon of leadership, which itself is presumed to have a stable ontology.

To commit to such an approach requires that leadership scholars either forget or ignore their own history and presume that an inevitable superiority is imbued in current knowledge. However, the historical fact of the repeated failure of different approaches to theorizing leadership surely demands a more circumspect view of its ontology, along with a greater acceptance of the epistemological limitations the favoured methods of inquiry carry with them. These irksome matters are only infrequently acknowledged as the field is characterized by the virtual absence of critical reflexiveness towards its own assumptions and predilections.[210] Consequently, at every point along the way leadership researchers have been able to find what they wanted to find, at least for a period of time, be it traits, standardized behaviours, contingent responses, charismatic, visionary transformers or, most recently, authentic leaders.

The production of leadership knowledge has consistently been over-determined by a prior conceptualization of leadership and its perceived value: leadership research thus typically functions to confirm researcher expectations rather than challenge them.[211] Consistently here we find a commitment to leadership understood as a vital source that can bring about an improved social and industrial order. Repeatedly, 'leadership', however it is conceived, is understood as carrying with it the promise of improvement, of 'progress', however that might be understood. 'Leadership', however conceived, is continuously connected with whatever is broadly understood as being desirable, with whatever is generally accepted as constituting an aspirational goal, a positioning which helps explain its enduring appeal and fascination. 'Leaders', however defined, are consistently depicted as persons warranting admiration, deserving of recognition and to whose guidance we ought to defer. Alternative perspectives have failed not only to dent the collective faith in the value of leadership, but even to bring about a more modest or cautious stance by mainstream leadership scholars.

Wider concerns to improve the human condition and, post-World War II, organizational performance, have also been crucial influences providing energy, funding and endorsement for the work of scholars whose stance has never been that of the disinterested scientist. While worker grievances, labour turnover and team and individual output were early matters to be correlated with leadership, as management concerns have shifted from control of workers' bodies to influence of their minds and selves, so too has leadership come to be correlated with organizational citizenship behaviours, employee satisfaction and other concerns now deemed relevant to the sought-after release of discretionary effort. The presumption of the legitimacy of manager-leaders to influence worker-followers has increasingly been naturalized in the leadership discourse at the same time as the scope of that influence has been extended. Leadership knowledge has thus contributed in important ways to identifying mechanisms and processes which enable work intensification and a more complete colonization of worker subjectivity.

At the same time, the expectations placed on leaders have grown rapidly as the discourse functions to discipline both leaders and followers to adopt a prescribed set of attitudes, behaviours and subject positions. Initially, leaders could simply 'be themselves', as their innate superiority gifted them something which others could merely admire and never hope to replicate. When leader traits were deemed irrelevant, the expectation which then developed was for supervisor-leaders to adopt a standardized approach which balanced a concern with both output and amicable employee relations. Matters became more complex when supervisor-leaders were expected to conduct a careful diagnosis of their context before adopting a suitable response. When managers were rendered into visionary transformational leaders as their core identity, the expectations placed on them rose exponentially. Now, 'reality', 'meaning', 'values' and the 'vision' of the future to which all efforts were to be directed derived from leaders, were theirs to shape. Leaders were explicitly tasked with being role models for all that was thought good and desirable in the modern workplace. More recently, leaders are now being asked to manufacture their own authenticity so as to ensure its complete alignment with organizational needs and interests.[212]

Consequently, while leadership discourse has functioned to support work intensification and the greater control of worker subjectivity, leaders too have been more comprehensively disciplined by this discursive regime, and the demands placed on them have risen dramatically. 'Leaders' have been more fully defined, their actions, attitudes and sense of self more fully prescribed, while the expectation that they have the answer to whatever troubles us has been placed upon their shoulders.

Only rarely have concerns about the potential for abuse of their position by those favoured with such authority over others been considered a relevant topic for modern leadership scholars to explore.[213] Rather, leadership knowledge has typically been produced with instrumental outcomes in mind, in full acceptance of the norms and requirements of capitalist economics, without demur and without consideration of any risks of exploitation or domination by leaders of those they lead. While we might now talk of leadership as having a transformational potential, this capacity has not been intended to be directed toward any fundamental aspect of the broader economic system, but rather only to its advancement and our collective commitment to that.

Since World War II, consistent attempts have been made to establish and maintain the relevance of leadership knowledge to managerial interests. This in turn has made it necessary for those who would claim to speak to the truth about leadership to maintain a broader appreciation of developments in organizational life, along with a constant monitoring of the commercial, legal, economic, technological and political trends and events that affect the functioning of organizations.[214] This connectedness likely provides a broader contextual basis to inform the production of leadership knowledge, yet typically the methodological preferences that are deployed remove from view this broader knowledge which scholars may have. Instead, adherence to the methodological orthodoxy of the field seems to prevail over the making of comments which rely on interpretivist perspectives drawn from more ethnographically oriented interaction with practitioners. The norms governing the publication of texts sanctioned as authoritative by this discursive regime function to maintain a narrow account of leadership. Philosophical and political concerns are now largely absent, and the question of what all this leading and following is actually for is rarely examined.[215]

Even though 'new leadership' has dominated the field since the 1980s, trait, behavioural and contingency/situational perspectives have also continued to attract attention, right through to the present day.[216] With few exceptions,[217] effort has not gone into reconciling these competing perspectives: the visible presence of a fractured and inconsistent field of truth claims is accompanied by silence about this overall state of affairs.

In recent years, a variety of different perspectives, such as relational,[218] distributed,[219] discursive,[220] practice[221] and phenomenological[222] accounts of leadership, have developed at the edges of the field. Many of these developments are founded on a less scientistic epistemology, adopt a social constructionist perspective, favour qualitative methodologies and show greater sensitivity to issues of context and power. These developments point to a potentially very different future for what may be claimed as the truth about leadership at the same time as they intensify the fracturing of the field. Prominent scholars have openly abandoned the search for a general theory of leadership.[223] However, this poses no impediment to the continued production of research, as most scholars rely on the use of a specific theory, meaning that they can avoid grappling with these broader and deeper problems.

As things currently stand, theoretical proliferation, an incommensurability of perspectives and a splintering of the field into different 'camps' with little interaction between them are marked features of the contemporary archive. Leadership 'science' in this regard is a failed project, for it cannot establish its most basic truths even among its own community. This dilemma arises due to the inherent limitations of a project whose driving force has become that of ensuring its own continuance by avoiding any serious questioning of its own most deeply held assumptions. So long as 'leadership science' lacks a strongly felt, philosophically informed scepticism as to the nature, value and effects of its object of analysis, it likely ensures its continued failure as a science. The evidence to date demonstrates that the unquestioning faith in leadership which has provided the foundation upon which modern theories have been built is highly unlikely to produce a robust, reliable science. Moreover, so long as 'leadership science' continues to avoid treating the political values and effects of its utterances as central concerns, it will likely continue to offer a technocratic, functionalist account of leadership which ultimately serves organizational interests but not the interests of those who work in organizations. If philosophy and politics were brought into the centre of 'leadership science', perhaps the faith which has driven this discourse over the last 150 years might finally be questioned.

This analysis of the archive of modern leadership studies demonstrates that pre-World War II a mix of romantic, biological and eugenicist concerns shaped the truth about leadership. Since that time, a strict adherence to the scientific form, coupled with an ongoing inability to fulfil its core purpose of establishing the truth, has developed. What we have is knowledge production which has been increasingly dedicated to serving the interests of capitalist economics. As a result, leader and follower autonomy and subjectivity have been more and more extensively colonized. What now exists is a discursive regime in which both 'leaders' and 'followers' are packaged into neat and tidy bundles and expected to fulfil the increasingly demanding performance expectations placed upon them without demur. What is largely absent is a valuing of the contributions of the many as well as those of the few. What is typically missing is the desire to challenge our prejudices, romantic ideals and prior assumptions.

Does the recent emergence of 'authentic leadership' offer a solution to any of these concerns? I suggest that insofar as it offers yet another psychological account of the extraordinary individual as constituting the truth about leadership,[224] the emergence of authentic leadership discourse simply compounds the problem. At face value, of course, it holds considerable appeal, appearing to offer a solution to the problem of self-serving and corrupt leadership.[225] And insofar as the authentic leader is expected to consider information in a balanced fashion and take a transparent approach to dealing with others, along with knowing themselves and using their own moral compass,[226] we see here a less grandiose subject being constructed than in other 'new leadership' models.[227] However, through maintaining an account of the leader as one comprised only of praiseworthy and desirable attributes, offering a standard which followers are incited to replicate, authentic leadership discourse simply adds a new player to what is an old game.

CONCLUSION

When we consider the era of leadership science we see that what has been produced is, by and large, the utterings of those dedicated to preserving our faith that leadership is the answer, regardless of the question. It could perhaps be said, therefore, that Carlyle offered us both the earliest and the latest account of the modern truth about leadership when he argued 'there is no act more moral between men than that of rule and obedience',[228] for the view which still prevails today is that leadership is inherently virtuous and desirable and not inherently troublesome for both the leader and the led. Yet Carlyle was in many ways simply reviving an earlier account of the truth about leadership, for in the 16th century Lipsius had already argued, 'what greater thing is there among men than that one is at the head of many'.[229] And this, too, can also be read as echoing a much earlier proposition, for 2500 years ago Aristotle argued that 'to introduce order . . . is the work of a divine power – of such a power as holds together the universe'.[230]

While leadership science follows the methods and rituals of modern science, its key developments have been informed by socio-political factors and not evidence, while the main theoretical paradigms it has offered fail to meet the expectations normally applied to science of generating knowledge that is objective and progressive, in both senses of the word. Our dilemma is that the accumulation of more and more data offers no guarantee of progress, nor does it guarantee that what has been produced constitutes a soundly based science. This dilemma is the consequence of the recurring positioning of 'leadership' as inevitable, natural, potent and desirable, a positioning which inhibits our ability to think differently about leadership and from which we must liberate ourselves.

NOTES

1. Hodgson, 2005
2. Hodgson, 2005; Trethewey and Goodall Jnr, 2007
3. Fleishman, 1973; Schriesheim and Bird, 1979; Shartle, 1979
4. Taylor, 1919
5. Mayo, 1945, 1946 [1933]. Original date of publication is noted in square brackets
6. Jacques, 1996; Wren, 2005
7. Jacques, 1996; Bruce, 2006
8. Bruce, 2006; Bruce and Nyland, 2011
9. Shartle, 1979
10. Avery, 2004; Bass, 2008; Huczynski and Buchanan, 2006
11. See, for example, Jennings, 1960
12. See, for example, Fleishman, 1953a, 1953b; Katz, Maccoby and Morse, 1950; Likert, 1961
13. Fleishman, 1953a, 1953b, 1973; Schriesheim and Bird, 1979; Shartle, 1979
14. Fleishman, 1973; Shartle, 1979; Stogdill, 1948
15. Fleishman, 1973; Hollander, 1979; Shartle, 1979
16. Fleishman, 1973, pp. 7–8
17. Fleishman, 1973, p. 8

18. The Michigan State studies initially understood these two constructs as being at opposite ends of one spectrum, meaning that it was thought that a supervisor/leader could be *either* production oriented *or* employee oriented, but not both. In light of Ohio State's findings that a supervisor could score highly on both 'consideration' and 'initiating structure' or low/high, high/low or low/low, the Michigan State data were re-evaluated and the constructs were reconceptualized in a manner that replicated the Ohio State model (Bowers and Seashore, 1966)
19. 1939
20. See, for example, Blake and Mouton, 1964; Fleishman, 1953a, 1953b; Katz et al., 1950; Likert, 1961
21. See, for example, Fleishman, 1953a; Katz et al., 1950; Likert, 1961
22. See, for example, Blake and Mouton, 1964
23. Bruce, 2006; Bruce and Nyland, 2011
24. See, for example, Katz et al., 1950; Likert, 1961; Morris and Seeman, 1950
25. Hollander, 1979; Schriesheim and Bird, 1979; Shartle, 1979
26. See, for example, Fleishman, 1953a, 1953b; Likert, 1961, 1967
27. Alvesson, 1996; Alvesson and Deetz, 2000
28. Alvesson and Deetz, 2000
29. Hollander, 1979; Schriesheim and Bird, 1979; Shartle, 1979
30. See, for example, Blake and Mouton, 1964; Katz et al., 1950; Likert, 1961, 1967
31. Bass, 2008; Hollander, 1979; Shartle, 1979
32. Hendry, 1944, p. 385
33. Lewin, 1944, p. 394
34. Stogdill, 1948
35. Lewin, 1944
36. Stogdill, 1948, p. 65
37. Hollander, 1979; Schriesheim and Bird, 1979; Shartle, 1979
38. Shartle, 1979
39. 1979
40. 1979, p. 132
41. 1966, p. 240
42. 1973, p. 3
43. 1977 [1933]
44. Gillham, 2001
45. Adorno, Frenkel-Brunswik, Levinson and Sanford, 1950; Hodgson, 2005; Trethewey and Goodall Jnr, 2007
46. Benjamin, 2007
47. 1973
48. Bass, 2008; Bowers and Seashore, 1966
49. See, for example, Mayo, 1945, 1946; Bowers and Seashore, 1966
50. Bruce and Nyland, 2011; Likert, 1961; Mayo, 1945, 1946
51. 1919
52. 1930
53. Hollander, 1979; Korman, 1966
54. Benjamin, 2007
55. 1944
56. Lewin, 1944, pp. 392–393
57. Benjamin, 2007
58. Fleishman, 1973; Schriesheim and Bird, 1979; Shartle, 1979
59. Korman, 1966, p. 360
60. Hodgson, 2005; Trethewey and Goodall Jnr, 2007
61. Bowers and Seashore, 1966; Fleishman, 1973
62. See, for example, Blake and Mouton, 1964; Katz et al., 1950; Likert, 1961; Morris and Seeman, 1950
63. See, for example, Blake and Mouton, 1964; Fleishman, 1953a; Likert, 1961

64. See, for example, Blake and Mouton, 1964; Fleishman, 1953b; Katz et al., 1950
65. See, for example, Blake and Mouton, 1964; Katz et al., 1950; Likert, 1967
66. See, for example, Blake and Mouton, 1964; Fleishman, 1953a; Likert, 1961
67. See, for example, Blake and Mouton, 1964; Katz et al., 1950; Likert, 1961; Morris and Seeman, 1950
68. Bruce, 2006; Bruce and Nyland, 2011
69. Cornuelle, 1975; Hodgson, 2005
70. See, for example, Blake and Mouton, 1964; Katz et al., 1950; Likert, 1961, 1967
71. Likert, 1967
72. Gitlin, 1993; Hodgson, 2005
73. Gitlin, 1993; Hall, 2005; Hodgson, 2005
74. Hanisch, 1970
75. Gitlin, 1993; Hall, 2005; Hodgson, 2005
76. Hall, 2005; Hodgson, 2005
77. Gitlin, 1993; Hall, 2005
78. Capitman, 1973; Cornuelle, 1975; Roos, 1972
79. See, for example, Katz and Kahn, 1966
80. Benjamin, 2007
81. See, for example, Cornuelle, 1975; Fiedler, 1967; Whyte, 1963 [1956]
82. See, for notable examples, Fiedler, 1967; Hersey and Blanchard, 1974; House, 1971; Vroom and Yetton, 1973
83. See, for example, Fleishman, 1953a; 1953b; Tannenbaum and Schmidt, 1958
84. 1966
85. 1971
86. 1973
87. 1974
88. 1958
89. 1967
90. 1973
91. 1971
92. 1974
93. See, for example, Fiedler, 1967; Hersey and Blanchard, 1974; House, 1971; Vroom and Yetton, 1973
94. Vroom and Yetton, 1973
95. Kerr and Jermier, 1978; Lombardo and McCall, 1978
96. 1967
97. See, for example, Hersey and Blanchard, 1974; House, 1971; Vroom and Yetton, 1973
98. Vroom and Yetton, 1973
99. Vroom and Yetton, 1973
100. See, for example, Fiedler, 1967; Hersey and Blanchard, 1974; House, 1971; Vroom and Yetton, 1973
101. Vroom and Yetton, 1973
102. Kerr and Jermier, 1978, p. 375, italics in original
103. See, for example, Kerr and Jermier, 1978; Pfeffer, 1977; Salancik and Pfeffer, 1977
104. Calder, 1977
105. See, for example, Fiedler, 1967; Hersey and Blanchard, 1974; House, 1971; Vroom and Yetton, 1973
106. Vroom and Yetton, 1973
107. pp. 259–260
108. 1975, p. 200
109. 1977, p. 94
110. 1978, p. 3
111. 1967
112. 1971
113. 1974

114. Ackerman, 1975; Cornuelle, 1975; Roos, 1972
115. 1963
116. Reed, 2006; Wren, 2005
117. Benjamin, 2007
118. Reed, 2006; Wren, 2005
119. See, for example, Fiedler, 1967; Hersey and Blanchard, 1974; House, 1971; Vroom and Yetton, 1973
120. 1967, p. 36
121. See, for example, Fiedler, 1967; Hersey and Blanchard, 1974; House, 1971; Vroom and Yetton, 1973
122. See, for example, Fiedler, 1967; Hersey and Blanchard, 1974; House, 1971; Vroom and Yetton, 1973
123. Ackerman, 1975; Hodgson, 2005; Magaziner and Reich, 1982
124. Gitlin, 1993; Hall, 2005
125. See Burns, 1978
126. 1978
127. Bass, 1999; Hunt, 1999; Jackson and Parry, 2011
128. Burns, 1978, p. 4
129. Burns, 1978
130. Burns, 1978
131. 1977
132. House, 1977
133. Eisenstadt and Weber, 1968
134. See, for example, Conger, 1989; Conger and Kanungo, 1987; Shamir and Howell, 1999
135. 1978
136. 1978
137. 1978
138. 1977
139. 1978
140. 1982
141. 1985
142. 1985a
143. 1985a
144. Bass, 1999; Huczynski and Buchanan, 2006; Jackson and Parry, 2011
145. Avolio, Bass and Jung, 1999
146. Avolio et al., 1999
147. Avolio et al., 1999
148. 1978
149. 1985a
150. 1985a
151. 1985a
152. 1978
153. 1977
154. 1985a
155. 1985, p. 21
156. Alvesson and Sveningsson, 2012; Jackson and Parry, 2011; Sinclair, 2007
157. See 1985a
158. Bass, 1985a, p. 45
159. Bass, 1985a, p. 24
160. Bass, 1985a
161. See, for example, Bass, 1985a; Burns, 1978
162. Bass, 1985a; Burns, 1978
163. See Bass, 1985a; Burns, 1978
164. Bass, 1985a, p. 15
165. Heath, 1975; Hodgson, 2005; Roos, 1972

166. Heath, 1975; Hodgson, 2005; Roos, 1972
167. Ackerman, 1975; Capitman, 1973; Cornuelle, 1975
168. Ackerman, 1975; Magaziner and Reich, 1982; Peters and Waterman, 1982
169. See, for example, Bass, 1985a; Burns, 1978
170. See, for example, Bass, 1985a; Bennis and Nanus, 1985; Peters and Austin, 1985
171. Calás and Smircich, 1991
172. Bass, 1985a, p. 4
173. Hodgson, 2005; Trethewey and Goodall Jnr, 2007
174. Bass, 1985
175. Alvesson and Spicer, 2011a; Alvesson and Sveningsson, 2012; Jackson and Parry, 2011
176. Gardner et al., 2010; Lowe and Gardner, 2000
177. See, for example, Avolio et al., 1999; Zhu et al., 2011
178. Bolden et al., 2011; Jackson and Parry, 2011; Sinclair, 2007
179. See, for example, Bass, 1985a, 1985b; Bennis and Nanus, 1985; Peters and Austin, 1985
180. See, for example, Bass and Riggio, 2006; Goleman et al., 2002; Kotter, 1988
181. Alvesson and Sveningsson, 2003a, 2003c
182. See, for example, Bass, 1985a; Goleman et al., 2002; Kotter, 1988
183. See, for example, Bass, 1985a, 1985b; Bennis and Nanus, 1985; Peters and Austin, 1985
184. Bass, 1985a
185. See, for example, Bass, 1985a; Goleman et al., 2002; Kotter, 1988
186. See, for example, Bass, 1985a; Burns, 1978; Peters and Austin, 1985
187. See, for example, Bass, 1985a; Burns, 1978; Peters and Austin, 1985
188. See, for example, Bass, 1985a; Goleman et al., 2002; Kotter, 1988
189. Bass, 1985a; Burns, 1978
190. Alvesson and Sveningsson, 2003a; Ford et al., 2008
191. See Carlyle, 1993
192. See, for example, Galton, 1892, 1970
193. Cowan, 1970
194. See, for example, Galton, 1892, 1970
195. Galton, 1892, 1970
196. Bass, 2008; Smith and Krueger, 1933; Stogdill, 1948
197. Stogdill, 1948
198. Stogdill, 1948
199. Alvesson, 1996; Hunter et al., 2007; Yukl, 1989
200. See, for example, Burns, 1978; Fiedler, 1967; Katz et al., 1950; Likert, 1961, 1967
201. See, for example, Bass, 1985a, 1985b; Bennis and Nanus, 1985; Likert, 1961
202. Alvesson, 1996; Antonakis et al., 2004; Bryman, 2004
203. Jackson and Parry, 2011
204. Alvesson, 1996; Alvesson and Sveningsson, 2012; Hunter et al., 2007; Sinclair, 2007
205. Bass, 2008
206. Alvesson and Deetz, 2000; Drath et al., 2008
207. Alvesson, 1996; Alvesson and Deetz, 2000; Alvesson and Skoldberg, 2000
208. Meindl et al., 1985
209. Calder, 1977
210. Alvesson, 1996
211. Alvesson, 1996; Alvesson and Skoldberg, 2000
212. Ford and Harding, 2011
213. See, for notable exceptions, Gabriel, 1997; Kellerman, 2004; Kets de Vries, 2003
214. See, for example, Avolio and Luthans, 2003; Bass, 1985a
215. Kempster, Jackson and Conroy, 2011; Ladkin, 2010
216. See, for example, De Neve et al., 2013; Kant et al., 2013; Kuvaas et al., 2012; Piccolo et al., 2012
217. See, for example, Goethals and Sorenson, 2006
218. See, for example, Uhl-Bien and Ospina, 2012
219. See, for example, Gronn, 2002

220. See, for example, Fairhurst, 2007
221. See, for example, Carroll, Levy and Richmond, 2008
222. See, for example, Ladkin, 2010
223. See Goethals and Sorenson, 2006
224. See, for example, George, 2003; Luthans and Avolio, 2003
225. Wilson, 2013b
226. Walumbwa et al., 2008
227. Wilson, 2013b
228. 1993, p. 171
229. Lipsius, 2004, p. 227
230. Aristotle, *Pols* 1626b: 30

7   Change and continuity in the truth about leadership

> [T]his was the proper task of a history of thought, as against a history of behaviours or representations: to define the conditions in which human beings 'problematize' what they are, what they do, and the world in which they live.
>
> (Foucault, 1985, p. 10)

INTRODUCTION

The preceding four chapters have focused on examining what Western scholars have claimed to be the truth about leadership in different epistemes, including our own. In this chapter, attention turns to examine what changes and continuities are notable when comparing these discourses. To do this, the analysis now moves back and forth across the whole gamut of leadership discourses previously examined. Changes in thought which are of particular interest here are those that are unexpected, which run counter to the normal expectation and assumption that what we have today is superior to that of the past. Similarly, the continuities in thought of particular interest here are also those which run counter to the normal expectation that the present is significantly different from the past. Identifying these possibly unexpected changes and continuities extends the scope of my earlier analysis by identifying connections between the present and the past in leadership discourse, consistent with Foucault's concept of the 'history of the present'.[1]

The examination undertaken here offers insight into the historical influences embedded within current understandings. It also enables consideration of past truths no longer operant for their potential utility in respect of current concerns and values. Cumulatively, surfacing these matters could help provide us with a potential 'rallying point for the counterattack' to challenge current norms and understandings.[2] This focus on identifying both change and continuity in leadership thought calls into doubt conventional assumptions about the accumulation of knowledge. At the same time, it seeks to generate fresh insights into our present condition such that new possibilities may begin to become evident.

In addressing change and continuity in leadership thought, I retain my focus on the same themes addressed in the preceding analyses of each discourse. I begin by recapping the problems which leadership has been called on to address at various times, demonstrating its profoundly contingent nature. Next, I identify changes and continuities in how the person of the leader, the follower and their relationship have been understood in different leadership discourses. I then examine change and continuity in the social function of 'leadership' discourse before finally considering the underpinning issues of epistemology and methodology which scholars have relied on in making claims to speak the truth about leadership.

DIFFERENT PROBLEMS, BUT LEADERSHIP IS THE ANSWER

As we have seen, time and time again calls for 'leadership' have arisen as a response to moral, social, political and economic trends or events which are deemed problematic. 'Leadership', whatever form it may take, has been repeatedly proffered as a solution to matters that are understood as troublesome, threatening and in need of fixing. The particular form of 'leadership' proposed to deal with the issues of concern draws on existing values, norms, epistemologies and methodologies, thereby rendering what is said relevant and plausible to its intended audience. Leadership, repeatedly, is thus invented as the solution to the things that trouble us.

Specifically, the Classical Greek scholars examined were concerned with disorder, class conflict, war, moral degeneracy and a loss of respect for tradition and the gods.[3] Seeing these as the consequences of a democratic approach to governance led to the development of a particular leadership model in which standards of behaviour were to be imposed by a single leader whose only concern was to be community well-being.[4] Here, it was positioned as 'the business of the ruler to give orders and of the ruled to obey'.[5] In this model, upholding a specified set of social practices, norms and values, as well as attending to strategic and operational issues affecting the security and stability of the state all formed part of the leadership model that was proposed.[6] Here, leadership in the form of a wise and divinely gifted leader granted unlimited authority was presented as the answer to every problem facing the community.[7]

In response to the problems of political and religious conflict and self-serving or incompetent leader behaviour, the late medieval leadership model positioned the king as God's representative on earth, endowing him with God's power, authority, divinity and goodness.[8] The leader here was said to be 'more like a divinity than a mortal' upon whom 'the happiness of the whole people' depended.[9] This positioning bolstered the leader's legitimacy, thereby helping to maintain monarchical rule. However, the discourse also set out in extensive detail a standard of conduct to which leaders were expected to adhere, thereby addressing concerns about poor leader behaviour. The model incorporated specific policy advice on substantive issues of governance, thereby further shaping 'leadership' as a solution to issues threatening the stability of the existing social order. All the key components of this model were, thus, designed to provide answers to the problems of the day.

In the modern episteme, Carlyle initially deemed problematic what he saw as the excessive rationalism of Enlightenment thought and the effects of the Industrial Revolution, factors he believed were damaging the 'human spirit', morality, faith and social cohesion.[10] To remedy this, he proposed a model of heroic leadership which extolled the value of passion and religious fervour as more powerful and more truly human than reason alone. He also advocated hero worship, through which he claimed we could reconnect ourselves to the best of human nature and to God, as well as tighten the bonds of community. For Carlyle, 'there is no act more moral between men than that of rule and obedience'.[11] Here again, then, the formulation of the truth about leadership was tightly matched to the issues of present concern.

Next, underpinning the efforts of trait theorists, was the problem of ensuring that only those 'fit' to lead, in a social Darwinian sense, were selected for leadership positions.[12] This desire arose from the belief that social problems originate in a mismatch between people's 'natural talents' and their actual role and position in society, a problem which they claimed modern science could now remedy. Here, it was claimed that 'there can be no question of the fact of inequality'.[13] Leadership research was, thus, focused on establishing criteria for 'weeding out' those not suitable for 'leadership' by defining the traits of 'genuine' leaders. For some of those assuming that leader traits were inherited, eugenicist policies formed part of the solution, offering a programme for reforming the population through selective breeding practices. The overall aim for these thinkers was to 'produce a highly-gifted race of men by judicious marriage during several consecutive generations'.[14]

For behavioural theorists, issues of worker motivation, performance, absenteeism and workplace conflict, issues deemed problematic in the managerial discourse of the time, were an important source of influence.[15] All these issues were presumed amenable to resolution by way of leader intervention. The task here was to determine through careful analysis the particular pattern of leader behaviour which would have most effect in addressing these problems.[16] For a period of time, this pattern was widely believed to comprise 'behaviour indicating friendship, mutual trust, respect, a certain warmth and rapport between the supervisor and his group', in conjunction with behaviour that 'organizes and defines the relationships in the group' and 'tends to establish well defined patterns and channels of communication and ways of getting the job done'.[17]

Essentially, situational and 'new leadership' theorists have pursued this same basic formulation of a combined focus by leaders on both tasks and relationships deriving from the continued focus on worker performance being deemed a problem requiring a solution. However, each has also been informed by other factors deemed problematic and offered specific formulations of the truth about leadership as a result. With situational theory, bureaucratic inflexibility and enhancing leader responsiveness to contextual factors were deemed problematic,[18] meaning that leaders were now said to need the skill to diagnose a situation and respond accordingly.[19] The key was thought to be to 'match the leadership situation and the man'[20] so that leaders 'engage in behaviours that complement subordinates' environments and abilities in a manner that compensates for deficiencies and is instrumental to subordinate satisfaction and individual and work unit performance'.[21]

The initial emergence of 'new leadership' relied on recent economic, moral, cultural and social trends and events in late 1970s America being deemed to constitute a crisis of leadership.[22] The concerns were said to be caused by this crisis in leadership but also able to be solved by leadership, provided it was re-formulated so as to offer 'new answers to new questions … using a new paradigm or pattern of inquiry'.[23] In this new formulation, leadership that produced change became the key requirement and so a leader's 'visionary', 'charismatic' and 'transformational' capacities came to the fore.[24] Here, the achievement of change was overtly positioned as benefiting both followers and organizations, reinforcing the positioning of leadership as a force for the common good. The discourse has sustained itself over time through a continuous accounting of the modern world and its complex and ever changing nature as being so problematic and challenging that leadership is said to be vital if we are to have any hope of continuing to progress human society.[25] Throughout its history, followers have been continuously deemed problematic, unable to reach their full potential in the absence of 'new leadership'.[26]

What my case studies reveal, then, is the highly contingent nature of the 'truth' about leadership. In response to various issues being seen as problematic, leadership scholars have repeatedly invented a particular response that they contend will address the issues of concern, referencing current values, norms, beliefs, epistemologies and methodologies so as to render their ideas relevant and plausible. This is arguably no bad thing: needs, values and norms change, and adapting our ideas about leadership in response seems a valid and desirable move.

However, what we must not overlook is that there are political, moral, ethical and social choices being made, first, in what is deemed problematic and, second, in positioning (some variant of) 'leadership' as our favoured response to what is deemed problematic. When calls for 'leadership' constitute our default answer to every issue we consider problematic, then we may understand ourselves as rendered completely docile to the allure of leadership. When alternative ways of solving problems, methods such as education, the establishment of rules, rewards and penalties at governmental or organization level, collective effort, technological fixes and so forth, are rendered by default subordinate to 'leadership', we gift the right to shape our future to the few, potentially at the expense of the many. Leadership knowledge has such matters embedded within it and cannot be, therefore, an objective, value-free science.

However, what pre-eminent modern scholars who claim to be offering us an accurate, truthful and scientific account have been telling us is that leadership is a natural, enduring phenomenon and that the truth about leadership is, therefore, a matter for discovery. Recall Bass' claim that 'many leaders of world religions, such as Jesus, Mohammed, and Buddha, were transforming. They created visions, shaped values, and empowered change'.[27] The clear implication is that transformational leadership is both enduring and universal. Recall Bennis and Nanus: 'leadership competencies have remained constant, but our understanding of what it is, how it works, and the way in which people learn to apply it has changed'.[28] The analysis here demonstrates that the essentialist and universalist understandings which inform the work of mainstream scholars today are profoundly problematic. In Chapter 8, I will explore further the implications of this finding for theorizing leadership in the future.

CONTINUITY AND CHANGE IN THE TRUTH ABOUT LEADERS

As the problems to which the solution of 'leadership' arose changed, the notion of the true leader also changed. Yet some things have also

remained the same. In this section, I therefore examine both change and
continuity in what has been claimed to be the truth about leaders. This
includes examining ideas about the person of the leader and claims for
the role, responsibilities and rights of the leader.

Continuities: the Person of the Leader

Defining the personal characteristics of the true leader has been the
primary focus of the leadership discourses examined here.[29] With 'leadership' repeatedly being understood as something which emanates from
leaders, establishing who leaders 'really' are has been, and remains today,
a key concern for leadership scholars.[30] What my analysis has shown is
that, almost without exception, the leader is understood as being a person
of superior capability to others: think 'leader', think 'superior being' is
the most fundamental, enduring and dominant equation that prevails.

Illustrative of this, leaders were depicted by the Classical Greeks as
'possessed of great natural gifts' that were 'not altogether human but
divine'.[31] Even Aristotle, whom we today understand as a political
moderate compared with Plato or Xenophon's more conservative bent,[32]
claimed that 'from the hour of their birth, some are marked out for
subjection, others for rule'.[33] In the late medieval discourse, leaders were
'a sort of celestial creature',[34] made by God to 'sitte [sit] on his throne
and rule ouer [over] other men'.[35] Carlyle retained the notion of divine
intervention, claiming that the 'great men' he studied had been 'sent into
the world'.[36] Trait theorists drew on social Darwinist notions and
typically concluded that natural differences rendered leaders superior.[37]
Recall here Lehman's confidence about the 'fact of inequality'.[38]

Since World War II, proclaiming the superiority of leaders as an innate
quality has been politically tenuous, because of its tension with democratic values and its similarity to the ideas that gave rise to the Holocaust.
Instead, it is the leader's 'behaviours', 'style', 'skills' and 'attitudes'
which have been the focus, with scholars at pains to claim these are
learnable.[39] However, the growing interest in 'neuro-leadership'[40] and
other recent trait-focused studies[41] may yet herald a full return to the
overt declaration of innate differences being the discursive norm within
the field. As noted in Chapter 6, 'new leadership' has depicted leadership
as a deeply held and embedded set of values, attitudes and behaviours
and has, therefore, already brought us closer once again to treating
leadership as an innate quality than was the case with behavioural and
contingency/situational discourses (see Model 6.1).

In fact, for the last quarter century we have been fed a steady diet of
claims that leaders are those who can out-think, out-pace and exceed in

quality, quantity, intensity and impact on the efforts of non-leaders. Leaders are presented to us as quite simply a different, and better, class of person. With 'new leadership' discourse, leaders are the people who 'do the right thing', in contrast to those who are merely managers who 'do things right'.[42] 'New leadership' discourse claims 'the secret of transforming leadership' is that 'people can be lifted *into* their better selves' by leaders,[43] suggesting that an alchemic art constitutes the secret which only leaders truly understand. With 'new leadership', we are told that the leader is one who is capable of bringing about change in 'who rules and by what means; the work-group norms, as well as ultimate beliefs about religion, ideology, morality, ethics, space, time, and human nature'.[44] No ordinary mortal indeed.

The second factor which has also remained largely constant is that those personal characteristics and ways of living which are held at various times to be admirable, exceptional and powerful have been linked to the person of the leader and claimed to be part of their nature.[45] At every point in time, the attributes ascribed to leaders align with, and simultaneously reinforce, the widely accepted values, norms and expect- ations as to what constitutes an admirable person to whom deference is due by others lacking such gifts. Later, in my analysis of discontinuities in how leaders have been understood, I will focus on what the *specific* characteristics ascribed to leaders are and how they have changed. For now, the point is that *regardless* of what the characteristics of leaders were said to be, they were understood at the time of their enunciation as being worthy of admiration and deference, as exceptional and desirable. Think 'leader', think 'the good person/life' is, thus, the second key enduring equation.

Illustrative of this, in the Classical Greek discourse leaders were expected and said to possess 'excellence of character in perfection'.[46] In the late medieval discourse, leaders, at their best, were said to be 'complete with every single virtue'.[47] Carlyle's focus was on leader- heroes who took the form of gods, prophets, poets, priests, men of letters and kings, thereby covering off every kind of person he considered worthy of 'hero worship'.[48] Trait discourse, following Carlyle's lead, also focused on examining factors deemed admirable or desirable (see Table 5.2 which addresses this linkage). These characteristics of the leader were assumed by trait theorists to be 'part and parcel of his original nature'.[49]

In the post-World War II period, with the focus shifting to workplace leadership, factors which are said to enhance worker performance and, hence, organizational and even national success have been directly linked to leaders by behavioural, situational/contingency and 'new leadership' discourses.[50] However, 'new leadership' discourse has gone further than its immediate predecessors, connecting leaders with innovation and change, with strategy, vision and the empowerment of others, all factors now deemed admirable, desirable and even essential to sustain the viability of the modern organization.[51] In a culture where economic success is constantly heralded as desirable and admirable, leaders have been positioned as potent and vital influencers of this success, ensuring that today when we 'think leader' we think 'the good person/life'.

The third enduring characteristic of 'the leader' is his masculinity. In recent decades, the explicit discursive exclusion of women from 'leadership' has, finally, disappeared. However, the attributes ascribed to leaders across all the discourses examined here are those which repeatedly bear a strong connection to the attributes ascribed to idealized notions of masculinity then prevailing.[52] Today, leadership is associated with characteristics such as 'charisma', 'vision', 'drive' and 'moral strength', attributes more commonly associated with contemporary masculine ideals.[53] By contrast, leadership today is not often associated with characteristics such as 'caring', 'nurturing' and 'supporting', characteristics associated with contemporary feminine ideals. Think 'leader', think 'male' is thus the third equation which endures.

Table 7.1 provides the *dispositif* (see Method Notes) which summarizes these three key continuities in the discursive construction of leaders.

Table 7.1 Enduring characteristics of the leader

Equation in the discourse	Status of the equation
think 'leader' think 'superior being'	enduring, unbroken, dominant
think 'leader' think 'the good person/life'	dominant but has been broken at times; has been strengthened with new leadership discourse
think 'leader' think 'male'	enduring but now not explicit; embedded in characteristics deemed leader-like

Maintaining the equation of 'leaders' with 'superior beings' and 'the good', however understood, is critical for 'leadership' as an idea to continue to hold its mystique, promise and appeal: the outpourings of scholars enunciating on this topic have been a critical facilitator of this. Today, 'personal growth' is widely understood as desirable, admirable and potent. Little wonder then that the intense leader–follower relationship directed at achieving follower growth as promoted by 'new leadership' discourse seems so attractive. What is applauded today is embracing the performativity requirements and demands for constant change which come with our current economic system. 'New leadership' discourse endorses and reinforces this expectation in its account of what constitutes a leader.

As I have shown, this relationship between 'the good', 'the superior' and 'the leader' has a substantial history. At every step in the cases examined here, it has been dependent on an interconnecting suite of factors. This includes truth claims being accepted as valid. Constitutional and organizational arrangements have typically reinforced and sustained its enactment. As best as historians can determine and our own contemporary experience confirms, actual persons have striven and continue to strive to align their actions with whatever was claimed to be the truth about leadership. However, the mere fact of its apparent longevity is no guarantee as to its future, for this arrangement is a human one, not one determined by nature. Model 7.1 provides a visual depiction of this dynamic.

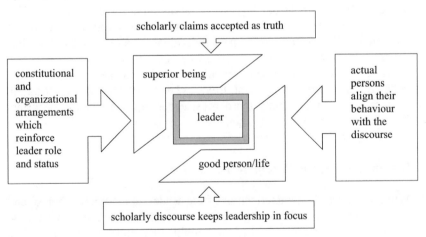

Model 7.1   The production of the perfect leader

On two occasions identified in this study, this linkage has broken down. The first was Locke's attempt to place the 'natural freedom' of all at the centre of his understanding of leadership, rendering it an impersonal concept expressed through the constrained exercise of legal authority.[54] Locke's account placed the person of the leader as one rightfully and wholly subservient to the higher authority of the law and largely regarded their personal characteristics as irrelevant, so long as they did not impede the proper exercise of legal authority. Locke's position depended on a basic mistrust of persons in positions of authority. He neither assumed the possibility of human perfection nor did he consider it desirable for society to be held sway to the personal preferences of the leader. With a less favourable view of the nature of leaders, and an emphasis on ensuring freedom from authority as critical to protecting 'natural rights', Locke thus broke the equation of 'leader', 'superior being' and 'the good'.

The other occasion this linkage was broken was post-World War II when leadership was theorized as constituting behavioural patterns focused on 'consideration' and 'initiating structure'.[55] These patterns were *not* attached to a broader conception of the leader persona. Because behavioural theory was seeking to distinguish itself from trait theory,[56] it carried with it no account of the leader as human subject. It also assumed an inherent capacity for reasonableness on the part of followers and a right to self-determination on issues of values.[57] This in turn meant that it proffered a limited scope for leadership action.[58] Developed at a time of heightened sensitivity to the potential dangers leaders could create, its claims were deliberately modest in scope. What it offered was an approach to '*doing* leadership work' rather than '*being* a leader'. The model was intended to be effective in enhancing workplace performance consistent with the need to respect individual freedoms and rights, thus limiting the scope of action of those in positions of authority.

As a point of historical coincidence, both Locke's approach and behavioural theory emerged at times when extremes of authoritarian, autocratic and quite simply murderous leadership had recently occurred. This likely contributed to their willingness or even desire to limit leadership to something rather modest in scope and impact.

Discontinuities: the Person of the Leader

While the overall characterization of the leader as a 'superior being' and a 'good person' who lives a 'good life' has remained largely constant, the specific characteristics ascribed to, sought after and admired in leaders have been remarkably changeable. Illustrative of this, for the Classical Greeks leaders were those possessed of 'manly virtue'[59] that ensured they were 'resolute in times of danger'.[60] They 'love truth',[61] possess a strong 'religious sensibility'[62] and 'revel in hard work and totally avoid idleness'.[63] A leader is said to be 'quick to learn' and 'have a good memory'.[64] He possesses 'natural gifts' and a 'natural bent for reason' which 'draw him toward philosophy',[65] this being the highest form of knowledge.[66] The picture that emerges in this discourse is of a warrior-philosopher who lives a devout and ascetic life focused on ensuring the well-being of the state and the people.

In 16th-century Europe, advanced knowledge of statecraft, warfare and religion were deemed critical for leaders to develop, complementing their divine birthright, enhancing their innate but tenuous 'majesty', and enabling them to combine virtue and prudence.[67] Contrary to the Classical Greeks, the accumulation and ostentatious display of wealth and power were now seen both to confirm the leader's favoured status in God's eyes and to help instil the fear and respect needed to render followers loyal and obedient. For Lipsius, the specific characteristics emphasized comprised prudence, virtue, majesty, clemency and modesty (see Model 4.2 for a fuller summary of his account of core princely virtues). Erasmus emphasized 'wisdom, a sense of justice, personal restraint, foresight, and concern for the public well-being'.[68] The key attributes of leaders highlighted by Calvin were 'integrity, prudence, clemency, moderation and innocence'.[69] Here, the picture that emerges is of someone possessed of extensive practical knowledge of all aspects of statecraft, grounded by their faith in God, 'majestic' in their demeanour and able to navigate in a complex context. Here, the leader is the dignified, masterful practitioner of *real*-politic whose power commands fear, respect and loyalty.

From Carlyle through to World War II, leaders were understood as possessing innate qualities which rendered them as such.[70] Qualities such as courage, determination, intelligence and an intensity of feeling were thought to be typical characteristics. (See Table 5.2 which summarizes Carlyle's account of Oliver Cromwell and its connection with later trait studies.) Leaders in this discourse were heroes, men of good breeding and usually good mannered, well educated, physically and mentally strong, determined and capable, and possessing a refined sensibility. They were the perfect Victorian gentlemen.

The characteristics attributed to leaders by behavioural theorists were a mix of behaviours focused on 'consideration' and 'structure' and which rendered someone able to gain the respect of a group, instil harmonious relations and secure willing compliance to the instructions issued.[71] For contingency/situational theorists, it was these approaches deployed in a manner suitable to the situation at hand.[72] Illustrative of these claims, Stogdill's 1974 meta-analysis of 52 studies published since 1945 concluded that

> leadership involves certain skills and capabilities – interpersonal, technical, administrative, and intellectual – enabling the leader to be of value to his group or organization. These skills allow him to maintain satisfactory levels

of group cohesiveness, drive, and productivity. He is further assisted in execution of the above functions if he possesses a high degree of task motivation, personal integrity, communicative ability, and the like.[73]

The picture of the leader that emerges here, then, is the well-rounded practical man of action, able to get along well with those he directs. This account of a thoroughly good chap seems to suggest a civilianized version of a military unit leader whose troops' morale is high and who would tackle any assignment with vigour.

With 'new leadership' discourse, it is the leader's ability to drive through rapid and dramatic change in organizational performance and 'culture' which has become the focus of attention.[74] Leaders are here understood as persons who are 'charismatic', who intellectually and morally stimulate others, encourage others' personal growth, and develop and pursue visions for a better future.[75] The image here is of the ideal Fortune 500 CEO, admired by employees, shareholders and market analysts alike, transforming the organization and those who work for it as he pursues his visionary strategy. Leadership scholars have crafted a mirror into which these persons can look and take pleasure in what they see glittering back at them.

Table 7.2 provides the dispositif which summarizes this analysis of change in what has been claimed to be the truth about leaders.

The analysis in Table 7.2 shows that what has been claimed to be the truth about the nature of leaders has changed repeatedly and significantly over time. Leaders have been variously constructed as warrior-philosophers, dignified and masterful practitioners of *real*-politic, heroic gentlemen, well-rounded practical men of action and visionary, change-focused CEOs. This suggests that no stable psychology of 'the leader' is likely to be found, for no 'human nature' exists in respect of leadership, if such a thing is assumed to be timeless and enduring. It further suggests that these truth claims are more usefully and plausibly understood as inventions designed to address different values and problems, rather than as discoveries about the true nature of leaders.

The alternative interpretation is that we have only just recently, finally, established the 'real truth' about leadership and that all that has come before is simply wrong. In this interpretation the constant changes in the conception of the leader, as noted in Table 7.2, are simply a record of past failures and errors. To hold to such a view requires a greater degree of confidence in positivist social science than I believe is warranted, as the limitations of this epistemology and its methods are well estab-lished.[76] However, the interpretation I favour does not constitute a body blow to leadership scholarship. Rather, it serves as an incitement to begin

Table 7.2 Key characteristics of the leader in different discourses

Classical Greek	16th-century Europe	Great man/trait theory (ca. 1840-WWII)	Managerial leadership (post-WWII)
divinely gifted; driven to serve others	divinely gifted; duty to serve and lead	driven/enabled by nature to lead others; 'nurture' enhances what 'nature' gifted	personal attributes plus acquired skills produce the desire and ability to lead
loves the gods; morally without fault	loves God; upholds Christian morality	assumed and expected to be good Christians	discourse is silent on issues of faith; leaders assumed and expected to act ethically
has perfect knowledge of what is right and wise; knowledgeable about all matters that affect community well-being	knows Christ's teachings; knowledgeable about worldly affairs of statecraft; possesses majesty; acts prudently	has sound judgement, foresight, strength of character, a 'can do' attitude, superior intelligence; is dependable, educated, courageous, socially active	knows how to motivate/change others to achieve higher levels of performance, commitment and personal growth
ascetic lifestyle – has restraint in eating, sleeping and sexual urges in order to serve better	combines majesty and prudent use of state funds so as to live in a manner consistent with their status and duties	lifestyle expected to be consistent with Christian values	committed to organizational goals; discourse silent on issues of lifestyle

future theorizing with an eye to developing a concept of leaders tailored to present concerns and values, rather than wasting further effort in the search to discover the 'true nature' of the 'true leader'.

A further shift in thought pertains to the attention given to the leader's body, something which has waned dramatically since World War II. The Classical Greeks' interest in leaders' bodies included, for example, concern about their exercise regime during their youth. An ascetic approach to eating, sleeping and sex was promoted. Illustrative of this, Xenophon tells us that, as an exemplary leader, Agesilaus 'would no more choose drunkenness than madness' and that 'he never used to eat the two portions he was served at feasts'.[77] We are told that Agesilaus 'treated sleep as the subject rather than the master of his activities'[78] and 'where sex was concerned, his self-control was masterful'.[79] In 16th-century European discourse, as discussed in Chapter 4, the leader's 'majesty' was embodied through their dress, their voice and their removal from the potentially damaging gaze of the masses. Illustrative of this concern about the body of the leader and how it was seen, Erasmus counselled that it was 'of considerable importance' that 'artists should represent the prince in the dress and manner that is most worthy of a wise and distinguished prince'.[80]

In the 19th century, both Carlyle and Galton were acutely interested in matters such as physical strength, facial characteristics and voice,[81] while various trait theorists explored a range of physical characteristics for their association with leadership in the decades leading up to World War II.[82] In the behaviour, contingency/situational and 'new' leadership paradigms, however, leaders have been presented to us in disembodied terms, as possessing minds, values, behaviours and emotions but no bodies. This development reflects, of course, the generally disembodied nature of the wider field of organizational studies during this same period.[83] Yet when set against the backdrop of the earlier emphasis given to the leader's body, this shift in attention constitutes a distinct discontinuity in leadership thought and is one which, I argue, serves simultaneously to maintain the positioning of leaders as superior beings, unencumbered by fatigue and immune to bodily weaknesses.

The Leader's Role, Responsibilities and Rights

Attention to the role, responsibilities and rights of leaders has also been a recurrent yet changing theme in the discourses examined here. As we have seen, in Classical Greece and 16th-century European thought, the leader's role was that of head of state. As part of this, leaders were held to have extensive rights and powers on matters deemed critical to the well-being of the people and the state, as the leader's primary responsibility was to safeguard these.[84] Illustrative of this, Plato argued that leaders were devoted to 'keeping their subjects safe' and 'doing all they can to make them better people than they were before'.[85] Lipsius claimed that 'the common interest has been placed in your lap by God and men; but indeed in your lap, in order that it be cherished'.[86]

In these discourses, leaders were expected to attend to issues such as the economy, state security, immigration, inter-state relations, infrastructure, education and moral and religious practices, and extensive advice was offered on these matters.[87] Complete obedience to the leader's instructions was also strongly endorsed. Aristotle tells us that leaders are those whom 'we ought to follow and obey'.[88] For Lipsius, maintaining society required 'a well-defined ordering of commanding and obeying'.[89]

For Carlyle, history was made by the gods, prophets, priests, poets, men of letters and kings who constituted the various forms of leadership he analyzed.[90] Regarding kingship as the highest and most modern form, Carlyle's expectation was, like the Classical Greek and medieval discourses before him, that such leaders would rule the state, promote religion and foster the development of the human spirit. Their role was to 'make what was disorderly, chaotic, into a thing ruled [and] regular'.[91] Later, trait theorists envisaged their Victorian gentlemen leaders as promoting virtuous behaviour and group cohesion through their efforts, advancing human society to a more advanced level.[92] Eugenicists' hope was to 'produce a highly-gifted race of men by judicious marriage during several consecutive generations'.[93]

However, the break here from earlier discourses was that neither Carlyle nor the trait theorists addressed themselves to the substantive issues of statecraft. Instead of engaging in the giving of advice on the leader's substantive role and responsibilities, as had Classical Greek and medieval scholars, the focus now was on elucidating the character and deeds of exemplary leaders. Carlyle's work, thus, marks the beginning of what later became an exclusive focus on the psychological domain of leadership, a distinct stepping away from the interest in public policy and statecraft which is such a strong focus of earlier discourses. In modernity knowing what the leader's role, rights and responsibilities are entails a focus primarily on issues in the psychological domain.

Consistent with this, the role claimed for leaders since World War II initially focused on a 'consideration' of the worker's needs and on 'structuring' the organization of work activities.[94] With the development of contingency/situational theories, the need to assess situational variables in determining a response was added to the leader's responsibilities.[95] Now, with 'new leadership' being the dominant discourse, the leader's role is seen as being the management of meaning[96] and ensuring a fundamental change is wrought upon followers' sense of self.[97] The expectation is that leaders are responsible for lifting follower performance and capability via the transformational process which is deployed in pursuit of the leader's visionary strategy. Today, the focus is placed on leaders' powers to change the psyche of followers, this being understood as both a potent and legitimate domain of action. Recall Bass' expectation that leaders produce transformational changes to 'the work-group norms, as well as ultimate beliefs about religion, ideology, morality, ethics, space, time, and human nature'.[98] Contemporary leadership discourse is largely silent as regards leaders' formal powers as these are matters now understood as being outside the domain of leadership scholarship. Instead, scholars with expertise in politics, law and human resource management (HRM) are left by leadership scholars to determine questions of formal authority.

The intense focus now given over to the psyche of followers is, meanwhile, one largely unconstrained by the legacy of the Enlightenment, with its focus on ensuring a balance of formal power, checks on authority, transparency of process and the right of appeal.[99] Consequently, while the visible, formal aspects of leaders' rights and powers have been severely constrained by means of formal rules and processes in the modern era,[100] in the domain of followers' psyche, the role, responsibilities, rights and powers of leaders have expanded and intensified dramatically in the last quarter century. Debate on boundary conditions as to the extent of appropriate leader influence has been marginalized because of the association made between 'leadership' and 'the good', with the follower's self treated as *terra nullius*, open for colonization.

An Unstable Ontology

What the foregoing analysis reveals is that leaders have been consistently positioned as superior beings, as good people who live good lives and, mostly, as men. The specific characteristics which define someone as a leader, as well as the roles, rights and responsibilities credited to leaders, have, meanwhile, undergone extensive change. At the level of basic ontology, while the Classical Greeks and 16th-century thinkers argued that leaders were rare,[101] today the vast sums committed to leadership development programmes[102] rely on the claim that many people possess the potential and ability to lead.[103]

The prevalence of a phenomenon is a key ontological characteristic requiring *explanation* if we are to claim a scientific grasp of that phenomenon, so the shift in understanding demands our attention. Why has leadership changed from something rare amongst the population to something now widely distributed? Perhaps it may be argued that certain aspects of modern society are more suited to releasing the leadership potential that otherwise lies dormant. This possibility warrants further research as it is not something leadership scholars have attended to thus far. Alternatively, the conflict could be dissolved by dismissing the Greek and medieval accounts altogether and arguing that 'true' knowledge commenced in 1978 or some other date when positivist social science achieved a firm grip on leadership. However, pending further research which can explain why leadership may have changed so markedly, this finding further demonstrates that leadership is an unstable, contingent invention.

CONTINUITY AND CHANGE IN THE TRUTH ABOUT FOLLOWERS

The 'follower', or more often 'followers' as a largely undifferentiated mass, appears as the necessary but typically problematic 'other' in the leadership discourses examined here.[104] Their existence is repeatedly invoked in justifying the necessity of leadership. The problems which followers are said to cause are a common focus of attention, be it lack of obedience and immoral behaviour in ancient and medieval times[105] or inadequate motivation, and task and moral 'immaturity' in modern times.[106] The nature of attention directed toward followers has, thus, largely been negative: followers are a problem to which leadership is the answer.

Followers have morphed over time from their ancient Greek and medieval European status as inherently and irremediably flawed beings[107] to their contemporary position as persons-of-unrealized-potential.[108] However, despite this, the follower's enduring position is as a fundamentally deficient being who requires the leader's intervention. It is arguably merely a change in social norms of what constitutes an acceptable way to speak of others rather than a fundamental change in the status of followers that has occurred.

So long as the equation of 'leader' with 'superior being' prevails in how leadership is understood, it is simultaneously a 'logical' necessity that followers be understood as lacking in some way deemed important: the leader cannot be rendered superior by definition unless the follower is also rendered inferior. Thus, this positioning of followers is used to prop up the necessity of leadership, the desirability of leadership and the rights and powers claimed for leaders.

Illustrative of this, Aristotle tells us that 'the lower sort are by nature slaves, and it is better for them as for all inferiors that they should be under the role of a master'.[109] Erasmus speaks of 'the low concerns and sordid emotions of the common people'.[110] For Carlyle, 'the subjects without king can do nothing'.[111] In the case of trait theory, followers simply lack the essential attributes that render one a leader. For situational/contingency theorists, recall that followers varied in their ability and willingness to perform. They might be enthusiastic, diligent and committed, but they could also be reluctant, hostile, suspicious or merely compliant.[112] With the development of 'new leadership' discourse, an apparently benevolent, empowering approach to followers was adopted. Here we are told that 'leaders see and act on their own and their followers' values and motivations'.[113] Yet this discourse also relies on the understanding that 'followers' attitudes, beliefs, motives and confidence need to be transformed from a lower to a higher plane of arousal and maturity'.[114]

A fundamental lack on the part of the follower thus continues even now to hold a dominant place in today's leadership discourse. This inequality is so embedded in the conventional way of understanding leaders and leadership that it can hide in plain sight and yet not attract comment, other than from non-conventional perspectives such as that being advanced here. So entranced have we become by the promise that the leader shall transform us into something better than we believed possible that this Faustian pact, which demands the subjugation of the follower in the name of their very salvation, goes largely unrecognized.

Repeatedly, leadership discourse has relied on a belittling, patronizing account of followers to sustain its claims. However, here again Locke and the behavioural theorists of the post-World War II period offer variations that move us away from this norm. Locke reversed the prevailing assumptions by adopting a suspicious, even hostile attitude toward leaders, seeking to limit their scope of action.[115] For him, this was absolutely vital to safeguard the 'natural freedom' he saw as being the birthright of all humanity. For Locke, leadership was more a danger than a solution, meaning that the rights and powers of leaders ought to be clearly prescribed, so as to protect from their interference the more important rights and powers of everybody else.

More recently, behavioural theorists understood followers as persons in possession of both rights and needs, assuming they possessed a natural inclination toward rational thought and action.[116] They were also highly sensitized toward limiting the scope for authoritarian leadership and disinclined toward any account of leadership as an innate capacity,[117] intent as they were on distancing themselves from trait theory and all that that potentially implied in a post-holocaust world. Taking these factors into account, behavioural theorists promoted patterns of behaviour for those in supervisory positions which took for granted managerial rights in decision-making, but did not go that extra step of assuming followers were, by definition, deficient and leaders superior. Instead, the focus was on behaviours, separated from any wider account of the human subject.

In ancient and medieval texts, the inadequacy of followers is thought to be overcome through demanding follower obedience to the leader's commands and warranting the use of force should such compliance not be forthcoming.[118] In contemporary texts, the approach to addressing followers' inadequacies has shifted to that of 'motivating the follower' through appeals to their values, to group goals, and, as part of 'new leadership', offering inspiring visions, support for personal growth and using 'corrective' actions such as variable rewards dependent on follower performance.[119] The aim has been to capture the hearts and minds of followers and engage these in pursuit of the leader's vision. The techniques are designed to persuade rather than coerce the follower to adopt the course of action sought by the leader.

The abolition of physical coercion reflects the modern boundaries on formal authority arising from the Enlightenment emphasis on the rule of law and the rights of persons.[120] Governmentality, the intensive monitoring and measuring of the self of another by those in positions of authority as a means of ordering society, is now the norm.[121] These developments have informed the widespread use of formalized procedures and rules in organizational life so as to limit the scope for personal whim. However, while the means of influence today exclude the use of force, the ends that are being sought remain essentially the same, namely follower compliance to the leader's will. The focus of attention has shifted over time from followers' obedient bodies and devout souls in ancient and medieval times to the productivity of their bodies in the post-World War II period and on to the commitment of their psyche to corporate interests in recent decades. This is the progress we have achieved via our truths about leadership.

Followers' alleged practical, intellectual or moral inadequacy has also rendered them dangerous at times. Both Classical Greek and 16th-century texts see followers en masse as potentially disruptive of social order and emphasize the need for constant leader vigilance. Illustrative of this, Aristotle claimed that 'a very great multitude cannot be orderly', but that order was what 'holds together the universe' and the 'divine power' that produced this result was the role of leaders.[122] Recall Machiavelli's argument:

> [T]he following may be said generally about men: that they are ungrateful, changeable, pretenders and dissemblers, avoiders of danger and desirous of gain, and while you do them good they are wholly yours, offering you their blood, their property, their life and their children ... when the need is far off, but when it comes close to you they revolt.[123]

More recently, Fiedler's contingency model explicitly assesses leader and follower power as key variables in determining what type of leadership style is best suited to a given situation.[124] However, by and large the danger posed by followers, which can be found in ancient and medieval texts, has today been reduced to a potential for disruption or frustration of the leader's wishes.

The fact that followers have not been problematized as dangerous in recent decades may reflect the extent to which 'new leadership' discourse has been successfully positioned as positive, empowering and legitimate, rendering the idea of follower resistance as a potential danger to the leader's continued authority largely unthinkable as a problem. However, recent mass 'follower' resistance, be it to the austerity measures adopted by EU governments, to talks aimed at advancing globalization or as part of the 'Arab Spring', constitutes potent real-world examples of what can happen when leaders today lose their legitimacy in the eyes of followers. The growing scholarly focus on 'authentic leaders'[125] and on 'follower-ship', in which it is positioned à la Carlyle as a laudatory act,[126] can usefully be understood as responses to the increasing fragility of our faith in leaders.

Table 7.3 offers a dispositif which summarizes the basis on which followers have either been praised or critiqued in the different discourses examined here.

What Table 7.3 demonstrates is that the specific characteristics and expectations placed on followers have varied over time, in the same way that the specific characteristics ascribed to leaders have varied (see Table 7.2 for earlier and associated commentary). Despite this, barring Locke and the behavioural theorists, followers are generally positioned as problematic and troublesome. Follower compliance to, or support for, the leader's requests also constitutes a recurrent source of praise against which only Locke and the behavioural theorists offer alternatives.

If followers were to be understood as capable, either individually or collectively, of making decisions, motivating themselves, developing and executing visions, building their own moral compass, or whatever it is that various theorists argue 'leaders' with their special abilities bring to the table, then the requirement for leadership would very quickly come into question, as would the rights and powers claimed for leaders. While some scholars have explored 'substitutes for leadership',[127] perhaps not surprisingly this has not been an approach embraced by leadership scholars more generally. However, what this analysis reveals is that the whole intellectual edifice of the dominant understanding of leadership is tenuous: as soon as we concede that 'followers' possess the capacity to act as rational, reasonable adults, the necessity and desirability of 'leadership' as conventionally theorized suddenly seems much less cer-tain, while the authority and scope of influence now granted to leaders suddenly seem far too extensive and intrusive.

Table 7.3 Followers' merits and demerits

Discourse	Followers are criticized for:	Followers are praised for:
Classical Greek texts	being immoral, unruly, self-interested; lacking understanding of what is right and true	complete obedience to the leader and adherence to religious and social norms
16th-century texts	being unruly, immoral, ignorant, unreliable in their love and loyalty for the leader	love and loyalty to the leader; adherence to religious and social norms
Locke's model	not actively defending their liberty from interference by leaders and others in positions of authority	seeking as much independence as possible from the influence of leaders in how they think and act
Carlyle's model	being unruly, immoral, ignorant; not appreciating the excellence of the true leader	worshipping leaders, which improves followers' morality
Trait theory	not subject to criticism per se as not a topic of interest; attributes described in order to distinguish leaders from non-leaders	not subject to praise per se as not a topic of interest
Behavioural theory	a lack of motivation, absenteeism and poor productivity are positioned as problems but not located in the person of the follower; acknowledged but not criticized for having needs for 'structure' and 'consideration'	not subject to praise per se; actions are presumed as typically being reasonable and legitimate
Contingency/ situational theory	a lack of motivation, absenteeism, poor productivity; a possible threat to leader power (Fiedler)	responding positively to the leader in terms of perceived motivation to perform, reduced absenteeism and increased productivity
'New leadership'	being self-interested; having moral immaturity; lacking vision and a sense of higher purpose	sacrificing self-interest for the corporate interests of the group; enthusiastically supporting the leader and accepting their guidance; becoming more like a leader and less like a follower

THE LEADER–FOLLOWER RELATIONSHIP

Today, the leader–follower relationship is understood as being one of respect, trust and even intimacy in terms of the leader's expected understanding of the follower.[128] The close connection which leaders are now expected to have with their followers carries with it the impression of egalitarian values where all persons mingle freely and equally in the same social space. This experience of warmth and closeness is quite a recent occurrence and is generally understood as a progressive move away from old hierarchical models where leaders were much more remote.

As we have seen, Classical Greek thinking positioned the leader as head of state at a considerable remove from those he led.[129] The leader's focus here was understood as being the welfare of the state overall, with the concerns of individual followers being of very limited interest. The understanding the leader was expected to have of the follower was thus rather abstract and impersonal and their interaction was limited.

Sixteenth-century texts were at pains to ensure that the leader's 'majesty' was not damaged by being overly visible to the polluting gaze of the masses.[130] The relationship here was also distant and the leader was not expected to 'lower' themselves to attend to the mundane concerns of ordinary followers. The leader's immediate advisors were also regarded with some caution, as possibly prone to flattery or unsound advice until their loyalty and competence were proven.[131] Even then, the leader's divine status rendered him existentially distinctive and separate from all others.

For Carlyle and trait theorists alike, the value of 'hero-worship' or, later, learning from one's betters, meant that the leader constituted a role model for the follower, someone whom they should seek to copy.[132] At a group level, the leader served as guide and decision-maker. The distance between leader and follower here was in terms of ability, but regular interaction was now assumed to be both necessary and desirable. Leaders were now to be looked at in order that followers might learn from them.

Post-World War II, with the move to managerial leadership as the focus, the relationship between leader and follower has been understood as demanding regular, friendly interaction and a depth of leader under-standing of both the individual follower and the group.[133] This under-standing is expected to assist the leader in encouraging the follower's better performance and, more recently, their personal and moral growth.[134]

This understanding of the leader–follower relationship rejects the earlier fears that the leader might be polluted or distracted through close contact with followers. It replaces it with the expectation that the greater the contact between leader and follower, the more the leader's qualities will 'rub off' onto followers.[135] Thus, rather than being isolated so as to enact leadership through strategy and policy decisions, leaders should now be ever present, enacting leadership through working directly on the person of the follower. This development relies on the re-positioning of the follower noted earlier from fundamentally-flawed-being to person-of-unrealized-potential. It also relies on a shift of the leader from the divine and the rare to the extraordinary yet prevalent mortal, offering every employee the potential to benefit from exposure to a leader.

Consequently, the leader–follower relationship is now one which requires followers to expose their innermost self to the greatest degree possible so as to maximize the beneficial effects of the leader's influence.[136] This process of continuous revelation of the follower self in order that it may be re-shaped to better fulfil the leader's vision renders followers both vulnerable and dependent. Thus, not only do egalitarian concerns inform this greater closeness between leader and follower: a regime of governmentality provides the wider context for thought and practice of this nature.[137] This intensive, never-ending surveillance extends to the self-monitoring in which leaders are expected to engage[138] so as to meet the precise requirements of 'new leadership'.

The developmental focus of 'new leadership' discourse, based on an understanding of the follower as possessing hitherto unrealized potential, is central to the positioning of leadership today as a progressive, humanistic endeavour.[139] This unleashing of the follower's true abilities, which the leader is expected to facilitate, is critical to leadership being said to function for the good of the follower. Its entwinement with a focus on lifting follower performance arises from the simultaneous unitarist expectation that leaders and followers both serve organizational interests and in so doing benefit themselves.[140] The conflict inherent in a dual focus on developing followers for their own sake and on lifting follower performance to better serve the needs of the organization is rendered invisible through an appeal to the humanistic elements of this relationship.

While a move toward greater closeness in the leader–follower relationship has occurred, the reciprocity previously emphasized has become less of a feature in the discourse. For the Classical Greeks, the complete obedience due to the leader was matched by the leader's complete devotion to the well-being of the state, irrespective of how demanding that might be for the leader.[141] In the medieval discourse, the love, loyalty and obedience due to the leader were to be reciprocated by his unceasing diligence in safeguarding the well-being of the people and the state.[142] By the time we reach the trait theorists, the sense of duty the leader previously owed to the led has disappeared, leaving only the respect and admiration for the leader which the follower was expected to have.[143]

While followers are now expected to reveal themselves to the leader and then change that self in accordance with the leader's advice, the leader now seems to owe less and less to the follower by way of duty, obligation or self-sacrifice. Now, simply through expressing their leadership, leaders are thought to serve others, as leadership per se is presumed as a good, as inherently positive, irrespective of the specific goal it acts in aid of.[144] Moreover, while follower self-interest is held automatically to be problematic and wrongly directed until it comes under the leader's influence,[145] leader self-interest is presumed benign unless proven otherwise; in such a case, the individual leader's status as such is then rendered doubtful, inauthentic, false, yet all the while 'leadership' as an ideal remains intact.[146]

If we directly contrast Classical Greek with 'new leadership', then the shift is from a relationship of obedience, subservience and distance, but with clear leader obligations for follower well-being, to one of intimacy in order to bring about a change in the self of the follower resulting in enhanced performance. The change is from a reciprocal relationship between unequal parties to one where the follower is now both end and means to an end, human and human resource, and where the duty of all is the achievement of enhanced performance. What seems lost is the sense of what the leader might owe to the follower by way of duty or obligation. What is instead emphasized is what the leader is able to bestow upon the follower, the process and experience of being transformed to become more like the leader.[147] This is now the service which leaders are expected to offer.

The parental nature of the leader–follower relationship that we saw in Classical Greek discourse has, meanwhile, become something much more ambiguous in the 'new leadership' discourse. This is because of the dependency leaders have in this discourse in expressing their very selves through achieving change in followers.[148] This requirement entwines leaders and followers in a dynamic where 'success' implies the possibility of mutual psychic extinction: if leaders succeed in transforming followers into leaders, as is promoted here, then their raison d'être is extinguished while followers cease to exist as such. This discourse demands that followers pass over their selves and their lives to leaders, to exist in a state in which leader self-expression is realized through follower self-denial.

The results sought and expected from the leader–follower relationship in Classical Greek and 16th-century thought were nothing short of the maintenance of social order and the saving of souls.[149] Locke's interest was in freedom in the earthly realm in order that we might determine our own conscience and course in life.[150] To achieve this he sought to limit the leader–follower relationship, but Carlyle then resurrected the earlier concern with saving society and souls via the potency of leadership.[151] Today, that focus has moved to the maintenance of the economic order through the realization of continuous improvements in performance.[152] This is said to occur through the unleashing of follower potential in pursuit of the leader's vision. This process is depicted in terms acceptable to the norms of modern social science. Yet inherent in the very notion of 'transformation' is that of a fundamental change in the very nature of a thing. Like the miracle in which water becomes wine, 'new leadership' carries with it an appeal to supernatural forces that will relieve us of our worries and bless us with their divinity.

THE SOCIAL FUNCTION OF LEADERSHIP DISCOURSE: THE PROMOTION OF ORDER, INEQUALITY AND THE EXTRAORDINARY

In terms of its social function, three recurrent features of leadership discourse are evident. The first is that 'leadership' is associated with the upholding of order as a vital social good. For the Classical Greeks, leadership was seen as an ordering force which was so fundamental and so powerful that it 'holds together the universe'.[153] Here, leadership stood between civilized society and a slide into anarchy, degeneracy, licentiousness, disrespect of the gods and social customs, immorality and a war of all against all. Similarly, in the medieval discourse, leadership was positioned as crucial to the maintenance of social order and public morality.[154] Carlyle argued that the worship of leaders enhanced the morality of followers and created bonds of affection which maintained social order.[155] He saw leaders as shaping and directing human history, creating order and progress where otherwise chaos and a lack of progress would prevail. Trait theorists, in assuming leadership was an innate personal quality, positioned leaders as responsible for ensuring social order.[156] Since World War II, with the shift to a workplace focus, the order that is now the centre of attention is ensuring the efficient production of goods and services in conjunction with worker/follower satisfaction and, more recently, transformational change.[157] This in turn is understood as contributing in important ways to the maintenance of social order more broadly.[158] Implicit in all these accounts is the belief that without the leader's steadying, guiding hand, disorder will prevail.

At various times leadership discourses, while still promoting the upholding of social order generally, have sought to reform the existing social system, to critique the status quo and challenge accepted norms. As we saw, the Classical Greek leadership discourse constituted an alternative model to that of Athenian democracy, arguing for the superiority of a single, wise, appointed leader and against what it saw as the unstable, unreasoning, unwise nature of collective, democratic governance.[159] Carlyle also had a reforming agenda, seeking to counter what he perceived as the problematic legacy of Enlightenment ideas which promoted reason and collective participation.[160] Some trait theorists such as Galton,[161] Cattell[162] and Ellis,[163] through their association with the eugenics movement,[164] also pursued a reformist agenda built on their conception of leadership as an inherited quality and their belief in the potential value of selective breeding practices.

In contrast, the leadership discourse of the 16th century was fully integrated into, aligned with and reinforced the existing social system of monarchical rule.[165] Since World War II, leadership discourse has played a similar role, taking as a given the requirements of capitalist economics.[166] It has promoted and supported the ceaseless search for enhanced productivity and performance as being something which is natural, normal and inevitable.[167] Contemporary leadership discourse has also been a key player in the broader shift in management discourse from a focus on producing compliant bodies to a focus on producing compliant minds.[168] To do this, it has appealed to now widely accepted beliefs about human potential and to the tradition of the leader as exceptional being. These are linked to an acceptance of the demand for a constant improvement in performance. Consequently, leadership discourse currently functions to uphold order in the workplace and to uphold the existing economic system more broadly. It thus serves to reinforce the current order of things, just as 16th-century texts served to reinforce Christian monarchy.

The second recurrent feature of the social function of leadership discourse is that it has continuously, barring Locke, offered a justification for the unequal distribution of rights, power and authority between leaders and followers.[169] Mostly, this arises from the positioning of followers as deficient while leaders are rendered superior. Behavioural theorists offer an exception to this because they base the differentiation of rights, power and authority solely on positional authority rather than on the superiority/inferiority thesis. However, that thesis at all other points provides a critical building block from which the advocacy of unequal rights, power and authority can readily be advanced. As we saw, both the Classical Greeks and medieval scholars regarded the majority of people as unruly and typically lacking in the capacity for right action, without the leader's direction. Today, the deficiency in followers is recast in the language of 'unrealized potential' which *only* the leader can release, but the overall effect remains a justification for the unequal distribution of rights, power and authority.

Associated with the positioning of leaders as superior comes the third recurring social function of leadership discourse: the promotion of leadership as something extraordinary, something supernatural. The divinity of the leader was clear cut and overtly stated in both Classical Greek and 16th-century texts. Carlyle also saw leaders as having been sent by God.[170] Thus, for much of the Western tradition leaders have been connected with the divine, essential, immortal and supernatural realm, separated from and superior to the mundane, prosaic and ordinary. From Galton onwards, the discourse became overtly secular and scientific in tone. Yet, despite this shift, again barring behavioural theory, there remains a reverential, admiring tone to the mainstream of leadership discourse which positions leaders at a remove from the mundane and ordinary.[171] 'New leadership' discourse has intensified and heightened this long-standing trend.

In the Western tradition, then, to speak of leadership is to speak about the maintenance of social order, the deficient nature of most people and the exceptional, supernatural leader. The direct link made between a fear of chaos, direct access to the extraordinary and leadership likely accounts for its enduring appeal. This linkage simultaneously presents us with the problem and the solution to the problem. It simultaneously takes us down to contemplate the worst of all scenarios, the breakdown of society, and lifts us up, so that we may see the spark of the divine made accessible to us in human form. Today, the seductive appeal[172] of this has been intensified, because it is now claimed that everyone has within them the potential to lead. Moreover, with existential fears growing about the survival of the planet, terrorism and the ongoing economic crisis, the necessity for leadership is readily presented to us as being greater than ever. My question is, must we persist with an understanding of leadership which relies on the assumption that most people are inadequate?

Whether leadership discourse has functioned to support or reform the existing social system with the exception of Locke, it has repeatedly offered an account which serves elite, anti-democratic interests. The combination of a positioning of order as a critical social good with followers rendered deficient and leaders as superior beings constitutes the three key enduring elements of the Western tradition. Changing any of these elements thus constitutes a potentially potent basis for reconceptualizing leadership; I will return to explore this further in the next chapter.

PRODUCING THE TRUTH ABOUT LEADERSHIP: WHAT HAVE WE GAINED AND LOST ALONG THE WAY?

The epistemological and methodological basis on which claims to speak the truth about leadership are made has changed dramatically over time. These changes largely mirror major developments in the Western intellectual tradition,[173] reflecting the influence those developments have had on leadership scholars. Hence we find a shift from an analytic philosophy reliant on both reasoning and myth in Classical Greece[174] to a renaissance philosophy in the 16th century, this being a blend of ancient Greek and Roman traditions and medieval Christian thought.[175] Over the course of the last century, the trend has been toward an increasingly empirical, quantitative and scientistic mode of reasoning and inquiry.[176]

We would normally understand these developments to mean that our knowledge today is superior to that of the past because it is grounded in more robust, reliable premises and methods of discovery. However, as I showed in Chapters 5 and 6, the major theoretical developments in modern leadership knowledge have not arisen from scientific discoveries but, rather, as inventive responses to varying problems. The modern account of leadership is also much closer in nature to those developed in both the Classical Greek and medieval epistemes than is normally understood. I have, therefore, already argued that the 'progress' made may not be as great as we might have expected. Having done that, here I am interested in focusing on what we might have lost as a result of these developments, further challenging the normal expectation that what we have achieved today is a superior access to the truth.

The truth about leadership in both Classical Greek and renaissance European literature was, as detailed in Chapters 3 and 4, multidimensional. As we have seen, this meant that the leader's childhood experiences constituted an important topic which leadership scholars considered they ought to know about and comment on.[177] As identified earlier, the leader's private life, including his eating, sleeping and sexual habits, his clothing and housing arrangements, his friends and his use of money, all these matters have in earlier times demanded attention in establishing the truth about leadership. As noted, the care and use of the leader's body were issues of interest in the past. Spiritual and religious aspects of life were also previously matters of considerable importance in understanding leadership.

These dimensions of life which used to constitute important aspects of knowledge about leadership in the past are today largely excluded and ignored. Generally, this is not because these matters have been scientifically proven as being irrelevant. Rather, current social norms place leadership in the public domain and treat the private domain as irrelevant to leadership knowledge. I am not advocating here that such matters ought to be resurrected as domains of inquiry for leadership scholars, but I do think we should be debating the boundaries we operate within and not simply taking them for granted. Our knowledge of leadership is narrower today than in the past and this is not what we would expect to be the case.

One consequence of our current boundaries is that the private lives of business leaders, the focus of the contemporary literature considered here, remain largely unexamined by scholarly researchers. This space has instead been dominated by autobiographers and biographers offering us hagiographic accounts.[178] Depending on whether privacy is considered more important than a broader understanding of the lived experience of leaders, or followers for that matter, this limitation may not be seen by some as a problem. Politically, of course, independent scholarly research which examined the lifestyles and benefits some leaders achieve might be considered inconvenient, especially if compared with that of followers. However, this is not a valid reason for ignoring these issues.

Another consequence of current boundaries is that both leaders and followers normally appear in our contemporary discourse as disembodied beings. Only rarely do leadership scholars seek to examine the embodied experience of leadership,[179] yet effective interpersonal communication, a key element of mainstream models, entails the use of voice, gaze and bodily stance. Why bodies have become largely off-limits for leadership knowledge warrants further investigation. To reiterate, the claim here is not that these matters are definitively important to our understanding of leadership: that remains to be debated. Rather, the concern is that the domains of leadership knowledge have narrowed and the field is not today debating its boundaries.

Classical Greek and 16th-century knowledge was also profoundly substantive in its orientation, while current knowledge is essentially processual and behavioural. As we have seen, knowledge of issues as diverse as town planning, crop management, trade policy, warfare and statecraft comprise central features of Classical Greek and 16th-century leadership knowledge.[180] To establish their credibility as experts in leadership demanded that these scholars understood and could provide advice on the substantive issues with which leaders had to contend. Today, because of the orientation toward producing knowledge which is claimed to be universally applicable, along with the specialization expected of scholars, the emphasis has moved completely away from an understanding of what all this leading and following is actually for. Instead, the emphasis has switched to the processes and behaviours of leading that are said to be transferable to any context, relevant to any issue.

As part of this move, questions of philosophy and politics are now routinely placed in separate domains of knowledge from leadership knowledge. Barring those scholars who are advocating for a central place for ethics in leadership knowledge,[181] the actual issues that leaders and followers come together to work on are not a matter of active debate within mainstream leadership literature. Today, we have the 'how', but our texts are typically missing the 'of what', 'where', 'who for' and 'why' of leadership.[182]

Important, inherently contestable choices and consequences are ignored when what leadership scholars offer up is a recipe for changing others without any assessment as to who actually benefits from that change. What is largely being produced is knowledge whose political effects are hidden, in which leadership is portrayed as a matter of technique whose aim is enhancing human potential. This apparently benign account ignores the micro and macro political and ethical issues that are inevitably associated with a relationship based on inequality. It assumes that the actual issues that leader and followers contend with are amenable to a global approach. It is hard to see how this narrowing of the debate constitutes an overall advancement of knowledge.

Despite these profound changes in the foundation, nature and scope of leadership knowledge, what has remained constant is the optimistic tenor of the discourse vis-à-vis the positive effects of leadership. The belief that a person of outstanding ability can have a positive impact on others always lies at the core of the discourse.[183] At every point, the aim has been to articulate an account of leadership that will achieve beneficial results for followers. The specific results that are sought vary, but the desired outcome is always to benefit followers. What we repeatedly see in the archive is the production of a disciplinary regime which seeks to govern and inform the actions of leaders, ensuring that their conduct and decisions are conducive to what is said to be in the best interests of followers. Consistently, then, leadership as a topic of inquiry creates for scholars a sense of labouring for the betterment of all, a worthy aim without doubt. However, insofar as the discourse remains reliant on the belittling of the follower its effects likely remain problematic.

CONCLUSION

This and the preceding four chapters now cumulatively constitute the detailed answers I offer to the questions informing this research. As this chapter has shown, our present understanding of leadership is just the latest variant in a long process of both change and continuity, but one where the overall distance travelled is much shorter than we might have expected. Plato might not recognize our contemporary methods of searching for the truth, but he would likely applaud the attention now being given over to the transformational visionary to whom all others should defer judgement. Where this leaves us is alarmingly close in our supposedly scientific, modern and progressive thinking to Plato's defence of totalitarian rule.

Positioning leadership as the answer to every question, as we have done (yet again) over the last quarter century, is not only destined to result in disappointment as actual, real human beings fail to meet such grandiose and naïve expectations.[184] It also encourages a dangerous passivity from the great majority of people. As 'followers', they are positioned as limited creatures who are to rely on leaders, in most cases managers let us not forget for guidance and motivation on who to be, how to act and what to think. To position leaders as we now do as ideal persons without fault is both to ask the impossible of them and to incite them to develop a distorted, narcissistic sense of their own capabilities. To position followers as we now do as merely latent, unrealized potential is to absolve the majority of adults from self-responsibility. With this, the motivation (and freedom!) to be had from pursuing one's own goals, thoughts and dreams along with the requirement to grow up are removed, rendering followers perpetual adolescents. In the ideal world as implied by 'new leadership' theory, the important decisions and the constant monitoring needed to keep these immature followers on track is to be left in the hands of a small, non-elected group of manager-leaders: Plato's *Republic* is just down the road from here.

The basic facts and chronology of the developments documented in the foregoing case studies are readily accessible in the archive for those who care to look. The interpretation I have placed on those basic facts and chronology is, of course, my own and open to challenge. However, for most of the last 150 years leadership scholars have shown remarkably little interest in this history. Lacking the broader perspective an appreciation of our history can bring, the field has assumed it possesses a modern worldview and is producing new knowledge. Yet in many ways it is reworking old ground. Absent a concern with the problematic nature of power, it has also naïvely assumed its outputs will have progressive political effects.

What my incursions into past truths demonstrate is that leadership theory can readily be entwined with substantive knowledge of a diverse range of matters. The effect of this has, in other times, been to produce leadership knowledge that is not merely processual or behavioural in orientation, but is also concerned with both substantive issues and with questions about the ends and not simply the means of leadership. If we were today to turn our minds to these matters, leadership studies could be radically re-invented. If we were to focus attention on the actual challenges facing leaders and followers, on the outcomes being sought and the ends we seek, as well as the means deployed to achieve them, then we could seek to build a new approach to theorizing leadership. In Chapter 8, I will explore where this way of thinking could take us.

NOTES

1. 1977, p. 31
2. Foucault, 1978, p. 157
3. Cartledge, 1993; Finley, 1963; Morris and Powell, 2006
4. See, for example, Aristotle, 2009; Plato, 1995, 2007; Xenophon, 1997, 2006
5. Xenophon, *Mem* 3.9.11
6. See, for example, Aristotle, *Pols* 1326a
7. See, for example, Plato, *St* 296e, 309a
8. See, for example, Calvin, 2010; Erasmus, 2010; James VI, 1950; Lipsius, 2004; Luther, 2010; Machiavelli, 2005
9. Erasmus, 2010, pp. 26–7
10. 1993
11. 1993, p. 171
12. See, for example, Cattell, 1906; Clarke, 1916; Galton, 1892, 1970; Lehman, 1966; Sorokin, 1925; Taussig and Joslyn, 1932; Thorndike, 1936; Visher, 1925
13. Lehman, 1966, p. 7
14. Galton, 1892, p. 45
15. See, for example, Mayo, 1945, 1946
16. See, for example, Blake and Mouton, 1964; Bowers and Seashore, 1966; Fleishman, 1953a, 1953b; Katz et al., 1950; Likert, 1961, 1967; Shartle, 1979
17. Fleishman, 1973, pp. 7–8
18. See, for example, Capitman, 1973; Cornuelle, 1975; Roos, 1972; Whyte, 1963
19. See, for example, Fiedler, 1967; Hersey and Blanchard, 1974; House, 1971; Tannenbaum and Schmidt, 1958; Vroom and Yetton, 1973
20. Fiedler, 1967, p. 248
21. House, 1996, p. 323
22. See, for example, Ackerman, 1975; Burns, 1978; Heath, 1975; Magaziner and Reich, 1982; Peters and Waterman, 1982
23. Bass, 1985a, p. 4

24. See, for example, Bass, 1985a; Bennis and Nanus, 1985; Burns, 1978; Conger, 1989; House, 1977
25. See, for example, Avolio and Luthans, 2003; Bass and Riggio, 2006; Goleman et al., 2002; Kotter, 1996; Kouzes and Posner, 2007
26. See, for example, Bass and Riggio, 2006; Burns, 1978
27. Bass, 2008, p. 618
28. 1985, p. 3
29. See, for example, Bass, 1985a; Carlyle, 1993; Fiedler, 1967; Fleishman, 1953a; Galton, 1970; Lipsius, 2004; Plato, 1995
30. See, for example, Avolio and Luthans, 2003; Zhu et al., 2011
31. Xenophon, *Oec* 21.12
32. Annas and Waterfield, 1995; Everson, 2009; Lane, 2007
33. Aristotle, *Pols* 1254a: 20
34. Erasmus, 2010, p. 26
35. James VI, 1950, p. 25, text in square brackets added
36. 1993, p. 3
37. See, for example, Cattell, 1906; Galton, 1970; Taussig and Joslyn, 1932; Thorndike, 1936
38. 1966, p. 7
39. See, for example, Bass, 1985a; Fleishman, 1953a; House, 1971; Likert, 1961
40. See www.neuroleadership.org (retrieved 20/02/2013)
41. See, for example, De Neve et al., 2013; Kant et al., 2013
42. Bennis and Nanus, 1985, p. 8
43. Burns, 1978, p. 462, italics in original
44. Bass, 1985, p. 24
45. See, for example, Bass, 1985a; Carlyle, 1993; Erasmus, 2010; House, 1971; Likert, 1967; Thorndike, 1936; Xenophon, 2006
46. Aristotle, *Pols* 1260a: 15
47. Erasmus, 2010, p. 26
48. 1993
49. Thorndike, 1936, p. 339
50. See, for example, Bennis and Nanus, 1985; Fiedler, 1967; Likert, 1961
51. See, for example, Bass, 1985a; Bass and Riggio, 2006; Kotter, 1988; Peters and Austin, 1985
52. See, for example, Bass, 1985a; Carlyle, 1993; Fiedler, 1967; Fleishman, 1953a; Machiavelli, 2005; Plato, 1995; Visher, 1925
53. Calás and Smircich, 1991; Fletcher, 2004; Sinclair, 2007
54. 2010
55. See, for example, Fleishman, 1953a; Katz et al., 1950
56. Fleishman, 1973; Shartle, 1979
57. See, for example, Blake and Mouton, 1964; Likert, 1961
58. See, for example, Fleishman, 1973
59. Xenophon, *Ag* 11.6
60. Xenophon, *Ag* 11.10
61. Plato, *Rep* 485c
62. Xenophon, *Ag* 3.5
63. Xenophon, *Ag* 5.3
64. Plato, *Rep* 494b
65. Plato, *Rep* 494e
66. See, for example, Plato, *Rep* 494d
67. See, for example, Erasmus, 2010; James VI, 1950; Lipsius, 2004
68. 2010, p. 5
69. 2010, p. 53
70. See, for example, Cattell, 1906; Galton, 1970; Thorndike, 1936
71. See, for example, Blake and Mouton, 1964; Fleishman, 1953a; Katz et al., 1950
72. See, for example, Fiedler, 1967; House, 1977; Vroom and Yetton, 1973

73. Stogdill, 1974, p. 96
74. See, for example, Bass and Riggio, 2006; Kotter, 1988; Peters and Austin, 1985
75. See, for example, Bass, 1985a; Bennis and Nanus, 1985; Burns, 1978; Conger, 1989
76. See, for commentary and analysis, Alvesson and Deetz, 2000; Austin, 1962; Russell, 1984
77. 5.1
78. 5.2
79. 5.4
80. 2010, p. 58
81. Carlyle, 1993; Galton, 1970
82. Smith and Krueger, 1933; Stogdill, 1948
83. Sinclair, 2007; Wolkowitz, 2006
84. See, for example, Aristotle, 2009; Erasmus, 2010
85. Plato, *St* 297a
86. 2004, p. 229
87. See, for example, Lipsius, 2004; Plato, 1995, 2007
88. Aristotle, *Pols* 1325b: 1
89. 2004, p. 295
90. 1993
91. 1993, p. 175
92. See, for example, Cattell, 1906; Clarke, 1916; Thorndike, 1936
93. Galton, 1892, p. 45
94. Fleishman, 1973; Shartle, 1979
95. See, for example, Fiedler, 1967; House, 1971; Vroom and Yetton, 1973
96. Smircich and Morgan, 1982
97. See, for example, Bass, 1985a; Burns, 1978; Conger, 1989
98. Bass, 1985, p. 24
99. Hampson, 2001; Morrow, 2005
100. Morrow, 2005; Russell, 1984
101. See, for example, Aristotle, 2009; Erasmus, 2010
102. Jackson and Parry, 2011
103. See, for example, Bass and Riggio, 2006; Bennis and Nanus, 1985; Goleman et al., 2002
104. See, for example, Bass, 1985a; Carlyle, 1993; Fiedler, 1967; Fleishman, 1953a; Galton, 1970; Lipsius, 2004; Plato, 1995
105. See, for example, Machiavelli, 2005; Plato, 1995, 2007
106. See, for example, Burns, 1978; Fiedler, 1967; Hersey and Blanchard, 1974
107. See, for example, Aristotle, 2009; Erasmus, 2010
108. See, for example, Bass, 1985a; Burns, 1978
109. Aristotle, *Pols* 1254b: 20
110. 2010, p. 24
111. 1993, p. 197
112. See, for example, Fiedler, 1967; House, 1971; Tannenbaum and Schmidt, 1958
113. Burns, 1978, p. 19
114. Bass, 1985, p. 3
115. 2010
116. See, for example, Fleishman, 1953a; Katz et al., 1950
117. See, for example, Fleishman, 1973; Shartle, 1979
118. See, for example, Lipsius, 2010; Plato, 1995, 2007
119. See, for example, Bass, 1985a; Bass and Riggio, 2006; Bennis and Nanus, 1985; Burns, 1978
120. Hampson, 2001; Morrow, 2005; Russell, 1984
121. Foucault, 1977, 2010
122. Aristotle, *Pols* 1326a: 30
123. 2005, p. 91
124. 1967

125. See, for example, Avolio and Luthans, 2003; Gardner et al., 2011; Walumbwa et al., 2008
126. See, for example, Kellerman, 2012; Riggio, Chaleff and Lipman-Blumen, 2008
127. See, for example, Kerr and Jermier, 1978; Pfeffer, 1977
128. See, for example, Bass, 1985a; Bass and Riggio, 2006; Bennis and Nanus, 1985; Burns, 1978
129. See, for example, Aristotle, 2009; Plato, 1995, 2007
130. See, for example, Erasmus, 2010; James VI, 1950; Lipsius, 2004
131. See, for example, Erasmus, 2010; Lipsius, 2004; Machiavelli, 2005
132. See, for example, Carlyle, 1993; Taussig and Joslyn, 1932; Visher, 1925
133. See, for example, Fleishman, 1973; Katz et al., 1950; House, 1971
134. See, for example, Bass, 1985a; Burns, 1978; Hersey and Blanchard, 1974
135. See, for example, Bass, 1985a; Burns, 1978
136. Burns, 1978
137. Foucault, 1977, 2010
138. See, for example, Bass and Steidlmeier, 1999; Goleman et al., 2002; Kouzes and Posner, 2007
139. See, for example, Bass, 1985a; Bennis and Nanus, 1985; Burns, 1978
140. See, for example, Bass and Riggio, 2006; Kotter, 1996; Kouzes and Posner, 2007
141. See, for example, Plato, 1995, 2007; Xenophon, 1997, 2006
142. See, for example, Erasmus, 2010; James VI, 1950; Lipsius, 2004
143. See, for example, Clarke, 1916; Sorokin, 1925; Thorndike, 1936
144. See, for example, Avolio and Luthans, 2003; Bass and Riggio, 2006; Kotter, 1996
145. See, for example, Bass, 1985a; Burns, 1978
146. See, for example, Bass and Steidlmeier, 1999
147. See, for example, Bass, 1985a; Bass and Riggio, 2006; Burns, 1978
148. See, for example, Bass, 1985a; Bass and Riggio, 2006; Burns, 1978
149. See, for example, Aristotle, 2009; Plato, 1995, 2007; Erasmus, 2010; Lipsius, 2004
150. 2010
151. 1993
152. See, for example, Bass, 1985a; Bass and Riggio, 2006; Bennis and Nanus, 1985
153. Aristotle, *Pols* 1320a: 30
154. See, for example, Erasmus, 2010; James VI, 1950; Luther, 2010
155. 1993
156. See, for example, Galton, 1970; Lehman, 1966; Thorndike, 1936
157. See, for example, Bass, 1985a; Fleishman, 1953a; House, 1971
158. See, for example, Bass and Riggio, 2006; Kotter, 1988; Peters and Austin, 1985
159. See, for example, Plato, 1995, 2007; Xenophon, 1997, 2006
160. 1993
161. 1892, 1970
162. 1906
163. 1904
164. Cowan, 1970; Gillham, 2001; Godin, 2007
165. Allen, 1951; Craigie, 1950; Jardine, 2010
166. Trethewey and Goodall Jnr, 2007; Western, 2007
167. See, for example, Bass, 1985a; Bennis and Nanus, 1985; Peters and Austin, 1985
168. Alvesson, 2001; Ford and Harding, 2007; Parker, 2002
169. See, for example, Aristotle, 2009; Bass, 1985a; Erasmus, 2010; House, 1971
170. 1993
171. See, for example, Bass, 1985a; Bennis and Nanus, 1985; Conger, 1989
172. Calás and Smircich, 1991
173. Morrow, 2005; Russell, 1984
174. Cartledge, 1993; Grant, 1991
175. Allen, 1951; Cameron, 2001; Skinner, 2002
176. Bass, 2008; Morrow, 2005; Russell, 1984
177. See, for example, Erasmus, 2010; Plato, 1995, 2007

178. See, for example, Branson, 2002; Welch and Byrne, 2001
179. See, for exceptions, Melina et al., 2013; Sinclair, 2007
180. See, for example, Aristotle, 2009; James VI, 1950
181. See, for example, Ciulla, 2004; Ladkin, 2010; Sinclair, 2007
182. Although, for an exception to this, see Kempster et al., 2011
183. See, for example, Aristotle, 2009; Bass, 1985a; Erasmus, 2010; House, 1996; Likert, 1961
184. See, for example, Alvesson and Sveningsson, 2003a, 2003b, 2003c; Ford et al., 2008

8   Conclusion and future trajectories

> Never before has so much attention been paid to leadership, and the fundamental question we must ask is, what do we know and what should we know about leaders and leadership? (Avolio et al., 2009, p. 423)

> There are times in life when the question of knowing if one can think differently than one thinks, and perceive differently than one sees, is absolutely necessary if one is to go on looking and reflecting at all. (Foucault, 1985, p. 8)

INTRODUCTION

So, what do we now know about the truth about leadership, how this truth is formulated and what it does for and to us? And how can we now think differently about leadership? In this chapter, I offer concluding comments on what this research has revealed, consider the implications of the findings and offer a new approach to theory building, along with examples of how it could be deployed. I begin by recapping the rationale for the study, my review of the literature, the questions I have addressed and the approach taken to addressing those questions. Next, I provide a series of tables summarizing the key findings in regards to the secondary questions, before turning to offer my key conclusions in respect of the primary question guiding this study: why has our understanding of leadership come to take the form it now does? I then turn to the future, demonstrating how the insights gained from this study could be put to use so as to enable us to think differently about leadership.

RECAPPING THE RATIONALE AND APPROACH TAKEN IN THIS STUDY

While Avolio et al. report with enthusiasm that 'never before has so much attention been paid to leadership',[1] this study has taken a critical step back to ask why this is even happening. Why has leadership come to be seen as the answer to every problem? Why has our understanding of leadership come to take the form it now does? The super-human expectations we now have of leaders, the permission now extended to these manager-leaders to change the psyche of their follower-employees, the assumption that most people are somehow deficient in the absence of leadership are key features of the current mainstream scholarly discourse on leadership which demand scrutiny.[2] The heavy focus now given over to strategy, vision and change in leadership discourse along with the disregard for the ordinary and mundane aspects of organizational life which occupy most of the people, most of the time, are matters which need explaining.

Critically oriented scholars have begun the task of scrutinizing this now normalized, disciplinary discourse. The results of these efforts reveal that despite its surface-level benevolence and apparent scientificity, troubling assumptions inform 'new leadership' and concerning consequences arise for people trying to enact its prescriptions.[3] These studies point to the potential value of further critical examination of 'new leadership', and so as part of my review of the literature I set out my own critique of the key assumptions underpinning mainstream leadership studies (see pages 27–31).

However, despite the promise of critical studies of leadership, thus far precious little research has focused on examining why the current understandings came about. Only rarely have contemporary leadership scholars seriously investigated the history of the field in order to better understand why we got *here*.[4] Consequently, one key contribution of this study is that it extends the critical 'history of leadership studies' literature in scope and thematic focus.

My review of the literature revealed that research into the problems which have informed the development of leadership discourses warranted further attention. So too did the key assumptions underpinning leadership discourses, the subjectivities and relationships they produced, and their social function. Analysis of change and continuity in leadership discourse was the final key matter in need of further research and so from this, and taking into account the theoretical and methodological framework guiding the study, emerged the questions to drive this research.

The approach taken to tackle the research questions was to deploy the Foucauldian strategy of de-familiarizing the present in which we are normally embedded, seeing this move as 'absolutely necessary if one is to go on looking and reflecting at all'.[5] This approach was chosen as Foucault's own studies demonstrated the utility of his methods for examining both past and present expert discourses and for addressing the issues of interest here.

The specific approach taken deployed Foucault's Archaeological method to examine the form of discourses and their conditions of possibility, revealing key underpinning assumptions shaping claims to speak the truth about leadership. The Genealogical method was used to examine processes of formation, beginning with identifying the issues deemed problematic in response to which claims to speak the truth about leadership have developed. These two methods were also combined in order to examine the social function and subjectivity and relationship effects arising from these discourses. Case studies which span different epistemes were used to support the de-familiarization strategy and from which an analysis of both change and continuity could be derived. This resulted in three points of focus: Classical Greece, 16th-century Europe and modern leadership studies, beginning in the 1840s.

Through these methodological moves and through its deployment of Foucault's key concepts of discourse, power, power/knowledge and subjectivity, the study sets forth a detailed and multi-faceted explanation for why we got *here*. It offers, I hope, a 'history of the present',[6] revealing why and how present understandings of leadership are problematic and, moreover, that these understandings are no modern scientific discovery. They are, rather, deeply informed by ideas from the past and their development is founded in certain issues being deemed problematic, from which 'leadership' in its varying forms then emerges as a response.

The study shows that, contrary to conventional understandings, 'new leadership' thinking is profoundly problematic but, being a contingent construction and not something grounded in nature or science, this situation is open to change. To substantiate this argument the case studies reveal how 'new' and other forms of leadership arose, and the underpinning assumptions and effects arising from these accounts of the truth about leadership. The cases have also brought to light both changes and continuities in leadership thought, providing examples from which, later in this chapter, I draw in order to create and demonstrate an approach for ensuring we can think differently about leadership as a consequence of this research.

SUMMARY OF KEY FINDINGS

In this section, I provide a series of tables which summarize my key findings for each of my secondary questions. Where relevant, I incorporate my own propositions arising from this research. I then turn to consider the overall research question: why has our understanding of leadership come to take the form it now does?

What Problems Have Informed the Development of the Leadership Discourses Examined Here?

Table 8.1   The problematics informing leadership discourses

Discourse	What was deemed problematic	Solution
Classical Greek	Disorder, class conflict, war, moral degeneracy, loss of tradition and respect for the gods linked to democratic governance	Standards of behaviour to be imposed by a single leader head of state whose only concern is community well-being
16th-century Europe	Political and religious conflict; the disorderly nature of the people; self-serving or incompetent leader behaviour	Leader as God's representative on earth, head of state, possessing God's power, authority, divinity and goodness. Set out standards of conduct for leaders to adhere to and provided policy advice to mitigate leader incompetence
Carlyle	Excessive rationalism of Enlightenment thought and the effects of the Industrial Revolution damaging to 'human spirit', morality, faith and social cohesion	Heroic leadership in which passion, religious fervour and bold deeds lift the human spirit and improve human society. Worship of hero leaders will build faith and morality, enhance social cohesion and bring out the best in human nature
Trait theory	Only those 'fit' to lead in a Darwinian sense should be selected, as social problems arise when there is a mismatch between a person's 'natural talents' and their role in society	Identify traits of leadership and only place people with those traits in leadership positions. For eugenicists, adopt selective breeding practices to improve the quality of the population
Behavioural theory	Ensuring managerial control of the problems of workforce motivation, performance, absenteeism and conflict so as to help sustain America's new dominance and continued progress	Leader behaviour focused on 'consideration' and 'structure'
Contingency/ situational theory	Social context challenges old modes of authority and seeks an end to bureaucratic inflexibility so leadership must become situationally contingent	Match leader behaviour to situational variables

'New leadership'	Initially a crisis in leadership in 1970s America. Sustained through problematizing the modern world as needing leadership which produces change. Followers have potential but this can only be released through leadership	Visionary, charismatic, transformational leadership

What Key Assumptions Have Informed These Discourses?

Table 8.2   Key assumptions informing leadership discourses

Discourse	Key assumptions
Classical Greek	Leader is superior by divine nature; follower is deficient by nature; the truth is established through the use of reason and by reference to traditional knowledge
16th-century Europe	Leader is superior by divine nature; follower is deficient by nature; the truth is established through examining ancient and biblical sources and the use of reason
Carlyle	Leader is superior by divine nature; follower is deficient by nature; the truth is established through reason, examining biblical sources, studying the life history of leaders and the science of faces
Trait theory	Leader is superior by nature; follower is deficient by nature; the truth is established through statistical analysis of bodily, social and psychological 'traits' and biographic and demographic data about leaders' family backgrounds, personal characteristics and achievements
Behavioural theory	Leadership is behavioural and is therefore learnable; the truth is established through statistical analysis of survey results through which various 'constructs' are tested to determine the one best way to lead
Contingency/ situational theory	Leadership is behavioural but also influenced by context; those who can adapt their behaviours to different needs are superior and best able to remedy the deficiencies of followers; the truth is established through conceptual models which are then tested by the statistical analysis of survey results to determine the appropriate way to lead in a variety of different situations
'New leadership'	Leaders are superior and this is likely due to a combination of nature and nurture; followers have potential but need the leader to unleash this; the truth is established through testing precise theoretical propositions using complex statistical analysis in order to develop a prescriptive model for universal application

Table 8.2 (continued)

Discourse	Key assumptions
My proposition	What we understand as constituting 'leadership' is a social construction with an unstable ontology and hence is open to adaption; contextual factors are critical; assumptions of superiority and inferiority are problematic; the political dimensions of leadership knowledge are unavoidable

What Subjectivities and Relationships are Produced by These Discourses?

Table 8.3   The subjectivity of the leader produced by these discourses

Discourse	Leader subjectivity
Classical Greek	Masculine warrior-philosopher who lives a devout and ascetic life focused on ensuring the well-being of the state and the people; divinely gifted
16th-century Europe	Divinely gifted; devout; learned but practical expert in all aspects of statecraft; majestic; masterful practitioner of *real*-politic; can also be imprudent, lacking in virtue, self-serving and manipulated by flattery
Carlyle	Divinely gifted; heroic man of good breeding; devout; well-educated; physically and mentally strong; determined and capable; possessing a refined sensibility; perfect Victorian gentleman
Trait theory	Man of good breeding and possibly superior genes; devout; well-educated; physically and mentally strong; determined and capable; possessing a refined sensibility; perfect Victorian gentleman
Behavioural theory	Behaviour is skilful in relating to people and organizing tasks; well-rounded, practical man of action
Contingency/ situational theory	Skilful and considered diagnostician of worker/follower behaviours; able to respond variably to the demands of different situations
'New leadership'	Visionary, charismatic, strategic, able to change others; the perfect CEO
My proposition	Leaders are as we invent them to be; scholars must carefully address the risk of producing an ideal which is impossible to uphold and which renders leaders superior and grants them excessive power; there need not be a defined 'leader' in every model of leadership we develop

Table 8.4   *The subjectivity of the follower produced by these discourses*

Discourse	Follower subjectivity
Classical Greek	Prone to immorality and unruly behaviour; lacks understanding of what is right and true; self-interested; needs the leader's intervention to live a good life
16th-century Europe	Prone to being unruly, immoral, ignorant and unreliable, but can also be loyal, loving and obedient
Carlyle	Prone to being unruly, immoral and ignorant in the absence of a focus on the leader as role model
Trait theory	Lack whatever it is that leaders possess to render them such
Behavioural theory	May have needs for support or direction but naturally inclined to reasonable action
Contingency/ situational theory	May have needs for support or direction; may be reasonable but can also be difficult
'New leadership'	Possess unrealized potential which needs the leader's intervention
My proposition	Followers are as we invent them to be; scholars must carefully address the risk of producing an ideal which renders followers inferior, passive or weak; there need not be a 'follower' in every model of leadership we develop

Table 8.5   *The leader–follower relationship produced by these discourses*

Discourse	Leader–follower relationship
Classical Greek	Distant; demands follower obedience; leader is simultaneously master, servant and slave to the people; relationship is akin to cloning as leader seeks to make followers more like himself
16th-century Europe	Followers are the subjects of leaders and owe him love, loyalty and obedience; relationship is distant so the leader's 'majesty' is not harmed by followers' gaze; the leader's key duty is to protect the well-being of followers
Carlyle	Followers worship leaders; leaders offer themselves as role models from whom others can learn
Trait theory	Leaders are admired by followers who look to them for guidance, advice and direction; leaders offer this service to others
Behavioural theory	Friendly; respectful; focused on achieving organizational results and entails leader guidance and, if needed, support to the follower

Table 8.5   (continued)

Discourse	Leader–follower relationship
Contingency/ situational theory	May be friendly, respectful but can also be challenging; requires a watchfulness on the part of the leader
'New leadership'	Close and intense; the leader works on the follower's psyche to unleash their potential
My proposition	The relationship varies with the different models we develop

What is the Social Function of These Discourses?

Table 8.6   The social function of leadership discourses

Discourse	Social function
Classical Greek	Leadership discourse functions to undermine the legitimacy of democracy and to position a singular 'warrior-philosopher' leader as the only thing that stands between order, morality and chaos
16th-century Europe	Leadership discourse functions to maintain the legitimacy and status of monarchical leadership and to simultaneously prescribe to monarchs how best to lead, setting a standard for their conduct
Carlyle	Leadership discourse functions to promote romanticist, aristocratic values, undermining the push for greater democracy and promoting the worship of heroic individuals as vital for morality and social cohesion
Trait theory	Leadership discourse functions to promote the naturalness of inequality and to provide a 'scientific' basis for weeding out those not 'fit' to lead, reinforcing social Darwinian and eugenicist discourses
Behavioural theory	Leadership discourse functions to advance organizational and managerial interests and does this by promoting the value and necessity of leadership and prescribing the one best approach to leading in the workplace that will secure enhanced productivity and willing compliance from follower-employees. The discourse also functions to protect followers' rights and dignity by attempting to ensure that leaders act in a reasonable manner
Contingency/ situational theory	Leadership discourse functions to advance organizational and managerial interests and does this by promoting the value, necessity, highly skilled and variable nature of workplace leadership, seeking to secure enhanced productivity and willing compliance from follower-employees

| 'New leadership' | Leadership discourse functions to advance organizational and managerial interests and does this by promoting vision, strategy and constant change as the hallmarks of the modern age and the modern leader, offering leaders an attractive identity script and seeking to secure the active engagement of follower-employees in allowing the leader to work on changing their psyche |
| My proposition | Leadership discourse ought to function as a sceptic in respect of its own utterances, seeing itself as a contingent invention and not a discourse of truth, and evincing an ethical and political awareness in respect of the interests it serves and the effects its proposals produce |

What Changes and Continuities are Notable when Comparing These Discourses?

Table 8.7   Change and continuity in leadership discourses

Issue	Changes	Continuities
Problems	What is deemed problematic varies so that, in conjunction with extant values, norms, epistemologies and methodologies, a specific, tailored form of leadership then emerges	Calls for leadership arise as a response to moral, social, political and economic trends or events which are problematized
Leader	The specific characteristics ascribed to leaders have undergone constant adaptation. There is no stable persona to be found and hence no stable ontology. The leader's responsibilities and rights have also changed from head of state to manager and while now constrained by laws and rules, the right to work on the self of followers has expanded with new leadership discourse	Think 'leader', think 'superior being', 'the good person/life' and 'male'
Follower	The follower has morphed over time from an inherently and irremediably flawed being to being a person of unrealized potential	Followers are a problem to which leadership is the answer

Table 8.7   (continued)

Issue	Changes	Continuities
Leader–follower relationship	The relationship has become much closer and more intensely focused on changing the follower's psyche	The leader is more powerful and capable than the follower who needs the leader's help, guidance, support and direction
Social function	The focus has shifted from heads of state to managers, whose depiction as leaders functions to enhance their status and influence at the same time as it increases the expectations placed on managers	Functions to uphold existing institutional and structural arrangements and the values and norms of the ruling class of the day, typically by rendering the unequal leader–follower relationship as something that is natural, necessary and good for followers
Epistemology and methodology	Mirrors shifts in the Western tradition from philosophy plus traditional knowledge to Christian philosophy through to Darwinian and then modern positivist social science	An optimistic and idealistic attitude is adopted toward leaders and the potential of leadership to solve problems of concern

Why Has Our Understanding of Leadership Come to Take the Form it Now Does?

My study reveals that our current understanding of leadership has not come about because we have been successful in producing something more scientific, enlightened and truthful than anything that has come before. We have not rid ourselves of idealistic, contingent constructions of leadership, informed by contemporary problems and underpinned by the epistemic and methodological preferences of our age, any more successfully than those who came before us. Indeed, just like those scholars of the past, those of today also work consistently from a basis of deeply held concerns about what is going on around them, hoping that their account of leadership will be one that brings about positive results. Good intentions have paved this road in abundance.

The sheer proliferation of 'new leadership' discourse and its repeated endorsement by scholars of note are important factors which help to explain why this particular formation dominates current understandings of leadership. Its form is also tailored to focus on the issues of the day and it offers, at the surface, an apparently benign, developmental approach which aligns well with current values and norms. 'New leadership' discourse is infectiously optimistic: it is excited and bold about what we can achieve. It speaks both to our fears and to our hopes.

The incorporation of 'new leadership' discourse into everyday practitioner usage[7] has been critical in supporting its naturalization and normalization. In a society where 'management' was already naturalized and normalized,[8] layering 'new leadership' into and onto this was not an especially difficult task. However, this has had the critical effect of adding a material, structural basis to 'new leadership', embedding it into the way our workplaces are organized and run. In the same way that the 16th-century discourse was reinforced by, and acted to reinforce, the system of monarchical rule, so too is 'new leadership' now reinforced by, and acting to reinforce, managerial structures as the preferred mode of organizing work. 'New leadership' may have overtaken mere management in status terms, but it nonetheless relies heavily on managerial structures to sustain and continuously normalize it. This entwinement likely helps explain the struggle to advance distributed models of leadership as an alternative to 'new leadership'. Now, when we challenge what 'leadership' is and how to do it, we find ourselves immediately caught up in arguments about managerial rights and authority, taking us directly to the heart of what is arguably the most pervasive power system in contemporary society.[9]

By focusing 'new leadership' discourse on issues of 'strategy', 'vision', 'charisma' and 'transformation', what has been put to managers is a compelling means of lifting themselves out of the often mundane nature of managerial work and positioning themselves as someone much more powerful, attractive and capable.[10] That their alleged right to work on, let me be blunt, to manipulate, the self of followers, that this is presented as enabling the follower's development, only adds to the appeal. How could any manager who wants to be successful in an age which cherishes the ideal of progress and which is obsessed with the continuous improvement of performance resist these claims to speak the truth about leadership? When we live in a world of constant and unsettling change, when we are told that realizing our potential is both our birthright and our duty, and when we are told that just along the corridor sits our manager ready, willing and able to help us meet these challenges, who could reject such an offer?

In its specific formulation of the truth about leadership, 'new leadership' discourse has drawn on a much longer tradition, some parts of which I have explored here with the specific aim of foregrounding these very links. Using this tradition it has told us, yet again, that leaders are superior to followers. The value of this tactic is that we are culturally attuned to such messages.[11] The idea does not shock us in the slightest but, rather, has a familiar and even reassuring ring to it. At a time when we spend so much of our lives inside organizations, which themselves are overwhelmingly organized hierarchically, deference to our 'superiors' is hammered into us from an early age. So here again is the leader, coming to save us from ourselves, coming to tell us what to do: situation normal in the Western tradition of the truth about leadership.

However, this time, responding to the issues and values of the day, the leader will strategize, envision and transform both us and our world in the process of saving us. This time, the leader is kind and friendly: they realize we have potential and they want to help us achieve that. That the greatest potential we are said to have by this discourse is to become more like the leader does not cause dismay, for the leader is our idealized model. Here, our success, our salvation, our greatest achievement is said to lie in striving to become a clone of our manager. This is what is being presented to us as science, as truth, as enlightened and modern thinking.

In his study of sexuality, Foucault concluded that we had mistaken modern thinking as a form of liberation, when in fact we had become increasingly subjected to 'that austere monarchy of sex, so that we become dedicated to the endless task of forcing its secret, of exacting the truest of confessions from a shadow'.[12] He proposed that the demand that we speak of sex and seek to find ourselves in it was simply a modern adaption of the medieval practice of confession. He also concluded from his study of the development of the modern prison system that it is a mistake to believe ours is a society more free and humane simply because torture has by and large been abolished. This is because what has developed in its place is a society where 'the judges of normality are present everywhere': there is a 'new modality of power' in which we are endlessly surveilled and made docile.[13]

Taking inspiration from these ideas and reflecting on my findings, I suggest that the mistake we have made with 'new leadership' is to believe that achieving our potential relies on subjecting ourselves so utterly to the guidance of our manager. I think we have mistakenly come to believe that unleashing what lies within demands first that we place ourselves in their hands, that it is both legitimate and helpful to allow ourselves to be so colonized, to be made so docile in the name of personal growth and enhanced workplace performance. If this is so, then 'new leadership' might be more usefully understood as constituting a modern, secularized, workplace-based confessional practice on the part of the follower, through which they more completely align themselves with the requirements of the organization. This formation could also be understood as extending managerial surveillance into the self of both the leader and the follower, with the leader simultaneously the workplace judge of our normality, the agent who promotes and assures our docility.

In the case of the leader, 'new leadership' can also be understood as a form of devotional practice in which leaders constitute our priestly caste, dedicating and subjecting themselves to adopting its prescriptive requirements, its specified rituals of strategizing, visioning and transforming others. The call to service for would-be leaders is to imagine that we might be the one capable of bestowing the gift of our vision, our strategy, our transformational capacities, upon others, hence the ready supply of those presenting themselves for consideration. That, and perhaps also the rewards we now heap upon leaders.

In seeing 'new leadership' in these terms, what becomes apparent is that 'new leaders' have become more and more powerful servants not of God, and not of the people, but of the modern organization, and that both they and their followers are called into being to serve that. Here, Foucault's advice is vital lest we become dismayed with where we have come to, for despite its presently entrenched state this 'does not mean it cannot be altered, nor that it is once and for all indispensable to our kind of society'.[14]

IMPLICATIONS FOR FUTURE RESEARCH

If the findings of this research were accepted as valid, then significant implications arise for future research. For a start, 'new leadership' theory would as a minimum require a fundamental reassessment to determine if its troubling assumptions and effects can actually be overcome. The essentialist ontology which underpins most of the theories, 'new' or not, which are still under active research would also need to be put aside and substituted with the contingent, constructed understanding of the ontological nature of leadership which my findings indicate.

A third implication is that leadership theorizing and research ought, most usefully, to commence with a contextual assessment of the problems for which leadership, in whatever form it takes, is being considered as constituting part of the response. Grounding our theorizing and research in specific problems overtly positions leadership scholars as interested parties, not neutral observers, and, thus, renders our efforts more open to scrutiny for the interests our propositions serve. As part of this, the substantive issues to which leadership is directed ought then to take a more central place in leadership research, thereby demanding a multi-disciplinary approach. This has implications in turn for the content of leadership-focused degrees, shifting the field away from the current dominance of psychology as the base discipline of most leadership researchers.

The findings here could also be regarded as the tentative beginnings for a renewed focus on examining the history of leadership thought as a source for new ideas, and to help us more fully understand the present in which we are normally embedded. There are many times and places from the past which are crying out for attention, most especially, I think, those from beyond the Western tradition with its typically individualistic orientation. The final major implication for further research is that the conceptual componentry and approach to theory building which I set out later in this chapter could form the basis of a new research approach.

Lest the reader be alarmed, I do not actually think that these fairly dramatic implications will eventuate. Too many entrenched interests are in place to sustain the current version of the truth about leadership and how this ought to be produced for one little book to, oh how ironic, 'transform' the field with its new 'vision' and 'strategy' for the future of leadership research. However, social constructionist approaches to leadership are having a growing influence and so this book serves to reinforce the potential utility of approaching leadership as something that is open to invention and re-invention.

FUTURE TRAJECTORIES

> The point was to learn to what extent the effort to think one's own history can free thought from what it silently thinks, and so enable it to think differently. (Foucault, 1985, p. 9)

The critical influence of assumptions and what is deemed problematic in giving shape to a conception of leadership relevant to current concerns and values has been brought into sharp focus by this study. Rather than treating leadership as a naturally occurring phenomenon whose enduring truth we must seek to discover by means of the scientific method, I have proposed that we understand leadership as an invention, one which history demonstrates can be tailored to respond to different priorities and be informed by different values and norms. In this last section, therefore, I work from this perspective to explore leadership for a 21st-century context.

My analysis identified a number of conceptual components which have repeatedly formed part of the Western tradition. I propose that these components can be used, adapted or rejected in seeking to develop forms of leadership relevant to our current needs and values. Each form of leadership which I have examined in this study has configured some or all of these component pieces in a specific way, supported by a particular set of epistemological and methodological assumptions: it is this insight which I propose constitutes a model for theory building. In the preliminary theory building which I offer here, I adopt a social constructionist epistemology and ontology and make the assumption that the models I propose could be, and ought to be, subjected to empirical assessment via a range of social scientific methods.

In what follows, I firstly provide an overview of these components before examining each in detail. I consider briefly how each component has been previously understood, what a different understanding might comprise and how this component might be deployed in a different way to that which has occurred to date, depending on what we choose to value and prioritize. After that, I sketch out two new models of leadership by drawing on these components, demonstrating how this approach offers a means for future theorizing.

My aim here is simultaneously bold and modest. It is bold insofar as I seek to demonstrate a new approach to leadership theory building which both draws on and breaks with the past. However, my aim is also modest insofar as I am interested in building theories of leadership which are tailored to contend with quite specific, limited problems rather than purporting to be the answer to every problem. Moreover, I also assume that leadership can only ever constitute part of the solution to that which concerns us and never a complete response. What I aim to demonstrate here is that theories of leadership can be developed which are humble and human, moving us away from the historical tendency to proffer grandiose accounts of perfection.

CONCEPTUAL COMPONENTRY FOR INVENTING LEADERSHIP

In no particular or fixed order of priority, the key conceptual components I have identified in the various forms of leadership considered in this study are as follows:

- contextual issues, problems, values and norms deemed of salience to leadership
- the purpose of leadership
- domains of leadership activity
- leader personal attributes, behaviours, rights, responsibilities and roles

- follower personal attributes, behaviours, rights, responsibilities, roles
- the leader–follower relationship.

In what follows, I propose some ideas for how each of these could be deployed in building new theories of leadership.

Contextual Issues, Problems, Values and Norms

My analysis has shown that leadership theories have repeatedly arisen as a response to the social context of their time. This process is not easily understood if leadership is assumed to be a natural phenomenon. The relevance, credibility and attractiveness of the various theories examined here has, however, relied heavily on the extent to which they claimed to be offering a solution to issues of current concern and accorded with existing norms and values.

The contextual issues I identified as repeatedly being deemed of salience to leadership have been moral, social, political and economic trends or events which are seen as problematic, usually because they are thought to pose some kind of threat to the existing social order. As we have seen, these concerns are time and again linked to the troublesome characteristics attributed to followers. Strong claims are repeatedly made about the effectiveness of leadership which arise from the superiority gifted to the person of the leader, positioning the leader and leadership as a comprehensive solution to the issues of concern. Associated with this, the focus has been on developing leadership theories which are claimed to have broad, even universal, application.

An alternative approach to all this is, firstly, to focus leadership theories on contending with much more tightly specified 'problems'. By way of example, potential 'problems' on which leadership theorizing could focus include creativity in the knowledge-intensive workplace, or leadership in a start-up business context. Secondly, leadership could also be positioned as offering a partial solution to these 'problems'. This would mean efforts would be needed, both theoretically and practically, to connect 'leadership' with other sources of influence, such as policy, legislation, procedures, systems and rules, or shared values, norms and behaviours thought conducive to addressing the problem at hand. This focused and multi-faceted response to contextual challenges would, thus, see the particular form of leadership as having targeted rather than universal application and position leadership as comprising only part of the solution. This approach to theorizing begins with the context and works from there, rather than beginning with the assumption that leadership will provide the answer regardless of the problem.

Values and norms are also important contextual factors. Those which have informed leadership theorizing have typically been conducive to upholding the status quo, but this need not necessarily be the case. Instead, challenge to existing norms and values could be incorporated into models of leadership. For example, blending leadership, economic, political and environmental theories, 'sustainable workplace leadership' could be theorized as a particular form, focused on securing a substantive balancing of employer, employee, shareholder, customer and community interests and, consistent with this, requiring distributed decision-making rights and responsibilities. This form of leadership would require supportive policies, procedures, behaviours, etc., to enhance its effectiveness: employee share ownership could be one such mechanism, while conflict management could be positioned as a key skill. Another leadership form designed to challenge the status quo could be 'environmental leadership', where environmental sustainability is prioritized as the overarching goal, and only those decisions and practices which had a neutral or positive environmental impact would be deemed consistent with such a model. Organizations, nation states and/or individuals could be assessed for their alignment with such a model. Again, political, economic and environmental knowledge and theory combine with leadership theory here, to produce an enriched, substantive form of leadership knowledge.

Importantly, there exists a vast set of choices as to which matters, among the many problems, norms and values which form part of our wider context, we choose to deem as being of relevance to leadership. We can continue to treat leadership as the answer to every problem and to develop models which claim universal relevance but lack sensitivity to contextual specifics. We can continue to separate leadership theory out, taking it away from substantive issues. Or, we can be more selective in the problems we hold as being amenable to some form of a leadership response, develop leadership models that focus on addressing specific issues or upholding specific values and norms, and fortify these by combining them with other types of interventions.

A significant implication of such an approach is the development of leadership models in which substantive knowledge of particular matters becomes a key component. Thus, 'environmental leadership' would likely require knowledge of such matters as climate change science, 'green' technologies, local and international policy and political developments on environmental issues, as well as particular methods for influencing others on environmental issues. Contextually driven leadership theorizing could, I propose, be endlessly inventive, and connect theory building much more intimately with practical problem solving. It would also help direct leadership studies away from the search for universals, which my analysis shows is founded on faulty ontological assumptions. Beginning with the context as the source for our thinking about leadership has the particular benefit of positioning leadership as something demanding continuous adaptation at the same time as it allows us to create forms of leadership uniquely tailored to current needs and values, rather than being trapped by the past.

Purpose of Leadership

The purpose of leadership has commonly been positioned as safeguarding and enhancing community and follower well-being, albeit that this has usually relied on assumptions of follower inadequacy. As we have seen, this broad brush, universalizing tendency has been a common feature of theorizing about the purpose of leadership. However, more choices exist for theory building if we 'play' with the theoretical componentry gifted to us by history.

Abandoning the assumptions of follower inadequacy and leader superiority is one way to shift our thinking about the purpose of leadership. This, in turn, directs us toward a processual focus, seeing the purpose of leadership as that which supports and enables collective effectiveness. This is quite different from the current focus on changing the self of the follower-employee. Yet even in situations with highly capable individuals, where there is a need to work together to achieve results, process matters. A theory in which the purpose of leadership is to enable collective effectiveness could be conceptualized in functional, processual and/or behavioural terms, but it need not attach itself to a conception of leaders or followers as persons with distinctive abilities.

Another approach is to adopt a more localized, specific notion of purpose, linked to the contextual issues on which, as proposed above, a given model is focused. Accordingly, the purpose of the 'sustainable workplace leadership' model sketched earlier could be to achieve a workplace where employment security is prioritized, where shareholder, community, employee and customer input is incorporated into the decision-making process and where securing the future of the enterprise is actively pursued. By providing a more localized conception of the purpose of leadership, substantive knowledge and associated interventions again rise up as of critical relevance in producing leadership knowledge that is of practical value, informed by a politics not wholly captured by shareholder interests.

Philosophical and political concerns about issues such as personal autonomy and the care and respect we might wish to show and expect from others are also matters that could inform our thinking about the purpose of leadership. Leadership models which abandon the assumption of leader superiority and follower inferiority serve different political purposes than those that promote follower subservience and dependency. Models which seek to limit the extent to which managers may reasonably act on the subjectivity of their employees are informed by different philosophical concerns about the nature of the self, its autonomy and its relations with others, and suggest a different purpose for leadership than the transformation of others.

Domains of Leadership Activity

What my analysis has shown is that up until quite recently leadership knowledge demanded attention be given to an extensive range of issues across the public, private, earthly and spiritual domains of life. As we have seen, for centuries to speak of leadership automatically and necessarily meant to speak of morality; of political, social, economic and military policy and strategy choices; of power and its legitimate uses; of the leader's self, body and personal life; of the divine; and of leader development from the cradle to the grave. Since World War II, the dominant focus of scholarly effort has narrowed dramatically to a focus on the workplace, concerning itself with issues affecting the productivity, performance and human relations of the modern organization and equipping 'leaders' to address those matters. This focus broadened somewhat when 'new leadership' brought in issues of strategy, vision and change. However, placed in the broader historical context considered here, what we have today is still a remarkably narrow approach to understanding leadership. Consequently, while this current focus now seems quite natural, history shows that there are choices to be made in leadership theorizing as to the domains of life to which attention is directed.

What is evident is that current leadership theorizing, while in some respects grandiose in the claims it makes about the leader-manager's rights to work on the self of their follower-employee, is also very narrowly focused on just one aspect of life: that of the workplace. As noted in Chapter 1, the mainstream of leadership studies, as channelled through *The Leadership Quarterly*, only rarely moves beyond the workplace domain. However, consistent with my foregoing propositions about how we might take a different approach to theory building, exploring different domains of life constitutes another opportunity to re-shape leadership theory.

Leader Personal Attributes, Behaviours, Rights, Responsibilities and Roles

Turning now to the leader, they can be conceived, consistent with the dominant Western tradition, as possessing a fairly fixed, conscious unity of self. Alternatively, drawing on postmodernist thought, the self of the leader can be understood as being more fluid and contradictory, as continuously produced in relation to others and events and not in full awareness of all its motives. Varying degrees of agentic power can be assumed relative to external factors.

Leaders can be conceived of as possessing certain personal attributes, the source of which we may postulate as being from nature and/or nurture. Alternatively, leaders can be thought of as persons in positions of authority which require certain learned skills, as with behavioural theory, meaning that their personality is of no particular relevance to our understanding of leadership. We could adopt an admiring, sceptical or even hostile stance in conceiving of those who seek to lead others. As relational, process and distributed theories of leadership[15] are already doing, we could also de-emphasize the leader, treating leadership as a co-produced or shared phenomenon, not something vested in individuals. If we do wish to have 'leaders' as part of our understanding of leadership, then the rights, responsibilities and roles we grant to them can be defined according to the values we hold about such matters as individual freedom, collective responsibility, privacy and the legitimate scope of leader action.

Follower Personal Attributes, Behaviours, Rights, Responsibilities and Roles

To break with the problematic tradition of denigrating followers, a leadership theory could deploy a conception of the follower as simply a positional ranking within an organizational hierarchy, and make no further assumption as to the attributes of such persons. This in turn might imply that the focus of leadership theorizing should be on matters of strategy, structuring work or facilitating group processes rather than on fixing the self of the follower. A strong reliance by adults on another person for leadership could be treated as problematic, thereby pushing us toward the development of an approach to leadership entirely directed toward enhancing 'follower' autonomy and self-reliance. We could take the stance that 'followers' are not inferior to leaders in any way that actually matters to us, but are, rather, equal partners. This would have implications for theorizing issues such as decision-making rights and processes and setting boundary conditions for leader activity so as to safeguard the equality of the partnership. Followers could be conceived of as being the people whom leaders must serve, thereby focusing attention on identifying what issues concern them, what expectations they have, what it is they want, reversing the current assumption that the leader is the one who knows best. What is apparent from all this is that as soon as we change the assumption that there is something lacking in followers our whole current conception of leadership loses its plausibility.

The Leader–Follower Relationship

If we develop theories of leadership in which there are no persons defined as leaders and no persons defined as followers, then logically enough there is no leader–follower relationship to be theorized about or researched. There may be manager–subordinate relationships or peer relationships, but if leadership is conceived of as a process, if it is distributed amongst many players, if it is understood as something co-produced or emergent, then the leader–follower relationship could be rendered conceptually redundant. Alternatively, we could draw from Enlightenment thinking in particular and seek to develop boundary conditions for governing this relationship, aiming to overcome the risks of exploitation, domination or manipulation. Rather than conceiving of this relationship as comprising transactional and transformational components as 'new leadership' discourse does, a focus on duty or mutual responsibilities could also be developed.

What the foregoing analysis demonstrates is that these key components of leadership theory can be deployed in many different ways. Model 8.1 offers a visual metaphor for this notion of *inventing* leadership by drawing on these conceptual building blocks, components which could be arranged in varying ways to meet varying needs.

In what follows, I sketch out two possible theorizations of leadership, drawing on the conceptual componentry identified above, in order to demonstrate my approach to theory building.

Model 8.1   Building blocks for thinking differently about leadership

INVENTING LEADERSHIP: TWO MODELS TO DEMONSTRATE A NEW APPROACH TO THEORY BUILDING

The proposition is, then, that we could be endlessly creative in formulating theories of leadership designed to inform practice in specific contexts. Rather than the normal 'mass production' model of leadership
theorizing which offers context-free prescriptions, the idea here is about
formulating local responses that are tailor-made, hand-crafted, as it were,
to specified situations, needs and values. Leadership theorists could
become partners to practitioners in formulating such theories, rather than
'educating' practitioners to conform to models which claim universal
applicability but which are blind to the practitioner's context. My aim
here is not to argue the merit of the theories which I offer, but rather to
simply set these out as samples of how rich and diverse our theorizing of
leadership could become through adopting this approach to theory

development. (See Wilson and Proctor-Thomson[16] for another example which is concerned with how we could generate a creativity-friendly leadership theory.)

Leadership as Facilitation of Group Effectiveness

One form of leadership that we could seek to invent is to conceive of leadership entirely in processual terms. The context I am particularly interested in addressing here is the challenge of organizing a group of colleagues to achieve a common goal, a situation many of us routinely encounter in our work.

The critical assumptions here are as follows:

- that co-ordination of the efforts of people with different responsibilities, skills and perspectives does not happen spontaneously but, rather, demands attention and effort
- that there are multiple methods for co-ordinating a group to perform effectively
- that common interests and shared goals are not always the case within a group
- that conflict within a group is inevitable
- that the potential for rational, reasonable behaviour by all exists and can be strengthened
- that the risk exists for some people to sometimes engage in unreasonable behaviour.

Taking these factors into account, leadership-as-facilitation would entail activities focused on supporting a group to function effectively. The 'leadership approach' taken might be highly inclusive, participative and fluid or more structured and formal, depending on the nature of the group and its collective responsibilities and aims. Responsibility for this leadership/facilitation work could be allocated to one person, rotated within the membership of a group or even potentially shared among multiple members. Leadership-as-facilitation would not automatically entail decision-making responsibilities in respect of substantive matters. Such responsibilities could be defined according to the preferences of the group members involved.

Reconceptualizing leadership as fundamentally a facilitative function reorients attention away from the person of the leader. By removing an idealized and prescribed identity script from our conception of leadership, this approach opens up a space for all persons to consider their leadership contribution in terms of how they can support their colleagues to achieve shared goals. In this, the presumption of leader control and superiority over others embedded in previous models is also removed. There is also no follower position in this model: instead there are simply group members. The problem to which leadership is directed here is that of group co-ordination, something assumed as common to groups and requiring no assumption of follower inadequacy.

Theorizing about leadership as primarily a facilitative function would shift our focus to *process* and away from the attributes of the leader. A conception of leadership which focuses on its facilitative functions also offers a model in which the holding of a formal position becomes a secondary consideration, thus embedding a more egalitarian assumption into our understanding of leadership. However, calling this facilitative work 'leadership' risks dragging in these extant conceptualizations which were clearly intended to deal with different needs and priorities and reflect different values.

Developing this form of leadership as a model would entail fleshing out both conceptually and empirically the techniques and skills which are of particular relevance to different group dynamics or settings. Criteria for different approaches to allocating the leadership role and assessing the effects of these approaches could also be the subject of research and conceptual development.

Leadership for Workplace Democracy

As I highlighted earlier, modern discourses have adopted an approach to speaking the truth about leadership in which the substantive issues to which leaders attend is typically ignored. Specifically, moral, political, religious, economic and governmental issues have been treated as issues separate from modern theories of leadership, which have offered trait, behavioural, situational and transformative accounts of leadership. Reversing this discursive closure, I propose a theory of leadership focused on enhancing workplace democracy as one warranting attention. This approach overtly blends political theory with leadership theory and proposes a model of leadership intended to challenge the status quo.

In this model, workplace leaders, managers, would be elected by the workforce. Constitutional models and processes could be developed to ensure that owners, shareholders and customers also form part of the electoral system. However, the goal of any such approach would be to have leaders who are formally and directly accountable to those to whom they claim to offer leadership. A duty to serve those interests is, thus, prioritized. From understanding *their* expectations, leaders would adopt a course that would be subject to ongoing validation by those who elect the leader. Opinion polls or other forms of gathering feedback would be critical tools for assessing leader effectiveness. Ensuring the success of fora which enabled ongoing dialogue between leaders and followers about issues of strategy, policy and execution would be a critical focus for leader attention. Leader behaviours which demonstrate respect for the rights and perspectives of others would become of critical importance. Speaking up and participating in debate would become a key expectation of 'followers'.

Such an approach no doubt seems idealistic and even fanciful at present. In the face of the failure of the current mainstream of leadership scholarship to explore a purpose for leadership beyond the colonization of the worker's psyche, enacted in the name of enhanced organizational performance, no doubt this is so. However, we should not forget that Burns, the so-called founding father of 'new leadership', originally offered up a model in which leaders were expected to serve and were accountable to followers.[17] His focus was leadership that 'emerges from, and always returns to, the fundamental needs and wants, aspirations, and values of the followers'.[18] Burns explicitly assumed that 'followers have adequate knowledge of alternative leaders ... and the capacity to choose among those alternatives'.[19] It was only when Burns' original conception was 'captured' by psychologists interested in workplace performance that the democratic ideal he promoted got swept aside. Perhaps now is a good time to recapture this ideal and try to put it to work properly, for as Foucault would have it, what is the point of studying the past if not to change the present?[20]

CONCLUSION

This book seeks to rise to Foucault's challenge of 'thinking differently' in regards to leadership. Through my analysis of the form and formation of different leadership discourses, it has become apparent that the confidence we might expect to have in contemporary knowledge produced under the auspices of science is not warranted in respect of 'new leadership' thinking. Despite its proliferation and repeated endorsements, it is an account no more grounded in truth and reason than any of its predecessors. Like them, it is a well-intentioned, carefully considered inventive response to specific issues being deemed problematic, relying on troubling assumptions and giving rise to unintended but nonetheless concerning consequences. Through this analysis, however, certain conceptual componentry that we might deploy in theorizing leadership has become apparent. In this chapter I have put these to use, demonstrating how they offer a fertile basis for inventing new forms of leadership, hopefully with greater attentiveness to the assumptions we make and the potential consequences that might flow from claims to speak to the truth about leadership. When all is said and done, the very simple proposition arising here is that leadership is what we make it to be. We should, therefore, make it with care, learning from the past in order to help bring about a future we actually want. We ought, in other words, to start thinking differently about leadership.

NOTES

1. 2009, p. 423
2. See, for example, Bass, 1985a, Bass and Riggio, 2006; Kouzes and Posner, 2007
3. See, for example, Alvesson and Sveningsson, 2003a, 2003b, 2003c; Ford and Harding, 2007, 2011; Ford et al., 2008
4. See, for example, Knights and Morgan, 1992; Trethewey and Goodall Jnr, 2007; Western, 2007
5. 1985, p. 8
6. Foucault, 1977, p. 31
7. As reported by, for example, Alvesson and Sveningsson, 2003a, 2003b, 2003c
8. Parker, 2002
9. Parker, 2002
10. See also Alvesson and Sveningsson, 2003c; Calás and Smircich, 1991
11. Meindl et al., 1985
12. 1978, p. 159
13. 1977, pp. 305–6
14. 1977, p. 305
15. See, for example, Crevani, Lindgren and Packendorff, 2010; Gronn, 2002; Ospina and Uhl-Bien, 2012
16. 2014
17. 1978
18. 1978, p. 3
19. 1978, p. 3
20. 1977

Method notes

> [A]fter all, what I have held to, what I have tried to maintain for many years, is the effort to isolate some of the elements that might be useful for a history of truth. Not a history that would be concerned with what might be true in the field of learning, but an analysis of the 'games of truth', the games of truth and error through which being is historically constituted as experience; that is, as something that can and must be thought. (Foucault, 1985, pp. 6–7)

INTRODUCTION

These notes are intended to help readers unfamiliar with the work of Michel Foucault to understand the key methods of inquiry and Foucauldian concepts which inform my analysis. To familiarize the reader with Foucault's approach, I offer an introductory overview of his intellectual position and the nature of his work before explaining the specific methodological and conceptual apparatus he developed and which I use in this study.

SITUATING FOUCAULT

Veritable lakes of ink have been spilt assessing Michel Foucault's work: he emerged as and remains a controversial figure.[1] His work falls within the broad tradition of European critical thought, with Kant, Nietzsche and Heidegger all important influences on his thinking.[2] While he typically rejected the labels others applied to his work, substantively and stylistically his approach can nonetheless be characterized as postmodern in its orientation.[3] Foucault has been described as both philosophical historian and historical philosopher, labels indicative of the complexity, sophistication and unique nature of his work.[4] Rather than simply rehearse the many debates about his work here, in what follows I set forth my own interpretation based on my reading of his key works and those of key commentators.

In terms of basic assumptions, Foucault is a nominalist, meaning he treats ideas (knowledge) about the world as a construction or interpretation and not as a direct representation of what actually exists.[5] Further, while ideas may develop through empirical observation, Foucault argues that what gets noticed and how it is interpreted is very strongly influenced by social norms, beliefs and values.[6] He further contends that discourses can bring into existence social practices and ways of being which later appear to be entirely natural.[7] In this sense Foucault proposes that what we 'know' is never simply a reflection of what exists, but rather is shaped by social norms and that knowledge is thus active in constructing what exists, including ourselves.[8]

Foucault's attention is, therefore, not directed toward discovering what really exists, for he eschews great scepticism about the existence of objective truths outside the realm of the physical sciences.[9] Instead, Foucault's focus is on what people regard as the truth at different times, including our own, on how this came about and what its effects are. His emphasis on the contingent, constructed and constructive nature of knowledge, and his critique of existing social practices and ways of being, mean that his approach falls within the social constructionist paradigm, according to Hacking's definition.[10] By this definition, a strongly social constructionist perspective not only seeks to bring to light the contingent, social foundations of practices typically understood as being 'natural', it also seeks to challenge the hidden politics of those practices and to encourage change.[11]

Dean proposes that Foucault focused on issues in three broad domains: (1) reason, truth and knowledge; (2) power, domination and government; and (3) ethics, the self and freedom.[12] Gutting claims that Foucault's goal 'was always to suggest liberating alternatives to what seem to be inevitable conceptions and practices'.[13] This, he suggests, was achieved by way of 'histories of ideas, histories of concepts, histories of the present, and histories of experience'.[14] In their analysis of his later works, Dreyfus and Rabinow argue that Foucault provides a method 'which replaces ontology with a special kind of history that focuses on the cultural practices that have made us what we are'.[15] Prado, however, cautions us that such is the diversity and nature of Foucault's oeuvre that it 'resists holistic interpretation'.[16]

Foucault proposes three reasons for undertaking historical analysis. Firstly, because he contends that knowledge is not innocent and removed from power but is rather entwined with power, he argues that we should seek to examine 'knowledge' for its origins and foundations so that we can better understand the workings of power and its effects.[17] Secondly, Foucault proposes that we should study the past because it may be influencing what we know and do today in ways not readily apparent to us.[18] Finally, Foucault contends that we should study the past because doing so enhances our ability to think differently about the challenges we face today, through exposing us to different ideas and even modes of thinking.[19]

Turning to Foucault's major historical analyses, these provide a contingent account of developments in expert knowledge and expert-informed social practices.[20] The contextual factors that were held to be problematic, to which a given discourse emerged in response, are identified. Socially constructed and historically situated ways of thinking and acting, events, chance, power, networks of influence and strategies are placed centre stage, rather than a progressive and teleological account in which truth, knowledge and ever greater enlightenment constitute the driving force for social change.[21] Foucault once described the task he had set for himself as 'to trace the history of the games of truth and error'.[22] However, in doing so he also shows how things have been different in the past, how arbitrary social change can be, and, therefore, he opens up space in which we can think differently about the present and our future.[23] The aim, Foucault says, is 'to know how and to what extent it might be possible to think differently, instead of legitimating what is already known'.[24]

Foucault's most famous works comprise detailed studies of the form and formation of expert discourses on madness,[25] crime and punishment[26] and sexuality.[27] In each of these studies, he offered an analysis which dramatically de-familiarized conventional understandings of both the past and the present. In examining madness, he challenged the allegedly modern and scientific basis of psychiatry, linking it back to medieval practices and beliefs.[28] His analysis of developments in the punishment of criminals threw doubt on whether modern approaches are really a positive, 'humane' advancement on the medieval practice of torture.[29] His analysis of sexuality showed that the conventional understanding that sex was until recently a taboo subject was deeply problematic and that present day understandings are best understood as an adaption of medieval confessional practices.[30] In each case, he was, therefore, able to demonstrate the influence of ideas from the past on current thought and practice and thereby change how we understand both the past and the present. Moreover, in his analyses Foucault points to the potentially problematic consequences for human freedom of expert knowledge, thereby calling into doubt our assumption that modern thought and practice are superior to that of the past, grounded in rationality, science and enlightened ways of thinking.

Over the last decade, a series of Foucault's lectures not previously published in English has become available.[31] Some of these date back to lectures given by Foucault in the early 1970s,[32] while others cover the very last of his lectures prior to his death in 1984.[33] What these texts point to is Foucault's enduring interest in questions about how we come to be as we are, how forces beyond ourselves act upon us, how we can come to know the truth and how we create an ethical, meaningful life.[34]

A sustained critique of modern systems of governing society and of the power of expert knowledge and its effect on our freedom is also a key focus in these works.[35] However, while these lectures offer further insights into Foucault's thinking and points of clarification, they do not indicate any fundamental shift in the primary methods and key concepts which he had been developing over the course of his life and which I address shortly, referencing earlier works.

THE FOUCAULDIAN METHOD USED IN THIS STUDY: INTERPRETIVE ANALYTICS

Foucault developed a range of methodological approaches over the course of his life, as he sought to respond to criticisms made of his earlier works.[36] The particular Foucauldian method to be used in this study is Interpretive Analytics. This is not a term which Foucault himself used; rather it was developed by Dreyfus and Rabinow[37] who had extensive dialogue with Foucault about his work. Interpretive Analytics seeks to understand and explicate both the form and formation of a body of knowledge, and its associated social practices, by way of a series of historical case studies.[38] In this research, I wish to understand and explicate both the form and formation of our contemporary understanding of leadership by way of a series of historical case studies. The starting point of such an analysis is an account of the '*problematizations* through which being offers itself to be, necessarily, thought'.[39] Hence, in each case, I start by identifying some key matters deemed 'problematic' which, I argue, informed the emergence of a particular understanding of leadership at the time of examination.

Discontinuous Histories

Interpretive Analytics is the term Dreyfus and Rabinow[40] use to describe the methodological approach taken by Foucault in his extended exploration of the history of sexuality.[41] Foucault intended to undertake six distinct but related case studies of the history of sexuality,[42] however only three were completed at the time of his death. Prior to these works, Foucault's histories typically commenced at a certain event or point in time which he held to be of direct relevance to the current day.[43] His analysis then concerned developments from that point forwards through to the present time. This approach I term a continuous history. In contrast, his approach from the second volume in his extended exploration of the history of sexuality was to select several times (and spaces) chronologically (and geographically) separated from each other for examination as the component parts of a broader study.[44] This approach I term discontinuous histories, and it is one key aspect of the Interpretive Analytics approach that I employ.

The strategic rationale for such an approach is to facilitate our ability to think differently, something Foucault regards as important but extremely challenging to achieve.[45] By choosing to examine how a given topic had been understood in different epistemes, Foucault hoped he might find different ways of thinking about that topic which could assist in addressing our present day concerns.[46] Equally, we may find surprising commonalities, traces of that past which inform our present.

At the detailed level of analysis of each individual case study, Interpretive Analytics involves the combined use of the main methodological approaches which Foucault had utilized largely in isolation of each other in his earlier work, namely Archaeology and Genealogy. In what follows, I discuss the key features of each of these methods, before turning to their combined use.

Foucault's Archaeological Method

Foucault's Archaeology comprises two components. First, it analyzes what the experts of a given period claim to be 'the truth' on a particular topic, paying particular attention to the assumptions and effects of those claims.[47] Second, it postulates the underlying 'structure of thought', or episteme, which make it possible for those 'truths' to be considered intelligible and plausible at the time they arose, even if they later came to seem nonsensical.[48] Archaeology thus seeks to identify and analyze the form of a set of claims to know the truth, a form which has two levels, that of particular truths about a specific topic and that of the general truth, which underpins and governs all truths in a given period.

Interpretive analysis is needed to identify the features and form of an episteme, as it operates at the level of taken-for-granted assumptions and values and is rarely explicitly enunciated.[49] Epistemes can and do change over time; however, such changes are not assumed to be inherently progressive or teleological, but rather are examined for their specific assumptions and effects.[50] In both its components, Archaeology focuses on what was said and done, specifically what was said by experts and done under their guidance. These Foucault termed 'discursive practices' and they constitute the primary data for Archaeology.[51] It is through the examination of discursive practices that one can discern the form of the specific and general 'truth' then operant.

Archaeology 'examines the "moment", however temporally extended that moment might be'; it 'provides us with a snapshot, a slice through the discursive nexus'.[52] Archaeology can be understood as a bounded piece of historical analysis; bounded by the particular 'truth' topic on which it focuses and bounded temporally by the episteme it exposes and examines.[53] One may, of course, conduct multiple archaeologies within the scope of one project by examining multiple epistemes.

Through its analysis of both the specific features of a given episteme and the truth claims made about a particular topic, Archaeology provides an account which reveals how a particular notion of what is 'true' was (or is) possible. With Archaeology, Foucault sidesteps ontology:[54] the aim is not to discover what really exists and what is really true, rather it is to assess the effects of what people claim to be true on who we are and how we live. Archaeology thus produces an analytics of truth.[55] Archaeology helps us figure out 'what is the shape of this truth' and 'what makes this truth possible' by way of reference to the epistemic underpinnings which render such an account of the truth as viable to begin with. Such accounts can be deeply disturbing, as they make our truths appear much more fragile than we would normally believe them to be. Archaeological analysis can, therefore, make the strange seem sensible and, at the same time, it can make what we see as sensible seem strange. It constitutes a de-familiarizing approach to analysis.

Foucault is known to have argued that epistemes determine what can be known, that we are, in effect, prisoners of our own episteme.[56] This view is both bleak and impossible to prove or disprove. Moreover, it is arguably a view he moved away from as his thought developed.[57] However, irrespective of this there remains no necessity to adopt a deterministic view of the influence of epistemic conditions. Rather, one can hold to a softer view, that due to the specific form of a given episteme, it is an influence rather than a determinant of what can be known or, alternatively, that all epistemes are influential rather than deterministic. I adopt a non-deterministic view. Moreover, I limit my epistemic analysis by keeping it focused on the topic of my inquiry, discourse on leadership, rather than venturing to offer a broader social analysis, as was Foucault's aim. Foucault was no strict disciplinarian when it came to methodology, including those methods he himself developed.[58] Accordingly, I suggest that these adaptations do no mortal damage to the Archaeological method.

Archaeology, therefore, analyzes what a particular episteme held to be the truth about a specific issue. It offers, also, an exposition of the underpinning intellectual conditions which made that account viable. What it leaves open is the question of 'how did this come about'? Foucault's other main method that contributes to Interpretive Analytics, Genealogy, attends to this.

Foucault's Genealogical Method

Genealogy provides a method which attends to how ideas and social practices change, develop and come to be seen as correct and truthful.[59] It does this without privileging individual actors as the source of change and without assuming that social change follows some natural progression to a higher state of perfection.[60] Instead, Genealogy looks to the social context in which discourses develop, looking for connections between what was seen as problematic at a given point in time and how discourses which claim to speak the truth form in response to these perceived problems.[61] Genealogy involves examining the networks of relationships, strategies and tactics that have facilitated certain ideas and practices coming to the fore.[62] There is no assumption of necessity or a pre-determined outcome or direction in Genealogy; instead, chance, opportunism and the capacity to dominate and to resist are treated as potential sources of social change.[63]

Power is central to such an analysis.[64] Attention goes to how social practices act to shape who we are, and how power relations influence how people use and experience their selves and their bodies.[65] Whatever effects or ways of being are created, constrained or disciplined in some way in a given discourse, and whatever is held up in that discourse as laudable or abominable, are matters of particular interest in a Genealogical analysis. It examines both the effects of a given discourse on persons and interpersonal relationships and how this situation developed.[66] It, too, is a de-familiarizing approach.

A Genealogy is an analytic history which traces the formation of knowledge about a certain topic over a given period.[67] It foregrounds how ideas and practices that may over time have come to be accepted as true, or right, actually developed, and in so doing helps us realize that things could have developed differently. Genealogy has been criticized because its heavy emphasis on power as the source of both change and stability makes it seem as if we can never escape from its clutches.[68] However, one need not adopt a deterministic account of power in order to conduct a Genealogical analysis; one can instead treat power as influential but not determinative.[69]

Archaeology and Genealogy Combined

Genealogy on its own leaves unanswered the question of how one can free oneself from the power/knowledge effects of one's own episteme and its claims to know the truth.[70] This question remains even if one adopts a less deterministic view of power. By combining Genealogy with Archaeology, and by conducting multiple, discontinuous histories, a broader analysis is created. It becomes possible to identify change and continuity in both the form and formation of knowledge about a particular topic in different epistemes.[71]

By combining these methods and applying them to multiple cases, we can see, for each case, both the substantive form of knowledge on the topic being examined and the formative processes which led to its creation. We can then compare across the cases. Consequently, Genealogy can change our understanding of how past developments in discourse arose, and its effects, while Archaeology can change our understanding of what renders a given form of knowledge intelligible, and its effects. Deployed in combination, the insights then gained from such an analysis can, thus, facilitate our capacity to better understand the past and the present and to develop new ideas to address issues of present concern. I put Genealogy and Archaeology to work to produce results and effects of this nature.

Change and Continuity in Thought

A specific outcome of an Interpretive Analytics study is the production of one or more dispositives, an analytic summary charting key commonalities and differences across the epistemic cases studied.[72] A dispositif, which here takes the form of an analytic table, identifies the key elements of a particular discourse in a given episteme compared with its articulation in a different episteme so as to identify both change and continuity. It constitutes a specific means of de-familiarizing our understanding of both past and present. To explicate this concept, Table 9.1 provides an extract from one of the dispositives which I have developed from my research, the substance of which I explain in Chapter 7.

Table 9.1   Sample dispositif: the person of the leader in different epistemes

Managerial leadership (post-WWII)	16th-century Europe	Classical Greece
committed to organizational goals; discourse silent on other issues of lifestyle	combines majesty and prudent use of state funds so as to live in a manner consistent with their status and duties	has an ascetic lifestyle – is restrained in eating, sleeping and sexual urges in order to serve others
discourse is silent on issues of faith; leaders assumed and expected to act ethically	loves God; upholds Christian faith and morality	loves the gods; morally without fault

In summary, there are five key aspects to the Interpretive Analytics method. As noted earlier, the starting point of any analysis is the identification of the issues deemed problematic to which a given discourse arose as a response. Archaeology is used to examine the form of a body of knowledge about a particular topic and identify the underlying epistemic framework which renders such knowledge claims possible and intelligible. It focuses on discursive practices, attending to both the rules which govern their existence and the effects of the discourse. Genealogy is used to examine the processes of formation of that body of knowledge, looking at how it came into being and its effects. It focuses on the impact of discourses on who we are and how we live and, thus, a concern with power is infused throughout a Genealogical analysis. Discontinuous histories are used to examine a given topic in different epistemes from which, finally, a dispositif can be developed to reveal both change and continuity over time. Model 9.1 identifies the key questions which shape an Interpretive Analytics study.

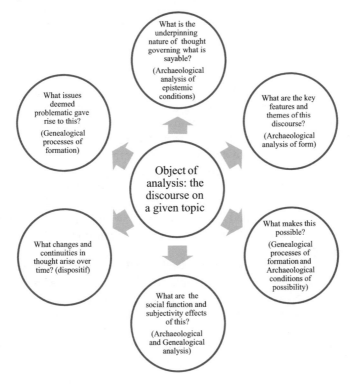

Model 9.1   Questions shaping an Interpretive Analytics study

Table 9.2 below explains the purpose of each component of an Interpretive Analytics study.

Table 9.2   Purpose of the components of an Interpretive Analytics study

Component	Purpose
Problems	Identify that which was deemed problematic to which a discourse emerged as a response
Archaeology	Describe the form of a discursive regime in a given period, its effects and its underlying epistemic conditions of possibility
Genealogy	Describe the formation of a discursive regime in a given period and its effects
Discontinuous histories (multiple cases)	Examine the same topic of interest in different epistemes
Dispositif	Identify change and continuity in how different epistemes have understood the same topic

FOUCAULT'S KEY CONCEPTS

In addition to his methods of inquiry, Foucault developed an extensive suite of concepts which constitute a further fundamental feature of his work and to which I now turn. Some of Foucault's concepts pertain to specific topics of inquiry. For example, his concept of 'scientia sexualis' denotes his assessment of the modern Western approach to sexuality.[73] Other concepts such as 'governmentality' explain a feature of modernity, a specific social system and historical period.[74] However, Foucault's key conceptual apparatus – *discourse*, *power*, *power/knowledge* and *subjectivity* – can be applied to potentially any topic and any historical context, and in what follows I explain these concepts and their application in my study.

For Foucault, social reality is continuously constructed through language, through our shared, and contested, interpretations of what exists, what is true and what is right.[75] However, *discourse*, arguably the most central of Foucault's concepts, comprises not only what is said and written.[76] It also includes social practices such as different ways of organizing time and space, of classifying and training persons, or of evaluating and ordering knowledge, which arise from our ideas about what is real, true and proper.[77] Consequently, both the ideational, or symbolic, and the material domains are captured by Foucault's understanding of discourse.[78] Moreover, this relationship is understood as being dynamically co-producing: language use shapes and informs the production of social practices, but so too can practices, when they are problematized, inform the development of new words and new language use. This, in turn, re-shapes our understanding of practices and helps to bring about changes in them.[79]

What Foucault proposes is that by analyzing discourses and their processes of development, we can come to understand how it is that we have been constructed into being who and what we are: from this analysis, we can begin to make choices for ourselves as to who and what we wish to become.[80] My study focuses on assessing scholarly discourse about leadership and tracking its development over time. Practitioner discourse is simply not accessible across all the epistemic cases, hence the focus solely on scholarly discourse. I look at who and what leaders and followers may become as a consequence of this scholarly discourse, as well as social practices associated with varying ideas about leadership for which documentary evidence is available.

Foucault conceives of *power* as being dispersed, potent and ever-present within the social system and as possessing both constructive and oppressive potential, depending on its specific deployment.[81] It is not expressed or possessed only via formal authority. Rather, power is a dynamic resource which permeates human interactions and relationships, informing the arrangement of social spaces, knowledge, bodies and selves. The use of power comprises both covert and overt acts: its exercise and effects can be harsh, visible and physical in orientation, or subtle, invisible and psychological.

For Foucault, power is a motive force in all social arrangements and developments.[82] By subjecting these arrangements and developments to an analysis which focuses on the operation and effects of power, Foucault argues that new insights can be obtained which call into question the veracity of conventional historical analyses that commonly assume social change to be inherently progressive. Foucault argues that we should focus on power not only because it is influential but because an analysis of this nature has the potential to disrupt existing power relations, possibly helping to trigger a shift to something more constructive.[83] Consequently, through deploying the Foucauldian conception of power in my analysis of scholarly discourse on leadership, I seek not only to expose its workings in the formation of claims to speak the truth about leadership but also to render the status quo more open to challenge.

Because leadership, especially when it is tagged to positions of authority, fairly self-evidently involves power, I do not see that any contribution is made by labouring this basic point in my analysis. Rather, what I focus on is how power is given specific, often subtle and multi-faceted expression in the form of different discourses, in the subjectivity effects produced by these discourses, in the social function they play and how its workings shape the process of formation and conditions of possibility informing different discourses. Consequently, the reader should understand that at every point when I am addressing these matters, which comprise the key elements of my analysis, what I am constantly pointing to is the detailed workings of power.

Closely connected to his concept of power is Foucault's concept of *power/knowledge*. With this concept, he proposes a co-producing relationship between power and knowledge, which strips knowledge of any claims to be 'pure' or apolitical.[84] Instead, power/knowledge draws our attention to the influence of power in both the development and deployment of knowledge, and the influence of knowledge in informing how, where, by whom, for what purpose and to what effect power is deployed. In my analysis, I examine how power has shaped the development and deployment of leadership knowledge and how leadership knowledge produces effects in terms of power. Here, the same proviso applies as that which concerns my use of power: the reader should understand that in dissecting leadership discourses my analysis proceeds on the basis of treating these as power/knowledge phenomena and that in tracing out their form and formation I am thereby constantly pointing to the workings of power/knowledge.

The end focus of Foucault's examinations of discourse, power and power/knowledge is to both identify and challenge the effects of these on human *subjectivity* and, thus, ultimately human society. For him, we are each the historically situated product of these factors acting on, enabling and constraining our sense of self, producing the limits of what is doable, sayable and thinkable.[85] Foucault claims that we are subjected to these forces, that we are subjectified by knowledge which has disciplinary effects, and yet simultaneously our very existence as the subjects we specifically are arises from these forces. To analyze discourse, knowledge and power/knowledge is thus to analyze the production of our very selves in order that we may critically reflect on that and potentially change it. In my study, I examine the production of the leader and follower as subjects about whom leadership scholars claim to speak the truth. I examine the effects of these discursively produced subject positions in order to challenge them.

A major benefit of the use of these concepts is that they enable analysis to occur at two levels. The first of these is what might be termed the 'micro' level, where the focus is on examining the effects a specific discourse, a specific configuration of power and power/knowledge, has at the level of individual subjectivity and of relationships between persons.

The second is what might be called the 'macro' level, where the focus is on examining the broader social function of a given discourse. In my analysis I examine both these micro and macro levels.

PRIMARY AND SECONDARY SOURCES

The nature of this study means that what might count in other studies as literature counts here as data. Selection of my primary sources was guided by the research questions and theoretical framework in determining what constituted relevant 'data'.[86] Given my focus on analyzing the dominant scholarly views of leadership, texts which credible sources confirmed as influential in their time and/or texts which offered an account of leadership which I assessed as being largely consistent with other contemporaneous texts were treated as primary sources of data. These texts were identified by various means including tracing references, using existing accounts of developments in leadership thought and drawing on my own prior knowledge of medieval and classical political thought. History texts were used both to identify possible primary sources as well as for the accounts they offered of the broader social context in which the primary sources were written. My sampling procedures were intended to achieve confidence[87] that the primary texts I compiled for analysis were sufficient to grasp in detail the dominant view of the time. The range of secondary sources I used to inform my data selection added independent support for those choices. Only texts available in English were used, although in some cases these were not in modern English. Where I sourced a recent edition of an older text for analysis, my chapter endnotes also note the original date of publication where this is known.

The norms of knowledge production and validation in modern social science favour journal publications over books. Books, however, are often used by scholars as their preferred means of advancing theoretical and conceptual positions ahead of empirical studies, and to reach a broader practitioner audience than can be achieved by journal publication alone. Taking these factors into account means that in Chapters 5 and 6, journal articles as well as books constitute both primary and secondary sources.

For the period prior to World War II, no consensus seems to exist as to what constitutes the most important studies, although Carlyle[88] and Galton[89] are clearly acknowledged as key influences.[90] I have therefore examined a range of texts which are illustrative of the use of trait theory which dominated at that time.[91] For the period since World War II, there is a solid degree of consensus amongst influential commentators as to the key theories, theorists and significant texts.[92] For Chapters 5 and 6, I also examined texts which offered broad reviews of the literature or which offer compilations of what was, at the time of publication, seen to be the most important issues and ideas then demanding scholarly attention.[93] Other primary texts on which this material is based are as cited throughout those chapters.

NOTES

1. Prado, 2009
2. Dreyfus and Rabinow, 1983; Miller, 1993; Wicks, 2003
3. Dean, 1994; Flynn, 1994; Wicks, 2003
4. Dean, 1994; Guttung, 1994; Wicks, 2003
5. Flynn, 1994; Blaikie, 2000
6. See, for example, 1977, 1978, 1980
7. See, for example, 1977, 1978, 1985
8. See, for example, 1980, 1986, 2005
9. See, for example, 1970, 1972
10. 1999
11. Hacking, 1999
12. 1994
13. 1994, p. 3
14. 1994, p. 7
15. 1983, p. 122
16. 2009, p. 3
17. See, for example, 1977, 1978, 1980
18. See, for example, 1985, 1986
19. See, for example, 1977, 1978, 1985
20. See 1970, 1977, 1978, 1985, 1986, 1989
21. Burrell, 1988; Dean, 1994; Prado, 2009
22. 1985, p. 8
23. Alvesson and Deetz, 2000; Alvesson and Skoldberg, 2000; Cummings and Bridgman, 2011
24. 1985, p. 9
25. 1989
26. 1977
27. 1978, 1985, 1986
28. Foucault, 1989
29. Foucault, 1977
30. Foucault, 1978, 1985, 1986
31. See Foucault, 2003, 2004, 2008a, 2008b, 2009, 2010, 2011
32. See, for example, 2008b
33. See, for example, 2011
34. See, for example, 2004, 2008a, 2011
35. See, for example, 2008b, 2009, 2010
36. Cummings and Bridgman, 2011; Dean, 1994; Dreyfus and Rabinow, 1983
37. 1983
38. Cummings and Bridgman, 2011; Dreyfus and Rabinow, 1983
39. Foucault, 1985, p. 11, italics in original
40. 1983
41. See Foucault, 1978, 1985, 1986

42. 1985
43. See, for example, 1977, 1989
44. See Foucault, 1978, 1985, 1986
45. 1985
46. 1985, 1986
47. See, for example, Foucault, 1970, 1972
48. Foucault, 1972, p. 191
49. Foucault, 1970, 1972
50. Cummings and Bridgman, 2011; Guttung, 1994; Kendall and Wickham, 1999
51. 1970, 1972
52. Bevis, Cohen and Kendall, 1993, p. 194
53. Burrell, 1988; Dreyfus and Rabinow, 1983; Kendall and Wickham, 1999
54. Cummings and Bridgman, 2011; Dean, 1994; Dreyfus and Rabinow, 1983
55. Dreyfus and Rabinow, 1983
56. See, for example, 1970, 1972
57. See, for example, Foucault, 1985, 2008, 2011
58. Guttung, 1994; Prado, 2009
59. See, for example, Foucault, 1977, 1978
60. Foucault, 1978
61. Cummings and Bridgman, 2011; Dean, 1994; Dreyfus and Rabinow, 1983
62. See, for example, Foucault, 1977, 1978
63. See, for example, Foucault, 1977, 1978
64. Alvesson and Deetz, 2000; Alvesson and Skoldberg, 2000; Dreyfus and Rabinow, 1983
65. See, for example, Foucault, 1977, 1978, 1980
66. See, for example, Foucault, 1977, 1978
67. Cummings and Bridgman, 2011; Dean, 1994; Dreyfus and Rabinow, 1983
68. See, for example, Hoy, 1986; Wicks, 2003
69. Wicks, 2003
70. Cummings and Bridgman, 2011; Hoy, 1986
71. Cummings and Bridgman, 2011; Foucault, 1985, 2011
72. Cummings and Bridgman, 2011; Dreyfus and Rabinow, 1983
73. 1978, p. 55
74. Foucault, 1977, 2003, 2011
75. See, for example, Foucault, 1970, 1972
76. See, for example, Foucault, 1970, 1977, 1978
77. See, for example, Foucault, 1977, 1985, 1986
78. Alvesson and Deetz, 2000; Dean, 1994; Kendall and Wickham, 1999
79. Foucault, 1978, 1985, 1986
80. See, for example, Foucault, 1985
81. See, in particular, Foucault, 1980, 1985
82. See, for example, Foucault, 1978, 1980, 1985
83. 1977, 1985, 1980
84. See, in particular, Foucault, 1980
85. See, for example, 1977, 1978, 1985
86. O'Leary, 2004
87. O'Leary, 2004; Silverman, 2005
88. 1993
89. 1970
90. See, for example, Clarke, 1916; Hook, 1945; Smith and Krueger, 1933; Taussig and Joslyn, 1932
91. See Bogardus, 1934; Carlyle, 1993; Clarke, 1916; Ellis, 1904; Galton, 1970; Lehman, 1966; Sorokin, 1925; Taussig and Joslyn, 1932; Thorndike, 1936; Visher, 1925
92. See, for example, Bass, 2008; Bedeian and Wren, 2001; Jackson and Parry, 2011
93. See Alvesson, 1996; Alvesson and Spicer, 2011a; Alvesson and Sveningsson, 2012; Antonakis, Cianciolo and Sternberg, 2004; Avery, 2004; Avolio et al., 2009; Barrow, 1977;

Bass, 2008; Bolden et al., 2011; Bowers and Seashore, 1966; Browne and Cohn, 1958; Bryman, 2004; Bryman et al., 2011; Caza and Jackson, 2011; Collinson, 2011; Day and Zaccaro, 2007; Fleishman and Hunt, 1973; Gardner et al., 2005, 2010, 2011; Goethals, Sorenson and Burns, 2004; Goethals and Sorenson, 2006; Greenwood, 1996; Grint, 1997; Gronn, 2003; Hollander, 1979; House, 1996; House and Aditya, 1997; Hunt and Dodge, 2000; Hunt and Larson, 1977; Jackson and Parry, 2011; Kelly, 2008; Korman, 1966; Lowe and Gardner, 2000; McCall and Lombardo, 1978; Northouse, 2004; Parry and Bryman, 2006; Rost, 1993; Schriesheim and Bird, 1979; Schriesheim and Kerr, 1977; Shartle, 1979; Sinclair, 2007; Smith and Krueger, 1933; Stogdill, 1948, 1977; Trethewey and Goodall Jnr, 2007; Western, 2007; Wren, 2005; Yukl, 1989, 1999, 2012.

References

Ackerman, R.W. (1975). *The social challenge to business*. Cambridge, MA: Harvard University Press.

Adair, J. (2002). *Effective strategic leadership*. London: Macmillan.

Adorno, T.W., Frenkel-Brunswik, E., Levinson, D.J., and Sanford, R.N. (1950). *The authoritarian personality*. New York: Harper.

Allen, J.W. (1951). *A history of political thought in the sixteenth century*. London: Methuen and Co.

Alvesson, M. (1996). Leadership studies: From procedure and abstraction to reflexivity and situation. *The Leadership Quarterly*, 7(4), 455–485.

Alvesson, M. (2001). Knowledge work: Ambiguity, image and identity. *Human Relations*, 54(7), 863–886.

Alvesson, M. (2003). Beyond neopositivists, romantics, and localists: A reflexive approach to interviews in organizational research. *Academy of Management Review*, 28(1), 13–33.

Alvesson, M., and Deetz, S.A. (2000). *Doing critical management research*. London: Sage.

Alvesson, M., and Kärreman, D. (2000). Varieties of discourse: On the study of organizations through discourse analysis. *Human Relations*, 53(9), 1125–1149.

Alvesson, M., and Kärreman, D. (2015). Intellectual failure and ideological success in organization studies: The case of transformational leadership. *Journal of Management Inquiry*. Online.

Alvesson, M., and Skoldberg, K. (2000). *Reflexive methodology: New vistas for qualitative research*. London: Sage.

Alvesson, M., and Spicer, A. (2011a). Theories of leadership. In M. Alvesson and A. Spicer (eds), *Metaphors we lead by: Understanding leadership in the real world* (pp. 1–30). London: Routledge.

Alvesson, M., and Spicer, A. (eds). (2011b). *Metaphors we lead by: Understanding leadership in the real world*. London: Routledge.

Alvesson, M., and Spicer, A. (2012). Critical leadership studies: The case for critical performativity. *Human Relations*, 65(3), 367–390.

Alvesson, M., and Sveningsson, S. (2003a). The great disappearing act: Difficulties in doing 'leadership'. *The Leadership Quarterly*, 14(3), 359–381.

Alvesson, M., and Sveningsson, S. (2003b). Good visions, bad micro-management and ugly ambiguity: Contradictions of (non-)leadership in a knowledge intensive organization. *Organization Studies, 24*(6), 961–988.

Alvesson, M., and Sveningsson, S. (2003c). Managers doing leadership: The extra-ordinarization of the mundane. *Human Relations, 56*(12), 1435–1459.

Alvesson, M., and Sveningsson, S. (2012). Un- and re-packing leadership: Context, relations, constructions, and politics. In M. Uhl-Bien and S. Ospina (eds), *Advancing relational leadership research: A dialogue among perspectives* (pp. 203–226). Charlotte, NC: Information Age Publishing.

Alvesson, M., and Willmott, H. (1992). On the idea of emancipation in management and organization studies. *Academy of Management Review, 17*(3), 432–464.

Annas, J. (2009). *Plato: A brief insight.* New York: Sterling.

Annas, J., and Waterfield, R. (1995). Introduction. In Plato, *Statesman.* Cambridge: Cambridge University Press.

Antonakis, J., Cianciolo, A.T., and Sternberg, R.J. (eds). (2004). *The nature of leadership.* Thousand Oaks, CA: Sage.

Antonakis, J., Schriesheim, C.A., Donovan, J.A., Gopalakrishna-Pillai, K., Pellegrini, E.K., and Rossomme, J.L. (2004). Methods for studying leadership. In J. Antonakis, A.T. Cianciolo and R.J. Sternberg (eds), *The nature of leadership* (pp. 48–70). Thousand Oaks, CA: Sage.

Aristotle. (2009). *The politics and the constitution of Athens.* S. Everson (ed.). Cambridge: Cambridge University Press.

Atwater, L., Mumford, M.D., Schriesheim, C.A., and Yammarino, F.J. (2014). Retraction of leadership articles: Causes and prevention. *The Leadership Quarterly, 25,* 1174–1180.

Austin, J.L. (1962). *How to do things with words.* Oxford: Oxford University Press.

Avery, G.C. (2004). *Understanding leadership: Paradigms and cases.* London: Sage.

Avolio, B.J., Bass, B.M., and Jung, D.I. (1999). Re-examining the components of transformational and transactional leadership using the multifactor leadership questionnaire. *Journal of Occupational and Organizational Psychology, 72,* 441–462.

Avolio, B.J., and Gardner, W.L. (2005). Authentic leadership development: Getting to the root of positive forms of leadership. *The Leadership Quarterly, 16*(3), 315–338.

Avolio, B.J., Gardner, W.L., Walumbwa, F.O., Luthans, F., and May, D.R. (2004). Unlocking the mask: A look at the process by which authentic leaders impact follower attitudes and behaviours. *The Leadership Quarterly*, *15*(6), 801–823.

Avolio, B.J., and Luthans, F. (2003). Authentic leadership: A positive developmental approach. In K.S. Cameron, J.E. Dutton and R.E. Quinn (eds), *Positive organizational scholarship* (pp. 241–261). San Francisco: Berrett-Koehler.

Avolio, B.J., Walumbwa, F.O., and Weber, T.J. (2009). Leadership: Current theories, research, and future directions. *Annual Review of Psychology*, *60*, 421–449.

Bannister, R.C. (1979). *Social Darwinism: Science and myth in Anglo-American social thought*. Philadelphia: Temple University Press.

Barber, J.D. (1992). *The presidential character: Predicting performance in the White House*. Englewood Cliffs, NJ: Prentice-Hall.

Barker, R.A. (2001). The nature of leadership. *Human Relations*, *54*(4), 469–494.

Barrow, J.C. (1977). The variables of leadership: A review and conceptual framework. *The Academy of Management Review*, *2*(2), 231–251.

Bass, B.M. (1985a). *Leadership and performance beyond expectations*. New York: Free Press.

Bass, B.M. (1985b). Leadership: Good, better, best. *Organizational Dynamics*, *13*(3), 26–40.

Bass, B.M. (1999). Two decades of research and development in transformational leadership. *European Journal of Work and Organizational Psychology*, *8*(1), 9–32.

Bass, B.M. (2008). *The Bass handbook of leadership: Theory, research and managerial applications* (4th edn). New York: Free Press.

Bass, B.M., and Riggio, R. (2006). *Transformational leadership*. Hillsdale, NJ: Lawrence Erlbaum.

Bass, B.M., and Steidlmeier, P. (1999). Ethics, character, and authentic transformational leadership behaviour. *The Leadership Quarterly*, *10*(2), 181–217.

Bedeian, A.G., and Wren, D.A. (2001). Most influential management books of the 20th century. *Organizational Dynamics*, *29*(3), 221–225.

Bejczy, I.P., and Nederman, C.J. (2007). Introduction. In I.P. Bejczy and C.J. Nederman (eds), *Princely virtues in the middle ages: 1200–1500* (pp. 1–8). Turnhout, Belgium: Brepols.

Benjamin, L.T. (2007). *A brief history of modern psychology*. Malden, MA: Blackwell.

Bennis, W.G. (1959). Leadership theory and administrative behavior: The problem of authority. *Administrative Science Quarterly*, *4*(3), 259–301.

Bennis, W.G., and Nanus, B. (1985). *Leaders: The strategies for taking charge*. New York: Harper and Row.

Bevis, P., Cohen, M., and Kendall, G. (1993). Archaeologizing genealogy: Michel Foucault and the economy of austerity. In M. Gane and T.
Johnson (eds), *Foucault's new domains* (pp. 193–215). London: Routledge.

Black, J. (2001). *Warfare, crisis and absolutism.* Oxford: Oxford University Press.

Blaikie, N. (2000). *Designing social research: The logic of anticipation.*
Cambridge: Polity Press.

Blaikie, N. (2007). *Approaches to social enquiry: Advancing knowledge*
(2nd edn). Cambridge: Polity Press.

Blake, R., and Mouton, J.S. (1964). *The managerial grid: Key orien-
tations for achieving production through people.* Houston, TX: Gulf
Publishing.

Bodin, J. (2009 [1576]). *On sovereignty: Six books of the Commonwealth.* Santiago: Seven Treasures Publications.

Bogardus, E.S. (1934). *Leaders and leadership.* New York: D. Appleton-
Century Company.

Bolden, R., Hawkins, B., Gosling, J., and Taylor, S. (2011). *Exploring
leadership: Individual, organizational and societal perspectives.*
Oxford: Oxford University Press.

Bowers, D.G., and Seashore, S.E. (1966). Predicting organizational
effectiveness with a four-factor theory of leadership. *Administrative
Science Quarterly, 11*(2), 238–263.

Branson, R. (2002). *Sir Richard Branson: The autobiography.* London:
Longman.

Braun, S., Peus, C., Weisweiler, S., and Frey, D. (2013). Transformational
leadership, job satisfaction, and team performance: A multilevel media-
tion model of trust. *The Leadership Quarterly, 24*(1), 270–283.

Briggs, R. (2001). Embattled faiths: Religion and natural philosophy in
the seventeenth century. In E. Cameron (ed.), *Early modern Europe:
An Oxford history* (pp. 171–205). Oxford: Oxford University Press.

Brock, M. (1973). *The Great Reform Act.* London: Hutchinson.

Browne, C.G., and Cohn, T.S. (eds). (1958). *The study of leadership.*
Danville, IL: Interstate Printers and Publishers.

Bruce, K. (2006). Henry S. Dennison, Elton Mayo, and human relations
historiography. *Management and Organizational History, 1*(2), 177–
199.

Bruce, K., and Nyland, C. (2011). Elton Mayo and the deification of
human relations. *Organization Studies, 32*(3), 383–405.

Brush, S.G. (1988). *The history of modern science: A guide to the second
scientific revolution, 1800–1950.* Ames, IA: Iowa State University
Press.

Bryman, A. (1986). *Leadership and organizations*. London: Routledge and Kegan Paul.

Bryman, A. (2004). Qualitative research on leadership: A critical but appreciative review. *The Leadership Quarterly*, *15*(6), 729–769.

Bryman, A., Collinson, D., Grint, K., Jackson, B., and Uhl-Bien, M. (eds). (2011). *The Sage handbook of leadership*. London: Sage.

Burns, J.M. (1978). *Leadership*. New York: Harper and Row.

Burrell, G. (1988). Modernism, postmodernism and organizational analysis 2: The contribution of Michel Foucault. *Organization Studies*, *9*(2), 221–235.

Calás, M.B. (1993). Deconstructing charismatic leadership: Re-reading Weber from the darker side. *The Leadership Quarterly*, *4*(3–4), 305–328.

Calás, M.B., and Smircich, L. (1991). Voicing seduction to silence leadership. *Organization Studies*, *12*(4), 567–602.

Calder, B.J. (1977). An attribution theory of behaviour. In B.M. Staw and G.R. Salancik (eds), *New directions in organizational behaviour* (pp. 179–204). Chicago: St Clair.

Calvin, J. (2010 [1559]). *On civil government*. H. Hopfl (ed.). Cambridge: Cambridge University Press.

Cameron, E. (2001). The power of the word: Renaissance and reformation. In E. Cameron (ed.), *Early modern Europe: An Oxford history* (pp. 63–101). Oxford: Oxford University Press.

Capitman, W.G. (1973). *Panic in the boardroom: New social realities shake old corporate structures*. Garden City, NY: Anchor Press and Doubleday.

Carlyle, T. (1993 [1840]). *On heroes, hero-worship, and the heroic in history*. M. Goldberg (ed.). London: Chapman and Hall.

Carroll, B., Levy, L., and Richmond, D. (2008). Leadership as practice: Challenging the competency paradigm. *Leadership*, *4*(4), 363–379.

Cartledge, P. (1993). *The Greeks: A portrait of self and others*. Oxford: Oxford University Press.

Cartledge, P. (2006). Introduction. In Xenophon, *Hiero the Tyrant and other treatises* (pp. vii–xx). London: Penguin.

Cattell, J.M. (1906). *American men of science*. New York: The Science Press.

Caza, A., and Jackson, B. (2011). Authentic leadership. In A. Bryman, D. Collinson, K. Grint, B. Jackson and M. Uhl-Bien (eds), *The Sage handbook of leadership* (pp. 350–362). London: Sage.

Ciulla, J.B. (ed.). (2004). *Ethics, the heart of leadership* (2nd edn). Westport, CT: Praeger.

Clarke, E.L. (1916). *American men of letters: Their nature and nurture*. New York: Columbia University.

Collins, J. (2001). *Good to great: Why some companies make the leap . . . and others don't*. New York: Harper Business.

Collinson, D. (2005). Dialectics of leadership. *Human Relations*, *58*(11), 1419–1442.

Collinson, D. (2006). Rethinking followership: A post-structuralist analysis of follower identities. *The Leadership Quarterly*, *17*: 179–189.

Collinson, D. (2011). Critical leadership studies. In A. Bryman, D. Collinson, K. Grint, B. Jackson and M. Uhl-Bien (eds), *The Sage handbook of leadership* (pp. 181–194). London: Sage.

Collinson, D. (2012). Prozac leadership and the limits of positive thinking. *Leadership*, *8*(2), 87–107.

Conger, J. (1989). *The charismatic leader: Behind the mystique of exceptional leadership*. San Francisco, CA: Jossey-Bass.

Conger, J. (1999). Charismatic and transformational leadership in organizations: An insider's perspective on these developing streams of research. *The Leadership Quarterly*, *10*(2), 145–179.

Conger, J., and Kanungo, R. (1987). Toward a behavioral theory of charismatic leadership in organizational settings. *Academy of Management Review*, *12*, 637–647.

Cornuelle, R. (1975). *De-managing America: The final revolution*. New York: Random House.

Cowan, R.S. (1970). Introduction to the second edition. In F. Galton (ed.), *English men of science: Their nature and nurture*. London: Frank Cass and Co.

Craigie, J. (1950). Introduction. In *Basilicon Doron of King James VI*. Edinburgh: William Blackwell and Sons.

Cresswell, J.W. (2003). *Research design: Qualitative, quantitative and mixed methods approaches* (2nd edn). Thousand Oaks, CA: Sage.

Crevani, L., Lindgren, M., and Packendorff, J. (2010). Leadership, not leaders: On the study of leadership as practices and interactions. *Scandinavian Journal of Management*, *26*(1), 77–87.

Cummings, S., and Bridgman, T. (2011). The relevant past: Why the history of management should be critical for our future. *Academy of Management Learning and Education*, *10*(1), 77–93.

Daunton, M.J. (2011). *Progress and poverty: An economic and social history of Britain 1700–1850*. Oxford: Oxford University Press.

Day, D.V., and Zaccaro, S.J. (2007). Leadership: A critical historical analysis of the influence of leader traits. In L.L. Koppes (ed.), *Historical perspectives in industrial and organizational psychology* (pp. 383–405). Mahwah, NJ: Lawrence Erlbaum Associates.

De Neve, J.-E., Mikhaylov, S., Dawes, C.T., Christakis, N.A., and Fowler, J.H. (2013). Born to lead? A twin design and genetic association study of leadership role occupancy. *The Leadership Quarterly*, *24*(1), 45–60.

Dean, M. (1994). *Critical and effective histories: Foucault's methods and historical sociology*. London: Routledge.

Drath, W.H., McCauley, C.D., Palus, C.J., Van Velsor, E., O'Connor, P.M.G., and McGuire, J.B. (2008). Direction, alignment, commitment: Toward a more integrative ontology of leadership. *The Leadership Quarterly*, *19*(6), 635–653.

Dreyfus, H.L., and Rabinow, P. (1983). *Michel Foucault: Beyond structuralism and hermeneutics* (2nd edn). Chicago: University of Chicago Press.

Eisenstadt, S.N., and Weber, M. (1968). *Max Weber on charisma and institution building: Selected papers*. Chicago: University of Chicago Press.

Ellis, H. (1904). *A study of British genius*. London: Hurst and Blackett.

Erasmus. (2010 [1516]). *The education of a Christian prince*. L. Jardine (ed.). Cambridge: Cambridge University Press.

Everson, S. (ed.). (2009). Introduction. In *Aristotle: The politics and the constitution of Athens* (pp. ix–xxxvii). Cambridge: Cambridge University Press.

Fairhurst, G. (2007). *Discursive leadership: In conversation with leadership psychology*. Thousand Oaks, CA: Sage.

Fairhurst, G. (2009). Considering context in discursive leadership research. *Human Relations*, *62*, 1607–1633.

Fairhurst, G., and Grant, D. (2010). The social construction of leadership: A sailing guide. *Management Communication Quarterly*, *24*(2), 171–210.

Fairhurst, G.T., and Putnam, L. (2004). Organizations as discursive constructions. *Communication Theory*, *14*, 5–26.

Fayol, H. (1930). *Industrial and general administration*. J.A. Coubrough (trans.). London: Pitman.

Feldman, D., and Lawrence, J. (eds). (2011). *Structures and transformations in modern British history*. Cambridge: Cambridge University Press.

Ferber, M. (2010). *Romanticism: A very short introduction*. Oxford: Oxford University Press.

Fiedler, F.E. (1967). *A theory of leadership effectiveness*. New York: McGraw-Hill.

Filmer, R. (2004 [1648]). *Patriarcha and other writings*. J.P. Somerville (ed.). Cambridge: Cambridge University Press.

Finley, M.I. (1963). *The ancient Greeks*. London: Chatto and Windus.

Fleishman, E.A. (1953a). The description of supervisory behaviour. *Journal of Applied Psychology, 37*(1), 1–6.

Fleishman, E.A. (1953b). The measurement of leadership attitudes in industry. *Journal of Applied Psychology, 37*(3), 153–158.

Fleishman, E.A. (1973). Twenty years of consideration and structure. In E.A. Fleishman and J.G. Hunt (eds), *Current developments in the study of leadership* (pp. 1–38). Carbondale, IL: Southern Illinois University Press.

Fleishman, E.A., and Hunt, J.G. (1973). *Current developments in the study of leadership*. Carbondale, IL: Southern Illinois University Press.

Fletcher, J.K. (2004). The paradox of postheroic leadership: An essay on gender, power, and transformational change. *The Leadership Quarterly, 15*(5), 647–661.

Flynn, T. (1994). Foucault's mapping of history. In G. Guttung (ed.), *The Cambridge companion to Foucault* (pp. 29–48). Cambridge: Cambridge University Press.

Ford, J., and Harding, N. (2007). Move over management: We are all leaders now. *Management Learning, 38*(5), 475–493.

Ford, J., and Harding, N. (2011). The impossibility of the 'true self' of authentic leadership. *Leadership, 7*(4), 463–479.

Ford, J., Harding, N., and Learmonth, M. (2008). *Leadership as identity: Constructions and deconstructions*. Basingstoke: Palgrave Macmillan.

Foucault, M. (1970). *The order of things: An archaeology of the human sciences*. London: Tavistock.

Foucault, M. (1972). *The archaeology of knowledge and the discourse on language*. A.M. Sheridan Smith (trans.). London: Tavistock.

Foucault, M. (1977). *Discipline and punish: The birth of the prison*. A. Sheridan (trans.). London: Penguin.

Foucault, M. (1978). *The history of sexuality, Vol. 1: The will to knowledge*. R. Hurley (trans.). New York: Random House.

Foucault, M. (1980). *Power/Knowledge: Selected interviews and other writings by Michel Foucault 1972–1977*. C. Gordon (ed.). New York: Pantheon.

Foucault, M. (1985). *The history of sexuality, Vol. 2: The use of pleasure*. R. Hurley (trans.). New York: Vintage.

Foucault, M. (1986). *The history of sexuality, Vol. 3: The care of the self*. R. Hurley (trans.). New York: Pantheon.

Foucault, M. (1989). *The birth of the clinic*. A.M. Sheridan Smith (trans.). London: Routledge.

Foucault, M. (2003). *Society must be defended: Lectures at the College de France, 1975–76*. D. Macey (trans.). London: Penguin.

Foucault, M. (2004). *The hermeneutics of the subject: Lectures at the College de France, 1981–1982*. F. Gros (ed.) and G. Burchell (trans.). New York: Picador.

Foucault, M. (2008a). *The birth of biopolitics: Lectures at the College de France, 1978–1979*. M. Senellart (ed.) and G. Burchell (trans.). Basingstoke: Palgrave Macmillan.

Foucault, M. (2008b). *Psychiatric power: Lectures at the College de France, 1973*. A. Davidson (ed.) and G. Burchell (trans.). New York: Picador.

Foucault, M. (2009). *Security, territory, population: Lectures at the College de France, 1975–1976*. M. Senellart (ed.) and G. Burchell (trans.). Basingstoke: Palgrave Macmillan.

Foucault, M. (2010). *The government of self and others: Lectures at the College de France, 1982–1983*. F. Gros (ed.) and G. Burchell (trans.). Basingstoke: Palgrave Macmillan.

Foucault, M. (2011). *The courage of truth (The government of self and others II): Lectures at the College de France, 1983–1984*. F. Gros (ed.) and G. Burchell (trans.). Basingstoke: Palgrave Macmillan.

Gabriel, Y. (1997). Meeting God: When organizational members come face to face with the supreme leader. *Human Relations, 50*(4), 315–342.

Galton, F. (1892 [1869]). *Hereditary genius: An inquiry into its law and consequences* (2nd edn). London: Macmillan.

Galton, F. (1970 [1875]). *English men of science: Their nature and nurture*. London: Frank Cass and Co.

Gardner, W.L., Avolio, B.J., and Walumbwa, F.O. (2005). Authentic leadership development: Emergent themes and future directions. In W.L. Gardner, B.J. Avolio and F.O. Walumbwa (eds), *Authentic leadership theory and practice: Origins, effects and development* (pp. 387–406). London: Elsevier.

Gardner, W.L., Cogliser, C.C., Davis, K.M., and Dickens, M.P. (2011). Authentic leadership: A review of the literature and research agenda. *The Leadership Quarterly, 22*(6), 1120–145.

Gardner, W.L., Lowe, K.B., Mossa, T.W., Mahoney, K.T., and Coglisera, C. (2010). Scholarly leadership of the study of leadership: A review of *The Leadership Quarterly's* second decade, 2000–2009. *The Leadership Quarterly, 21*(6), 922–958.

Gemmill, G., and Oakley, J. (1992). Leadership: An alienating social myth? *Human Relations, 45*(2), 113–129.

George, B. (2003). *Authentic leadership: Rediscovering the secrets to creating lasting value*. San Francisco: Jossey-Bass.

Gilbert, A.H. (1938). *Machiavelli's Prince and its forerunners: The Prince as a typical book de regimine principum.* Durham, NC: Duke University Press.

Gillham, N.W. (2001). *A life of Sir Francis Galton: From African exploration to the birth of eugenics.* Oxford: Oxford University Press.

Gitlin, T. (1993). *The sixties: Years of hope, days of rage.* New York: Bantam.

Godin, B. (2007). From eugenics to scientometrics: Galton, Cattell, and Men of Science. *Social Studies of Science, 37*(5), 691–728.

Goethals, G.R., Sorenson, G.J., and Burns, J.M. (eds). (2004). *The encyclopaedia of leadership.* Thousand Oaks, CA: Sage.

Goethals, G.R., and Sorenson, G.L.J. (eds). (2006). *The quest for a general theory of leadership.* Cheltenham, UK and Northampton, MA, USA: Edward Elgar Publishing.

Goldberg, M. (1993 [1840]). Introduction. In T. Carlyle, *On heroes, hero worship and the heroic in history* (pp. xxi–lxxx). London: Chapman and Hall.

Goleman, D., Boyatzis, R., and McKee, A. (2002). *The new leaders: Transforming the art of leadership into the science of results.* London: Little, Brown Book Group.

Goodin, R.E., and Klingeman, H.-D. (1996). *A new handbook of political science.* Oxford: Oxford University Press.

Gowin, E.B. (1915). *The executive and his control of men: A study in personal efficiency.* New York: Macmillan.

Gowin, E.B. (1918). *The selection and training of the business executive.* New York: Macmillan.

Gowin, E.B. (1919). *Developing executive ability.* New York: The Ronald Press Company.

Grant, M. (1991). *A short history of classical civilization.* London: Weidenfeld and Nicolson.

Gray, V.J. (ed.). (2007). *Xenophon on government.* Cambridge: Cambridge University Press.

Greenwood, R.G. (1996). Leadership theory: A historical look at its evolution. *Journal of Leadership and Organizational Studies, 3*(1), 3–16.

Grierson, H.J.C. (1977 [1933]). Carlyle and Hitler. *Essays and addresses.* Philadelphia: West.

Grint, K. (ed.). (1997). *Leadership: Classical, contemporary and critical approaches.* Oxford: Oxford University Press.

Grint, K. (2000). *The arts of leadership.* Oxford: Oxford University Press.

Grint, K. (2005a). Problems, problems, problems: The social construction of 'leadership'. *Human Relations, 58*(11), 1467–1494.

Grint, K. (2005b). *Leadership: Limits and possibilities*. Houndmills: Palgrave Macmillan.

Gronn, P. (2002). Distributed leadership as a unit of analysis. *The Leadership Quarterly*, *13*(4), 423–451.

Gronn, P. (2003). Leadership: Who needs it? *School Leadership and Management*, *23*(3), 267–290.

Grugulis, I., Bozkurt, O., and Clegg, J. (2010). *No place to hide? The realities of leadership in UK supermarkets* (SCOPE Research Paper No. 91) (pp. 1–20). Cardiff: Economic and Social Research Council Centre on Skills, Knowledge and Organisational Performance.

Gunn, S. (2001). War, religion, and the state. In E. Cameron (ed.), *Early modern Europe: An Oxford history* (pp. 102–133). Oxford: Oxford University Press.

Guthey, E., Clark, T., and Jackson, B. (2009). *Demystifying business celebrity*. London: Routledge.

Guttung, G. (1994). Michel Foucault: A user's manual. In G. Guttung (ed.), *The Cambridge companion to Foucault* (pp. 1–28). Cambridge: Cambridge University Press.

Hacking, I. (1999). *The social construction of what?* Cambridge, MA: Harvard University Press.

Hall, S. (2005). *Peace and freedom: The civil rights and anti-war movements in the 1960s*. Philadephia: University of Pennsylvania Press.

Hampson, N. (2001). The Enlightenment. In E. Cameron (ed.), *Early modern Europe: An Oxford history* (pp. 265–297). Oxford: Oxford University Press.

Hanisch, C. (1970). The personal is political. *Notes from the second year: Women's liberation.* Available at: http://carolhanisch.org/CHwritings/PIP.html (retrieved 20/02/2013).

Hargrove, E.C. (2004). History, political science and the study of leadership. *Polity*, *36*(4), 579–593.

Harvey, M. (2006). Leadership and the human condition. In G.R. Goethals and G.L.J. Sorenson (eds), *The quest for a general theory of leadership* (pp. 39–45). Cheltenham, UK and Northampton, MA, USA: Edward Elgar Publishing.

Hasian Jnr, M.A. (1996). *The rhetoric of eugenics in Anglo-American thought*. Athens, GA: University of Georgia Press.

Heath, J.F. (1975). *Decade of disillusionment: The Kennedy–Johnson years*. Bloomington: Indiana University Press.

Heifetz, R.A. (1994). *Leadership without easy answers*. Cambridge, MA: Harvard University Press.

Hendry, C.E. (1944). Foreword. *Journal of Educational Sociology*, *17*(7), 385.

Herodotus. (1998). *The histories.* C. Dewald (ed.). Oxford: Oxford University Press.

Hersey, P., and Blanchard, K.H. (1974). So you want to know your leadership style? *Training and Development Journal, 28*(2), 22–37.

Hobbes, T. (1996 [1651]). *Leviathan.* R. Tuck (ed.). Cambridge: Cambridge University Press.

Hodgson, G. (2005). *America in our time: From World War II to Nixon – what happened and why.* Princeton, NJ: Princeton University Press.

Hollander, E.P. (1979). The impact of Ralph M. Stogdill and the Ohio State leadership studies on a transactional approach to leadership. *Journal of Management, 5*(2), 157–165.

Hook, S. (1945). *The hero in history: A study in limitation and possibility.* London: Secker and Warburg.

Hopfl, H. (2010). Introduction. In M. Luther and J. Calvin (eds), *Luther and Calvin on secular authority* (pp. vii–xxvii). Cambridge: Cambridge University Press.

Hosking, D.M. (2007) Not leaders, not followers: A postmodern discourse of leadership processes. In B. Shamir, R. Pillai, M.C. Bligh and M. Uhl-Bien (eds), *Follower-centred perspectives on leadership* (pp. 243–264). Greenwich, CT: Information Age Publishing.

House, R.J. (1971). A path–goal theory of leader effectiveness. *Administrative Science Quarterly, 16*(3), 321–339.

House, R.J. (1977). A 1976 theory of charismatic leadership. In J.G. Hunt and L.L. Larson (eds), *Leadership: The cutting edge* (pp. 189–207). Carbondale, IL: Southern Illinois University Press.

House, R.J. (1996). Path–goal theory of leadership: Lessons, legacy, and a reformulated theory. *The Leadership Quarterly, 7*(3), 323–352.

House, R.J., and Aditya, R.M. (1997). The social scientific study of leadership: Quo Vadis? *Journal of Management, 23*(3), 409–473.

Hoy, D.C. (1986). Power, repression, progress: Foucault, Lukes and the Frankfurt School. In D.C. Hoy (ed.), *Foucault: A critical reader* (pp. 123–148). Oxford: Blackwell.

Hu, J., Wang, Z., Liden, R.C., and Sun, J. (2012). The influence of leader core self-evaluation on follower reports of transformational leadership. *The Leadership Quarterly, 23*(5), 860–868.

Huczynski, A., and Buchanan, D. (2006). *Organizational behaviour.* New York: Prentice-Hall.

Hunt, J.G. (1999). Transformational/charismatic leadership's transformation of the field: An historical essay. *The Leadership Quarterly, 10*(2), 129–144.

Hunt, J.G., and Dodge, G.E. (2000). Leadership déjà vu all over again. *The Leadership Quarterly, 11*(4), 435–458.

Hunt, J.G., and Larson, L.L. (1977). *Leadership: The cutting edge.* Carbondale, IL: Southern Illinois University Press.

Hunter, S.T., Bedell-Avers, K.E., and Mumford, M.D. (2007). The typical leadership study: Assumptions, implications, and potential remedies. *The Leadership Quarterly, 18*(5), 435–446.

Irwin, T. (1989). *Classical thought: A history of Western philosophy.* Oxford: Oxford University Press.

Jackson, B., and Parry, K. (2011). *A very short, fairly interesting and reasonably cheap book about studying leadership* (2nd edn). London: Sage.

Jacques, R. (1996). *Manufacturing the employee: Management knowledge from the 19th to 21st centuries.* London: Sage.

James VI. (1950 [1599]). *Basilicon Doron.* Edinburgh: William Blackwell and Sons.

Jardine, L. (2010). Introduction. In Erasmus, *The education of a Christian prince* (pp. vi–xxiv). Cambridge: Cambridge University Press.

Jennings, E.E. (1960). *An anatomy of leadership: Princes, heroes, and supermen.* New York: Harper and Bros.

Kant, L., Skogstad, A., Torsheim, T., and Einarsen, S. (2013). Beware the angry leader: Trait anger and trait anxiety as predictors of petty tyranny. *The Leadership Quarterly, 24*(1), 106–124.

Katz, D., and Kahn, R. (1966). *The social psychology of organizations.* New York: Wiley.

Katz, D., Maccoby, N., and Morse, N.C. (1950). *Productivity, supervision, and morale in an office situation.* Ann Arbor, MI: Institute for Social Research, University of Michigan.

Kellerman, B. (2004). *Bad leadership: What it is, how it happens, why it matters.* Boston: Harvard Business School Press.

Kellerman, B. (2012). *The end of leadership.* New York: Harper Business.

Kelly, S. (2008). Leadership: A categorical mistake? *Human Relations, 61*(6), 763–782.

Kempster, S., Jackson, B., and Conroy, M. (2011). Leadership as purpose: Exploring the role of purpose in leadership practice. *Leadership, 7*(3), 317–334.

Kendall, G., and Wickham, G. (1999). *Using Foucault's methods.* London: Sage.

Kerr, S., and Jermier, J.M. (1978). Substitutes for leadership: Their meaning and measurement. *Organizational Behavior and Human Performance, 22*(3), 375–403.

Kets de Vries, M. (2003). *Leaders, fools and impostors: Essays on the psychology of leadership.* Lincoln, NE: iUniverse Inc.

Kets de Vries, M. (2006). *The leader on the couch*. Chichester: Jossey-Bass.

Knights, D., and Morgan, G. (1992). Leadership and corporate strategy: Toward a critical analysis. *The Leadership Quarterly, 3*(3), 171–190.

Korman, A.K. (1966). 'Consideration', 'initiating structure' and organizational criteria: A review. *Personnel Psychology, 19*(4), 349–361.

Kotter, J.P. (1988). *The leadership factor*. New York: Free Press.

Kotter, J.P. (1996). *Leading change*. Boston, MA: Harvard Business School Press.

Kouzes, J.M., and Posner, B.Z. (2007). *The leadership challenge* (4th edn). San Francisco, CA: Jossey-Bass.

Kuhn, T.S. (1996). *The structure of scientific revolutions* (3rd edn). Chicago: University of Chicago Press.

Kuvaas, B., Buch, R., Dysvik, A., and Haerem, T. (2012). Economic and social leader–member exchange relationships and follower performance. *The Leadership Quarterly, 23*(5), 756–765.

Ladkin, D. (2010). *Rethinking leadership: A new look at old leadership questions*. Cheltenham, UK and Northampton, MA, USA: Edward Elgar Publishing.

Lane, M. (2001). *Plato's progeny: How Plato and Socrates still captivate the modern mind*. London: Duckworth.

Lane, M. (2007). Introduction. In Plato, *The Republic* (pp. xi–xl). London: Penguin Books.

Laslett, P. (2010). Introduction. In J. Locke, *Two treatises of government* (pp. 3–133). Cambridge: Cambridge University Press.

Lehman, B.H. (1966 [1928]). *Carlyle's theory of the hero: Its sources, development, history, and influence on Carlyle's work*. New York: AMS Press.

Lewin, K. (1944). A research approach to leadership problems. *Journal of Educational Sociology, 17*(7), 392–398.

Lewin, K., Lippitt, R., and White, R.K. (1939). Patterns of aggressive behavior in experimentally created 'social climates'. *The Journal of Social Psychology, 10*(2), 269–299.

Likert, R. (1961). *New patterns of management*. New York: McGraw-Hill.

Likert, R. (1967). *The human organization: Its management and value*. New York: McGraw-Hill.

Lipsius, J. (2004 [1589]). *Politica: Six books of politics or political instruction*. J. Waszink (ed.). Assen, the Netherlands: Royal Van Gorcum.

Locke, J. (2010 [1690]). *Two treatises of government*. P. Laslett (ed.). Cambridge: Cambridge University Press.

Lombardo, M.M., and McCall, M.W. (1978). Leadership. In M.W. McCall and M.M. Lombardo (eds), *Leadership: Where else can we go?* (pp. 1–11). Durham, NC: Duke University Press.

Lowe, K.B., and Gardner, W.L. (2000). Ten years of *The Leadership Quarterly*: Contributions and challenges for the future. *The Leadership Quarterly*, *11*(4), 459–514.

Luthans, F., and Avolio, B.J. (2003). Authentic leadership: A positive developmental approach. In K.S. Cameron, J.E. Dutton and R.E. Quinn (eds), *Positive organizational scholarship: Foundations for a new discipline* (pp. 241–258). San Francisco: Berrett-Koehler.

Luther, M. (2010 [1523]). *On secular authority*. H. Hopfl (ed.). Cambridge: Cambridge University Press.

Machiavelli, N. (2005 [ca. 1516]). *The Prince*. W.J. Connell (ed.). Boston: Bedford/St Martins.

Magaziner, I.C., and Reich, R.B. (1982). *Minding America's business: The decline and rise of the American economy*. New York: Harcourt Brace Jovanovich.

Mayo, E. (1945). *The social problems of an industrial civilization*. Boston: Harvard University Press.

Mayo, E. (1946 [1933]). *The human problems of an industrial civilization* (2nd edn). Boston: Harvard University Press.

McCall, M.W., and Lombardo, M.M. (eds). (1978). *Leadership: Where else can we go?* Durham, NC: Duke University Press.

McNeill, W.H., and Sedlar, J.W. (eds). (1969). *The Classical Mediterranean world*. New York: Oxford University Press.

Meindl, J.R., and Ehrlich, S.B. (1987). The romance of leadership and the evaluation of organizational performance. *Academy of Management Journal*, *30*(1), 91–109.

Meindl, J.R., Ehrlich, S.B., and Dukerich, J.M. (1985). The romance of leadership. *Administrative Science Quarterly*, *30*(1), 78–102.

Melcher, A.J. (1977). Leadership models and research approaches. In J.G. Hunt and L.L. Larson (eds), *Leadership: The cutting edge* (pp. 94–108). Carbondale, IL: Southern Illinois University Press.

Melina, L.R., Burgess, G.J., Falkman, L.L., and Marturano, A. (eds). (2013). *The embodiment of leadership*. San Francisco, CA: Jossey-Bass.

Mill, J.S. (1989 [1851]). *'On Liberty' and other writings*. Cambridge: Cambridge University Press.

Miller, J. (1983). *The glorious revolution*. London: Longman.

Miller, J. (1993). *The passion of Michel Foucault*. New York: Simon and Schuster.

Miner, J.B. (1975). The uncertain future of the leadership concept: An overview. In J.G. Hunt and L.L. Larson (eds), *Leadership frontiers* (pp. 197–208). Kent, OH: Kent State University Press.

More, C. (2000). *Understanding the industrial revolution.* London: Routledge.

Morris, I., and Powell, B.P. (2006). *The Greeks: History, culture and society.* Upper Saddle River, NJ: Pearson Prentice Hall.

Morris, R.T., and Seeman, M. (1950). The problem of leadership: An interdisciplinary approach. *American Journal of Sociology*, *56*(2), 149–155.

Morrow, J. (2005). *History of Western political thought: A thematic introduction* (2nd edn). Basingstoke: Palgrave.

Nicholson, H., and Carroll, B. (2013). Identity undoing and power relations in leadership development. *Human Relations*, *66*(9), 1225–1248.

Northouse, P.G. (2004). *Leadership: Theory and practice* (3rd edn). Thousand Oaks, CA: Sage.

O'Leary, Z. (2004). *The essential guide to doing research.* London: Sage.

Olechnowicz, A. (ed.). (2007). *The monarchy and the British nation, 1780 to the present.* Cambridge: Cambridge University Press.

Osborn, R.N., Hunt, J.G., and Jauch, L.R. (2002). Toward a contextual theory of leadership. *The Leadership Quarterly*, *13*(6), 797.

Ospina, S., and Sorenson G.J. (2007). A constructionist lens on leadership: Charting new territory. In G.R. Goethals and G.J. Sorenson (eds), *The quest for a general theory of leadership* (pp. 188–204). Cheltenham, UK and Northampton, MA, USA: Edward Elgar Publishing.

Ospina, S., and Uhl-Bien, M. (2012). Exploring the competing bases for legitimacy in contemporary leadership studies. In M. Uhl-Bien and S. Ospina (eds), *Advancing relational leadership research: A dialogue among perspectives* (pp. 1–42). Charlotte, NC: Information Age Publishing.

Parker, M. (2002). *Against management: Organization in the age of managerialism.* Oxford: Polity.

Parry, K.W., and Bryman, A. (2006). Leadership in organizations. In S.R. Clegg, C. Hardy, T.B. Lawrence and W.R. Nord (eds), *The Sage handbook of organization studies* (2nd edn) (pp. 447–468). London: Sage.

Peters, T., and Austin, N. (1985). *A passion for excellence: The leadership difference.* New York: HarperCollins.

Peters, T., and Waterman, R.H. (1982). *In search of excellence: Lessons from America's best-run companies.* Sydney: Harper and Row.

Pfeffer, J. (1977). The ambiguity of leadership. *The Academy of Management Review*, *2*(1), 104–112.

Piccolo, R.F., Bono, J.E., Heinitz, K., Rowold, J., Duehr, E., and Judge, T.A. (2012). The relative impact of complementary leader behaviors: Which matter most? *The Leadership Quarterly*, *23*(3), 567–581.

Plato. (1995). *Statesman*. J. Annas and R. Waterfield (eds). Cambridge: Cambridge University Press.

Plato. (2007). *The Republic*. M. Lane (ed.) (2nd edn). London: Penguin Books.

Porter, L.W., and McLaughlin, G.B. (2006). Leadership and the organizational context: Like the weather? *The Leadership Quarterly*, *17*(6), 559–576.

Prado, C.G. (ed.). (2009). *Foucault's legacy*. London: Continuum International.

Quatro, S.A., and Sims, R.R. (eds). (2008). *Executive ethics: Ethical dilemmas and challenges for the C-suite*. Charlotte, NC: Information Age Publishing.

Reed, M. (2006). Organizational theorizing: A historically contested terrain. In S.R. Clegg, C. Hardy, T.B. Lawrence, and W.R. Nord (eds), *The Sage handbook of organization studies* (2nd edn, pp. 19–54). London: Sage.

Riggio, R., Chaleff, I., and Lipman-Blumen, J. (2008). *The art of followership: How great followers create great leaders and organizations*. San Francisco: Jossey-Bass.

Roos, J. (1972). American political life in the 60s: Change, recurrence and revolution. In R. Weber (ed.), *America in change: Reflections on the 60s and 70s*. Notre Dame, IN: University of Notre Dame Press.

Roskin, M.G., Cord, R.L., Medeiros, J.A., and Jones, W.S. (2000). *Political science: An introduction* (7th edn). Upper Saddle River, NJ: Prentice-Hall.

Rost, J.C. (1993). *Leadership for the twenty-first century*. Westport, CT: Praeger.

Russell, B. (1984). *A history of Western philosophy*. London: Unwin Hyman.

Salancik, G.R., and Pfeffer, J. (1977). Constraints on administrator discretion: The limited influence of mayors on city budgets. *Urban Affairs Quarterly*, *12*, 475–498.

Sandberg, J., and Alvesson, M. (2010). Ways of constructing research questions: Gap-spotting or problematization? *Organization*, *18*(1), 23–44.

Schriesheim, C.A., and Bird, B.J. (1979). Contributions of the Ohio State studies to the field of leadership. *Journal of Management*, *5*(2), 135–145.

Schriesheim, C.A., and Kerr, S. (1977). Theories and measures of leadership: A critical appraisal of current and future directions. In J.G.

Hunt and L.L. Larson (eds), *Leadership: The cutting edge* (pp. 9–44). Carbondale, IL: Southern Illinois University Press.

Schruijer, S.G.L., and Vansina, L.S. (2002). Leader, leadership and leading: From individual characteristics to relating in context. *Journal of Organizational Behavior*, *23*(7), 869–874.

Shamir, B. (2007) From passive recipients to active co-producers: Followers' roles in the leadership process. In B. Shamir, R. Pillai, M.C. Bligh and M. Uhl-Bien (eds), *Follower-centred perspectives on leadership* (pp. ix–xxxix). Greenwich, CT: Information Age Publishing.

Shamir, B., and Howell, J.M. (1999). Organizational and contextual influences on the emergence and effectiveness of charismatic leadership. *The Leadership Quarterly*, *10*(2), 257–283.

Shartle, C.L. (1979). Early years of the Ohio State University leadership studies. *Journal of Management*, *5*(2), 127–134.

Silverman, D. (2005). *Doing qualitative research: A practical handbook* (2nd edn). London: Sage.

Sinclair, A. (1998). *Doing leadership differently: Gender, power and sexuality in a changing business culture.* Carlton South, VIC: Melbourne University Press.

Sinclair, A. (2007). *Leadership for the disillusioned: Moving beyond myths and heroes to leading that liberates.* Crows Nest, NSW: Allen and Unwin.

Sinclair, A. (2009). Seducing leadership: Stories of leadership development. *Gender, Work and Organization*, *16*(2), 266–284.

Skinner, Q. (2002). *Visions of Politics, Vol. 2: Renaissance virtues.* Cambridge: Cambridge University Press.

Smircich, L., and Morgan, G. (1982). Leadership: The management of meaning. *The Journal of Applied Behavioural Science*, *18*(3), 257–273.

Smith, H.L., and Krueger, L.M. (1933). A brief summary of the literature on leadership. *Bulletin of the School of Education, Indiana University*, *9*(4), 3–80.

Somerville, J.P. (2004). Introduction. In R. Filmer (ed.), *Patriarcha and other writings* (pp. ix–xxiv). Cambridge: Cambridge University Press.

Sorokin, P. (1925). American millionaires and multi-millionaires: A comparative statistical study. *Journal of Social Forces*, *3*(4), 627–640.

Stogdill, R. (1948). Personal factors associated with leadership: A survey of the literature. *Journal of Psychology*, *25*, 35–71.

Stogdill, R. (1974). *Handbook of leadership: A survey of theory and research.* New York: Free Press.

Stogdill, R. (1977). *Leadership abstracts and bibliography 1904–1974.* Columbus, OH: Ohio State University.

Strack, G.A. (2007). Piety, wisdom and temperance in 15th C Germany: A comparison of vernacular and Latin mirrors for princes. In I.P.

Bejczy and C.J. Nederman (eds), *Princely virtues in the middle ages: 1200–1500* (pp. 259–280). Turnhout, Belgium: Brepols.

Sutherland, N., Land, C., and Böhm, S. (2014). Anti-leaders(hip) in social movement organizations: The case of autonomous grassroots groups. *Organization, 21,* 759–781.

Tannenbaum, R., and Schmidt, W.H. (1958). How to choose a leadership pattern. *Harvard Business Review, 36*(2), 95–101.

Tarnas, R. (1991). *The passion of the Western mind: Understanding the ideas that have shaped our world.* New York: Ballantine Books.

Taussig, F.W., and Joslyn, C.S. (1932). *American business leaders: A study in social origins and social stratification.* New York: Macmillan.

Taylor, F.S. (1919). *The principles of scientific management.* New York: Harper and Bros.

Thorndike, E.L. (1936). The relation between intellect and morality in rulers. *American Journal of Sociology, 42*(3), 321–334.

Thucydides. (2006). *The history of the Peloponnesian War.* R. Crawley and D. Lateiner (trans.). New York: Barnes and Noble.

Tooley, M.J. (2009). Introduction. In J. Bodin (ed.), *On sovereignty: Six books of the Commonwealth* (pp. 9–42). Santiago: Seven Treasures Publications.

Tourish, D. (2014). Leadership, more or less? A processual, communication perspective on the role of agency in leadership theory. *Leadership, 10,* 79–98.

Tourish, D., Craig, R., and Amernic, J. (2010). Transformational leadership education and agency perspectives in business school pedagogy: A marriage of inconvenience? *British Journal of Management, 21,* 540–559.

Trethewey, A., and Goodall Jnr, H.L. (2007). Leadership reconsidered as historical subject: Sketches from the Cold War to Post-9/11. *Leadership, 3*(4), 457–477.

Uhl-Bien, M., and Ospina, S. (eds). (2012). *Advancing relational leadership research: A dialogue among perspectives.* Charlotte, NC: Information Age Publishing.

Uhl-Bien, M., and Pillai, R. (2007). The romance of leadership and the social construction of followership. In B. Shamir, R. Pillai, M.C. Bligh and M. Uhl-Bien (eds), *Follower-centred perspectives on leadership* (pp. 187–210). Greenwich, CT: Information Age Publishing.

Uhl-Bien, M., Russ, M., and McKelvey, B. (2007). Complexity leadership theory: Shifting leadership from the industrial age to the knowledge era. *The Leadership Quarterly, 18,* 298.

Van Knippenberg, D., and Sitkin, S.B. (2013). A critical assessment of charismatic–transformational leadership research: Back to the drawing board? *The Academy of Management Annals, 7*(1), 1–60.

Vernant, J.-P. (1995). Introduction. In J.-P. Vernant (ed.) and C. Lambert and T.L. Fagan (trans.), *The Greeks* (pp. 1–22). Chicago: University of Chicago Press.

Vernant, J.-P. (2006). *Myth and thought among the Greeks.* J. Lloyd and J. Fort (trans.). New York: Zone Books.

Verway, M. (2007). Princely virtues or virtues for princes: William Peraldus and his *de eruditione principus*. In I.P. Bejczy and C.J. Nederman (eds), *Princely virtues in the middle ages: 1200–1500* (pp. 51–72). Turnhout, Belguim: Brepols.

Visher, S.S. (1925). A study of the type of the place of birth and of the occupation of fathers of subjects of sketches in 'Who's Who in America'. *American Journal of Sociology*, *30*(5), 551–557.

Vroom, V.H., and Yetton, P.W. (1973). *Leadership and decision-making.* Pittsburgh: University of Pittsburgh Press.

Walumbwa, F.O., Avolio, B.J., Gardner, W.L., Wernsig, T.S., and Peterson, S.J. (2008). Authentic leadership: Development and validation of a theory-based measure. *Journal of Management*, *34*, 89–126.

Wang, X.-H., and Howell, J.M. (2012). A multilevel study of transformational leadership, identification, and follower outcomes. *The Leadership Quarterly*, *23*(5), 775–790.

Waszink, J. (2004). Introduction. In J. Lipsius (ed.), *Politica: Six books of politics or political instruction* (pp. 3–202). Assen, the Netherlands: Royal Van Gorcum.

Welch, J., and Byrne, J.A. (2001). *Jack: What I've learned leading a great company and great people.* London: Headline.

Western, S. (2007). *Leadership: A critical text.* London: Sage.

Whyte, W.H. (1963 [1956]). *The organization man.* Harmondsworth: Penguin.

Wicks, R. (2003). *Modern French philosophy: From existentialism to postmodernism.* Oxford: Oneworld.

Wilson, S. (2013a). Situated knowledge: A Foucauldian reading of ancient and modern classics of leadership thought. *Leadership*, *9*(1), 43–61.

Wilson, S. (2013b). The authentic leader reconsidered: Integrating the marvellous, mundane and mendacious. In D. Ladkin and C. Spiller (eds), *Authentic leadership: Clashes, convergences and coalescences* (pp. 55–64). Cheltenham, UK and Northampton, MA, USA: Edward Elgar Publishing.

Wilson, S., and Proctor-Thomson, S. (2014). Unleashed? Developing creativity-friendly leadership theory. In C. Bilton and S. Cummings (eds), *Handbook of creativity and management* (pp. 211–229). Cheltenham, UK and Northampton, MA, USA: Edward Elgar Publishing.

Wodak, R., Kwon, W., and Clarke, I. (2011). 'Getting people on board': Discursive leadership for consensus building in team meetings. *Discourse and Society*, *22*, 592–644.

Wolff, J. (2006). *An introduction to political philosophy*. Oxford: Oxford University Press.

Wolkowitz, C. (2006). *Bodies at work*. London: Sage.

Wren, D.A. (2005). *The history of management thought* (5th edn). Hoboken, NJ: Wiley.

Xenophon. (1997). *Memorabilia, oeconomicus, symposium, apology*. E.C. Marchant and O.J. Todd (trans.). Cambridge, MA: Harvard University Press.

Xenophon. (2006). *Hiero the Tyrant and other treatises*. P. Cartledge (ed.). London: Penguin.

Yukl, G. (1989). Managerial leadership: A review of theory and research. *Journal of Management*, *15*(2), 251–289.

Yukl, G. (1999). An evaluation of conceptual weaknesses in transformational and charismatic leadership theories. *The Leadership Quarterly*, *10*(2), 285–305.

Yukl, G. (2012). Effective leadership behavior: What we know and what questions need more attention. *The Academy of Management Perspectives*, *26*(4), 66–85.

Zaleznik, A. (1977). Managers and leaders: Are they different? *Harvard Business Review*, *55*(5), 67–80.

Zhang, A.Y., Tsui, A.S., and Wang, D.X. (2011). Leadership behaviors and group creativity in Chinese organizations: The role of group processes. *The Leadership Quarterly*, *22*(5), 851–862.

Zhu, W., Avolio, B.J., Riggio, R., and Sosik, J.J. (2011). The effect of authentic transformational leadership on follower and group ethics. *The Leadership Quarterly*, *22*(5), 801–817.

Index